S0-BBS-066

MANUFACTURING MELTDOWN

RESHAPING STEEL WORK

D.W. Livingstone,
Dorothy E. Smith
& Warren Smith

Fernwood Publishing • Halifax and Winnipeg

LIBRARY
FRANKLIN PIERCE UNIVERSITY
RINDGE, NH 03461

Copyright © 2011 D.W. Livingstone, Dorothy E. Smith and Warren Smith

All rights reserved. No part of this book may be reproduced or transmitted in
any form by any means without permission in writing from the publisher,
except by a reviewer, who may quote brief passages in a review.

Editing and design: Brenda Conroy
Cover design: John van der Woude
Printed and bound in Canada by Hignell Book Printing

MIX
Paper from
responsible sources
FSC® C013916

Published in Canada by Fernwood Publishing
32 Oceanvista Lane
Black Point, Nova Scotia, B0J 1B0
and 748 Broadway Avenue, Winnipeg, Manitoba, R3G 0X3
www.fernwoodpublishing.ca

Fernwood Publishing Company Limited gratefully acknowledges the financial support of the
Government of Canada through the Canada Book Fund, the Canada Council for the Arts, the
Nova Scotia Department of Tourism and Culture and the Province of Manitoba, through the
Book Publishing Tax Credit, for our publishing program.

Library and Archives Canada Cataloguing in Publication

Livingstone, D. W., 1943-
Manufacturing meltdown : reshaping steel
work / D.W. Livingstone, Dorothy E. Smith, Warren Smith.

Includes bibliographical references and index.
ISBN 978-1-55266-402-5

1. Steel industry and trade--Canada. 2. Iron and steel
workers--Labor unions--Canada. 3. Steel industry and
trade--Management--Employee participation--Canada.
4. Stelco Inc.--Management. I. Smith, Dorothy E., 1926-
II. Smith, Warren, 1947- III. Title.

HD8039.I52C3 2011   331.7'6691420971   C2010-908055-6

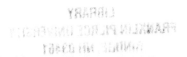
LIBRARY
FRANKLIN PIERCE UNIVERSITY
RINDGE, NH 03461

Contents

Preface

D. W. Livingstone, Dorothy E. Smith and Warren Smith

The first case study in this book, by D.W. Livingstone, began in the early 1980s in the wake of the first wave of mass layoffs in the Canadian steel industry. The study was part of a larger project to understand the coping strategies of steelworker families for dealing with disruptions to established employment conditions, household work relations and community activities.[1] The primary focus of the project was Hilton Works (a.k.a. Hamilton Works), Stelco's integrated steel plant in Hamilton, at the time the largest industrial worksite in the country. The original plan of that project was to gain the co-operation of both Stelco management and the local union, United Steel Workers of America (USWA) Local 1005 (now United Steelworkers of America [USW]). Stelco management consistently refused support. Local 1005's executive, stewards and a general membership meeting virtually unanimously supported the initiation of the project, and union leaders, for the most part, were helpful throughout. The basic results were given back to the local (e.g., Corman, Livingstone, Luxton and Seccombe 1985; Livingstone 1997, 1999b) as well as published more widely in book form (Corman, Luxton, Livingstone and Seccombe 1993; Livingstone and Mangan 1996; Seccombe and Livingstone 1999; and Luxton and Corman 2001). Chapter 1 is based on data on employment conditions gathered in the steelworker families project from 1982 to 1996, as well as further interviews and documentation up to Stelco's entry into bankruptcy proceedings in January 2004.

In the late 1990s, Livingstone initiated a research network to conduct an extensive series of surveys and case studies of work and lifelong learning in diverse settings.[2] Dorothy Smith developed one of these case studies to deal with the transmission and storage of knowledge between generations of the industrial working class. Local 1005 was a convenient research site. The results of this case study are reported in Chapter 2. Many people helped with this study, but chief among them are the eight people who were good enough to allow Dorothy and Stephan Dobson to interview them about their experience of learning (and teaching) steel at Stelco. Dorothy and Stephan consider them co-authors, since much of the discussion comes out of their analysis, but confidentiality agreements forbid naming them. Staff at the United Steelworkers of America Local 1005 were enormously helpful and Dorothy and Stephan are particularly appreciative of the support of Warren Smith, then president, and Bob Sutton, at that time editor of *Steel Shots*, without whose help they could not have gone forward with their work. They are also very appreciative of Frances Tolnai's transcriptive work, which produced remarkably accurate transcriptions from often less-than-perfect tape recordings. Livingstone's support and discussions — as well as access to his library and additional interview materials — are also much appreciated.

After Warren Smith's retirement from Stelco in 2005, he and Livingstone agreed to collaborate on a case study of the future prospects for jobs in integrated steel plants, informed by the experience of Stelco's Hamilton plant in emerging from the bankruptcy process. Once more, the support of Local 1005 leaders was valuable in providing access to records and members for interviews. Barb Fennessy was involved in gathering much of the data for this study (see Fennessy and Smith 2006; Fennessy 2009).

These case studies may be more fully appreciated in conjunction with the other findings of the steelworker families project. Wally Seccombe, Meg Luxton and June Corman, colleagues in that project, contributed detailed profiles of the changing employment patterns, household relations and community activities of Stelco workers and their partners after the mass layoffs of the early 1980s. Their research documented the end of the male breadwinner family and the juggling challenges these steelworker families faced as most of the women sought paid employment and men came to terms with the end of their job security.

Numerous members of Local 1005 provided invaluable support through the stages of these case studies. Cec Taylor and members of his executive strongly supported the inception of the steelworker families project. Alex Auchinvole, Chuck Emberson and Bob McSeveney offered wise counsel in the transition period after Taylor's departure. Bob Sutton, recording secretary of 1005 for many years, was the main contact during the presidency of John Martin, from 1988 to 1996. During Warren Smith's presidency, from 1997 to 2003, Bob continued to be the main contact with the local both for facilitating Dorothy's case study and for conducting further interviews. During Rolf Gerstenberger's presidency, 2003 to the present, several members of the executive, especially Gary Howe and Jake Lombardo, have been helpful in providing information to complete our final case study.

Among those who worked as research assistants on these case studies, Stephan Dobson deserves special recognition for editorial assistance. He participated in a number of interviews, transcribed many and edited all chapters of this book. Milosh Raykov provided several important statistical analyses of steel data sources and conducted extensive documentary and bibliographic searches. Barb Fennessy provided additional steel statistics in conjunction with her related dissertation study (2009). Maggie Breau, Katina Pollock and Reuben Roth assisted in bibliographic searches. Many others contributed to the research on the steelworker families project and are acknowledged in previous publications on that project. Colleagues who offered feedback on some of the chapters included Barb Fennessy, Mike Hersh, D'Arcy Martin, Jack Quarter, Peter Sawchuk, Wally Seccombe, Bob Sutton and Peter Warrian.

The three case studies differ in authorship, time frame and particular research approaches. But, taken together, they are intended to offer new insights into the labour and learning processes through which steelworkers have dealt with the major disruptions to their lives since the onset of the global steel crisis. These studies may also be suggestive for understanding the changing labour and learning processes in many other declining industries in the development of global capitalism.

Notes

1. The Steelworker Families Project was funded by the Social Sciences and Humanities Research Council (Grant No. 410–83–0391).
2. The research network, New Approaches to Lifelong Learning (NALL), was funded by the Social Sciences and Humanities Research Council (Grant No. 818-1996-1033).

Labour Displacement and the Enduring Significance of Steelwork

D. W. Livingstone

Labour Displacement in Capitalist Economies

This book focuses on the process and consequences of the displacement of labour in primary steel manufacturing. For most of human history, most of our labour was devoted to food production. The development of agriculture and large-scale human settlements permitted the growth of other occupations, but food production remained the primary labour of the majority of people until the rise of industrial capitalism in the nineteenth century. The development of industrial machinery stimulated both massive labour savings in agriculture as well as the massive expansion of manufacturing of all sorts. Many of those forced off the land were drawn into factories and increasingly became dependent upon purchase of agricultural commodities. Growing inter-firm competition and technological innovations for enhanced profits of manufacture served to stimulate agricultural production beyond basic domestic demand, to provoke trade wars in some goods and to reduce agricultural workers in developed industrial countries to a small fraction of the labour force. Much of the peasant population has also now been drawn off the land in less industrialized or developing countries. The exodus of labour from all forms of agriculture (including crop cultivation and livestock production) continues along with the commodification of more specialized forms of food. Other extractive resource industries such as mining, fishing and logging have followed similar paths.

The expansion of manufacturing continued into the mid-twentieth century. Steel, auto, petro-chemical and electrical industries created new mass-produced commodities that quickly became essential needs for urbanizing workforces. Similar processes of devising a marketable product and an efficient division of labour, then an expansion of product markets and labour forces, were replicated for many material manufactured goods across the globe.

But in recent generations, as automation has increased and market capacity has been exceeded, a spiral of mass layoffs of workers and the mergers or failures of remaining firms have occurred in many sectors. These processes have been evident for some time in the petro-chemical and auto industries but are also appearing in newer goods-producing industries such as electronics. Between 1970 and the early twenty-first century, the advanced capitalist countries lost significant numbers of manufacturing jobs, over a third of the total employment in this sector (Organisation for Economic Co-operation and Development [OECD] 2003; Pilat, Cimper, Olsen and Webb 2006). Even most newly industrialized countries have now joined this trend, with manufacturing employment declining in nearly all countries since 1990 (International Labour Organization [ILO] 2003); more than 10 percent of factory jobs were lost in the United States, China and Mexico alike between 1996 and 2002 (National Center for Policy Analysis 2003). We are now witnessing the general decline of employment in manufacturing in a way much more rapid than we saw in agriculture in the previous two centuries. Steel manufacturing provides one of the most extreme cases.

The Enduring Significance of Steelwork

Steel remains the most essential material for building the modern world. From thumb tacks to transport trucks, from tin cans to transmission towers — without steel, the world we know would not exist. Hundreds of millions of tons are produced annually, much of it now from recycled scrap steel. It is inconceivable that steel could be replaced any time soon as a vital material for maintaining modern societies. Just as with the transformation of agricultural production, the steel industry will likely become more and more capital intensive and less and less a source of employment. But a leaner, more efficient global steel industry will probably survive into the foreseeable future.

However, the loss of the capacity to control production of steel domestically is likely to have a negative impact on the health of national economies and their capacity to develop high-wage service jobs. Generally, as Cohen and Zysman have observed: "Manufacturing matters. Manufacturing is critical to the health of the economy; lose manufacturing and you will lose — not develop — high-wage service jobs.… Over time, you can't control what you can't produce" (1987: xii–iv). Manufacturing industries interact very strongly with service industries, both as providers and as users of intermediate inputs. The manufacturing sector remains a "flywheel," a main driver of innovation and technological innovation in other sectors, and still accounts for the bulk of business expenditure on research and development (R&D). The R&D undertaken by manufacturing firms has continued to be turned into patentable innovations, most often by the developed countries (Pilat et al. 2006). While conditions are changing rapidly in the global steel industry, with the emergence of leading Korean and Chinese firms, for example, as innovators rather than mere imitators, those developed countries that continue to control their own advanced manufacturing industries have the best prospects for healthy economies. The interactive centrality of manufacturing also means that the working conditions and wage levels of manufacturing workers have strong effects on those of the burgeoning numbers of service workers. Steelworkers were long regarded as leaders of the industrial core of the working class. This old industrial core is quickly dwindling. How its remaining members cope with capitalist restructuring initiatives in manufacturing industries is still vital to the economic prospects of the working classes of all advanced societies.

For some time, there has been a preoccupation on the part of analysts of changes in capitalist production systems with "new industrial spaces" (Scott 1988) and the "creative economy" based in communications and service industries (Florida 2002), both of which are now commonly seen to typify knowledge-based economies and to have more relevant, flexible employment relations as compared to older manufacturing centres. This preoccupation ignores the following four fundamental facts:

1) as just noted, manufacturing in advanced capitalism both sustains agricultural output and nurtures high-level service activities and often entails high levels of innovation;

2) in spite of locational shifts, the most technologically innovative global manufacturing still remains predominantly within the industrial regions established by early in the twentieth century (Storper and Walker 1989; Pilat, et al. 2006);

3) even as ownership of manufacturing firms and basic production zones shift away from older industrial sites, established forms of higher value-added production and access to lucrative consumer markets in developed manufacturing regions are likely to be maintained as long as these markets remain profitable (Peck 1996; Treado 2010); and

4) the remaining manufacturing industries in developed countries are more and more likely to be increasingly knowledge-based organizations. Computerized production systems emerged in the steel industry, for example, long before knowledge-based economy discourse become common, and steel is now a sophisticated material commodity, engineered to a wide variety of product characteristics and applications which communications and service industries, among others, intimately depend upon (Warrian 2010a).

There have been many obituaries of plant closures and their social consequences (e.g., Bluestone and Harrison 1982; Lerner and Somers 1989; Stock 2001; Cowie and Heathcott 2003). But aside from programmatic statements about the need for further research focused on manufacturing processes (e.g., Committee on New Directions in Manufacturing, National Research Council 2004), employment changes within existing worksites with relatively low capital mobility, such as resource and heavy manufacturing industries, have been given little recent attention by researchers (e.g., Barnes, Hayter and Grass 1990). Employment restructuring at established manufacturing sites may be as important as new employment processes in greenfields or new sectors might be for understanding current production relations in capitalist societies. Steel is the classic case.

The emergence of a "post-industrial society" or "knowledge-based economy" dominated by highly educated information service workers, the "creative class," has been heralded since the 1960s (see Bell 1973, 1989; Castells 2004; Florida 2002). However, such "knowledge workers" have remained a small minority of the entire labour force (see Livingstone 2002). What we are seeing more pertinently in recent societal change is the familiar story described above. Upheavals in established patterns of production have occurred throughout the history of Western industrial capitalism in one key sector after another: in agriculture during the nineteenth century, in energy generation and transportation in the early twentieth century, in manufacturing today and most likely in the service sector tomorrow. These periodic upheavals share the following basic features:

1) competitive capital investment in the key employment sector to the point of massive overproduction capacity relative to consumer markets, followed by extraordinary state intervention and increased concentration of ownership to maintain sector production;
2) rapid implementation of major existing technologies that can multiply productivity and drastically reduce operating costs of surviving enterprises; and
3) a huge reduction in the key sector's labour force, coupled with negotiations to revise the social contract between capital and labour.

In short, there has been a persistent tendency toward capital-intensive, labour-displacing forms of technological change for the enhancement of productivity and the assurance of profits in one sector after another. The recent upheaval in heavy manufacturing industries such as steel and the rapid expansion of less-secure service sector employment are the most current manifestations of the fundamental underlying dynamics of the industrial capitalist mode of production which have prevailed in Western societies for roughly two centuries — namely, inter-firm competition in pursuit of profits, competitive negotiations between employers and workers over profits and benefits, and continual revolutionizing of the forces of production.[1]

All productive capitalist enterprises are at least periodically impelled to invest in new technologies and new product lines and to undertake an intensive reorganization of their workforces in order to survive. The development of the capitalist labour process has entailed a wide variety of employer strategies and tactics in relation to their employees; these initiatives have usually revolved around profitability prospects of particular production processes and secondarily around concern about either controlling or deskilling workers.[2] Much of the recent literature heralding the "post-industrial society" — or somewhat more modestly arguing that "flexible specialization" production techniques are indicative of a "second industrial revolution" or that a "post-Fordist regime of accumulation" is imminent — tends to exaggerate both the pervasiveness and distinctive character of recent economic changes.[3] The recent changes are best understood as a fairly widespread implementation by employers of a new set of technologies utilizing much smaller, recombinable standardized components or modules (especially in microelectronics) along with strategies to motivate workers to use their discretion to operate these devices efficiently, all in order to ensure the profitable production and marketing of diversified commodities. Neither the changing sectoral composition of employment from manufacturing to services nor accelerating rates of change in employment conditions and commodity markets should obscure the continuity of these underlying dynamics. The same capitalist logic of incessant commodification and periodic labour intensification is still at work. The contradictions in this logic are only more evident within key sectors that have reached a condition of overcapacity in relation to available markets and extreme underemployment of labour, as has been the case in many advanced capitalist societies' manufacturing industries, most notably steelmaking, in the present generation.

In the last quarter of the twentieth century, the global steel industry of developed countries experienced the most massive employment losses in the history of manufacturing. About a million and a half jobs or *two-thirds* of the 1975 employment level were gone by the turn of the century. The United Kingdom and Germany, two of the oldest steel-producing countries, lost nearly 90 percent of their steel jobs (International Iron and Steel Institute [IISI] 2004a, 2004b). For well over a century, expanding steel production was integral to the expansion of industrial capitalism; global steel production and employment levels grew together. But since 1975, production levels have continued to grow while employment plummets. The global economy now has many more steel mills than it knows what to do with, a persistent overcapacity of around 20 percent or 300 million tons per year. Countries with the greatest overcapacity are making strenuous efforts to sell at low prices abroad; plant closures, bankruptcies and mergers abound in most advanced industrial countries; and the remaining steel producers are making keen efforts to survive through labour-saving technologies and still more layoffs. The rapid emergence of industrializing countries, notably China, as major steel importers created a temporary boom in global demand for steel. But as these countries become steel exporters, overcapacity problems in more industrialized countries are accentuated.

One largely ignored aspect of labour displacement has been the effect on workers' knowledge. Workers expelled from a declining sector are compelled to transfer their skills and learn new ones to get jobs in other industries. What of those remaining? Those in manufacturing restructuring regimes and industries with declining employment face intense new formal training initiatives. The connection of such formal initiatives to workers' actual prior knowledge is rarely addressed. There are growing numbers of studies beginning to examine the relations between formal education and informal learning more generally (see Livingstone and Sawchuk 2004a; Livingstone 2009, 2010). But the cumulative effect of mass layoffs of younger workers and extensive early retirements on the collective level and effective use of remaining workers' knowledge has scarcely been assessed. As the leading case of plummeting manufacturing employment, the steel industry offers deep object lessons, to be examined in this book.

Those in other manufacturing industries as well as those in the service sector — the remaining source of large-scale employment — should pay close attention to steel efforts to survive via enterprise restructuring and labour force renewal. The widespread failure to anticipate the aging of the remaining labour force and the underestimation of the strategic importance of transmitting informal as well as formal working knowledge to future generations of steelworkers could be fatal flaws for the sustainability of many industries.

The Case Studies

The three case studies in this book are all centred on the Hilton Works plant of Stelco located in Hamilton, Ontario. Throughout the last century, Stelco was Canada's largest steelmaker. Hilton Works remains one of the oldest surviving integrated steel plants in North America. In the early 1980s, it had the largest labour force of any plant in Canada. D.W. Livingstone's initial studies of Hilton Works began in the early 1980s as a major part of a research project on how steelworker families and Hamilton families generally were coping with the hard times related to the first mass layoffs in the Canadian steel industry (see Corman, Luxton, Livingstone and Seccombe 1993; Livingstone and Mangan 1996; Seccombe and Livingstone 1999; Luxton and Corman 2001). These studies provide most of the evidence up to the mid-1990s for the first case study. Dorothy Smith's case study was begun in the late 1990s as a project sponsored by the SSHRC research network on New Approaches to

Lifelong Learning (NALL) (see <nall.ca>) and involved interviewing workers at Hilton Works. The final case study, dealing with current conditions and future prospects for jobs in the steel industry, was conducted in conjunction with the SSHRC research network, The Changing Nature of Work and Lifelong Learning (WALL). We believe this book represents one of the most substantial bodies of evidence available on the effects of steel industry restructuring on labour conditions and on the use of workers' knowledge.

In Chapter 1, Livingstone presents an overview of changing conditions in the global steel industry between the 1970s and the turn of the century and summarizes global and Western-nation steel production, employment, organizational and technological changes. He paints a picture of the Canadian steel industry, of Stelco, and of Hilton Works situated in Hamilton, Canada's "Steel City." Canadian steelmakers had been relatively efficient at the outset of the global steel crisis. But when the global effects of overcapacity hit Canada in the early 1980s, the familiar pattern of labour displacement occurred. Young steelworkers were laid off, and early retirements were encouraged. This in-depth analysis of Hilton Works during the 1980–2003 period offers unique insights into the challenges and choices that labour force renewal has faced in virtually all sectors of capitalist production. On the basis of company and union documents and interviews with steelworkers, processes for reorganizing the workforce at Hilton Works are analyzed in detail. The remaining workforce entered the twenty-first century with most workers nearing retirement and virtually no new hires for a generation.

Chapter 2 by Dorothy Smith and Stephan Dobson is based on extensive interviews primarily with steelworkers who worked at Hilton Works during the period from the late 1970s to the mid-1990s, the period when traditional, largely informal processes of transmitting knowledge and skills to the next generation of workers were progressively displaced. Formal training initiatives, many involving the participation of community colleges, were disconnected from these vital informal learning processes, jeopardizing the reproduction of skills and knowledge based on the experience of the steel labour force. Most of these interviews were conducted in the period leading up to Stelco's entry into the bankruptcy process in early 2004.

In the final chapter, Livingstone and Warren Smith assess current global and local conditions in the steel industry, including a detailed account of the restructuring process at Hilton Works since the beginning of the bankruptcy process. They consider twenty-first century options for organizational restructuring and labour force renewal in developed countries' integrated steel industry[4] in general and for the remains of Stelco and Hilton Works in particular. Alternatives include different ownership options (further foreign takeovers; repurchase by domestic private capital; creation of government [or crown] corporations; worker ownership) and different models of management-labour relations (hierarchical or consultative management; industrial democracy or worker self-management). Stelco may be distinctive in terms of initiating, in 2004, a bankruptcy process while making record profits, as well as in its chronic incapacity to consult workers on either technological change or industrial relations problems. Indeed, some would suggest that the Stelco/U.S. Steel model now represents an extreme case of centralized hierarchical control with relatively limited sustainability prospects. But the insights of labour activists and other workers at Hilton Works as well as a review of recent general research literature and industry and union documents do identify some preferable and feasible alternatives for steelwork.

While their numbers drop, steelworkers still matter at the moment. The ways in which restructuring and labour force renewal occur in the steel industry can have profound implications for sustainable working-class employment in manufacturing and advanced capitalist economies generally. The case studies in this book offer insights into roles that steelworkers and their knowledge have played in shaping and could play in reshaping the modern steel industry.

Notes

1. The classic exposition of these essentially contradictory relationships in industrial capitalist production systems is in the writings of Karl Marx, particularly Volume 1 of *Capital* (Marx 1954). See also Castells (1980) and Livingstone (2009).

2. Most research on changes in the capitalist labour process since Braverman (1974) has focused on forms of management control (e.g., Edwards 1979) or issues of deskilling and reskilling (e.g., Wood 1989) in and of themselves. The contingent character of these specific relations in association with enterprise profitability prospects has very frequently been ignored, as is well documented by Cohen's (1987) critical review.

3. For a general critique of the "post-industrial society" thesis, which stresses its mystifying infatuation with new information technologies and its obscuring of underlying social relations of capitalist production, see Robins and Webster (1988). See also Hrynyshyn (2002). For a general critique of the related "flexible specialization" thesis, see Williams et al. (1987). Critical discussions of a "Fordist" regime or mode of development, and hence of the inadequacy of the concept of "post-Fordism," may be found in Foster (1988).

4. The integrated steel industry includes plants that begin the steelmaking process with coke and iron ore, as distinct from mini-mills that begin with scrap steel.

Chapter 1

Melting the Core Steel Workforce, 1981–2003

D. W. Livingstone

There really isn't any job security. Even with the seniority, you are still in doubt. You still don't really know. Sure, tomorrow I'm going to go to work, but you really don't know. The company may go belly up and it's been close. When I first started, boy, you got a good job for life, but no, the steel industry went for a dive, the economy went, everything else... I guess, well, nothing's for sure anymore. You can have the greatest job in the world, but no matter where you live, nothing's for sure. I think everyone knows that now. And it's not just Hamilton, it's everywhere.[1] — Skilled trades worker in Hamilton Works steel plant, over twenty-five years' seniority, 1994

This chapter[2] begins by describing the global steel crisis that started in the 1970s and the somewhat delayed development of this crisis in Canada. The primary focus is on Stelco's Hamilton Works.[3] In 1980, Stelco was the largest steel company in Canada, and Hamilton Works was the largest industrial worksite in the country. After providing brief profiles of Stelco and its home city, the chapter examines the processes of reshaping the core labour force at Hilton Works by a persistent combination of downsizing and job restructuring, periodic efforts to refashion industrial relations and formalistic initiatives to retrain remaining steelworkers. The evidence of Stelco management strategies and the responses of the unionized workforce in this flagship plant offer a revealing case study of the dramatic changes occurring within the Canadian steel industry between 1981 and the early twenty-first century.

The Global Steel Crisis

Between 1900 and 1974, global raw steel production grew almost continuously, with a greater than sixfold increase since World War II.[4] But the steel industry of the advanced capitalist economies entered a deep crisis in the mid-1970s. The recession triggered by OPEC oil price increases led to a drop of about 10 percent in world steel output in 1975. In spite of production gains in newly industrializing countries, total world output fluctuated below prior peak levels through the 1980s because of precipitous production declines in the European Community and especially in the United States.

In spite of this declining demand for steel, the big Western integrated companies continued to increase their production capacities until 1980 as a result of commitments to investment plans and optimistic projections presuming resumption of prior growth. Capacity utilization fell below 60 percent in many OECD countries (ISTC 1992a, 1992b). Facing chronic surplus capacity, with nearly saturated conventional markets for steel in the domestic motor and construction industries, and the prospect of increased competition from both offshore steel and substitute products such as plastics and aluminum, Western steel firms engaged in competitive price-cutting to maintain their market shares. As price wars spread and Western steel firms continued to experience a general fall in the level and rate of profit, there was growing acknowledgment of a need for substantial reorganization of the industry (Kutscher 1986).

But in a world of inter-firm competition and large fixed costs, few private steel firms have ever willingly reduced their production capacities. By the 1970s, the scale of production for integrated steelworks had become so immense that only the most powerful financial groups or the state could meet the capital investment requirements to establish such plants (see Howell et al. 1988 and Mény and Wright 1985). In most Western European countries, escalating capital costs led to a series of state loans and nationalizations designed to absorb industry debt burdens. Mergers and joint ventures, as well as diversification into other profitable industries, became favoured means for the remaining private firms to avoid bankruptcy. In spite of state agencies' efforts to co-ordinate industry restructuring,[5] over-optimism about their own steel market opportunities continued among remaining individual Western firms. As such, average capacity utilization rates in the 1980s remained lower than in the pre-1974 era (Barnett 1988; see also Marcus and Kirsis 1988; Keeling 1988).

Gross global steelmaking capacity remained at about a billion tons a year until the mid-1990s and still exceeded production by more than 200 million tons in 1995 (ISTC 1992a, 1992b; Marcus and Kirsis 1995). Newly industrializing countries built integrated steel plants as fast as the advanced capitalist countries shut them down. The volume of international trade in steel continued to increase, helping to keep steel export prices fluctuating mostly downward (Marcus and Kirsis 1995). Among Western steelmakers, plant mothballing, closures and mergers substantially reduced the gap between effective capacity and actual production levels. Average OECD capacity utilization climbed back over 80 percent by the mid-1990s (ISTC 1992a, 1992b). But, after subsidizing the downsizing of their national steel industries in the wake of the 1974 crisis, most fiscally challenged Western governments encouraged re-privatization (Moinov 1995). Revived competitive investment in international joint ventures with new technologies by the remaining integrated steel companies and the surging mini-mill sector (Mangum, Kim and Tallman 1996) again increased production capacity beyond secured future consumption levels. Competing firms with high fixed costs were again unwilling to cut back output even in response to an unprecedented "death spiral" in steel prices (Marcus and Kirsis 1995). In light of the continuing fluctuation in steel prices and escalating production costs, further bankruptcies and mergers of private steel companies became inevitable. For example, between 1999 and 2003, more than thirty steel companies, representing over half the industry capacity in North America, filed for bankruptcy protection (Considine 2005).

The major human consequence of this drive for profit and company survival were the most massive single-industry job-losses in the history of capitalist manufacturing, with widespread disruption of the communities that had grown up around the large integrated steel plants. Between 1975 and 2003, employment in the steel industries of the advanced capitalist economies was reduced by two-thirds, a loss of well over a million jobs (IISI 2004a: 19). The United Kingdom industry experienced the largest reduction, losing over 85 percent of its steelworkers, followed by France and the United States, which lost around three-quarters of their steel workforces; Japan eliminated nearly two-thirds of its steel jobs. The costs in human suffering in communities that experienced plant closures are incalculable.[6] The responses of steelworkers' unions and other community organizations varied widely, from plant takeovers, public demonstrations and government lobbying to acceptance of very limited buyouts and disillusionment (see High 2003). In any event, many of these previously secure steelworkers faced early retirement, prolonged unemployment or the prospect of much lower-paid temporary jobs, often far afield. Their household partners were increasingly compelled to seek generally low paying, often temporary jobs to attempt to reconstitute the "family wage." Governments, steel companies and trade unions began to co-operate in adjustment programs both to soften the social impact of unemployment and provide some job security for remaining workers (Houseman 1991).

These massive layoffs and the availability of new cost-cutting technologies also stimulated major ongoing efforts by integrated companies to restructure the long-established wage bargain in their steel plants. There were at least two common tactical features in employer initiatives to reshape the core workforce in steel:

1) persistent attempts to revise both contractual agreements and established work rules in the direction of greater flexibility among workers, without altering established managerial prerogatives; and

2) campaigns to convince workers and their communities of the company's enhanced interest in its remaining workers and their ideas.[7]

Integrated steel firm managements around the world came to the conclusion that "human resource management" was the key to their salvation.[8] In the context of persistent global overcapacity (Shalom 1991: D3), the remaining integrated steel firms left themselves little choice but to pursue the contradictory process just mentioned of reducing *and* nurturing their core workforces (see Scherrer 1991). By the mid-1990s, there were more former steelworkers than employed steelworkers in the active workforces of virtually all advanced capitalist societies (Moinov 1995). But the remaining core workers were increasingly regarded by management as valuable potential partners in their enterprise. As John Correnti, president of Nucor Corporation, the industry-leading mini-mill, put it:

> Fewer people have to produce more steel. In our company, we look at all our employees as businessmen. We're not there just to buy their backs or buy their hands and their arms; *we're there to buy their minds*. We put them in business for themselves. (1994, italics added)

The industrial relations problem for steel employers has remained essentially as it was when F.W. "Speedy" Taylor began his experiments in work redesign for U.S. steel companies over a century ago. The problem was how to overcome the collective resistance of steelworkers to the speed-up of work — speed-ups that resulted in reduced piece rates in the past and now serve to eliminate jobs.[9] From their origins, mass production systems — with their expensive capital equipment and interconnected workflows — have been dependent on reliable and attentive workers. From Taylor's time-and-motion studies and piece-rate incentive system to computerized continuous processing methods and extensive benefits packages, management efforts to develop the capital-labour relations of mass production have been constructed on a recognition that the attitudes and aspirations of workers are critical determinants of productivity. "Taylorism" in this sense has remained alive and well in the steel industry and elsewhere.[10] Industrial relations in integrated steel plants in particular have long been marked by the companies' formal and informal strategies intended for ensuring the allegiance of a stable core workforce (see Bowen 1976; Elbaum 1984; Stone 1974; Betheil 1978; Stieber 1980; Quinlan 1986). Specific industrial relations approaches have oscillated between emphases on tight control and relaxed supervision. The "new" philosophy of human resource management has placed increasing emphasis on workers' own initiative and team discipline because the combination of greatly reduced employment numbers with more expensive equipment has placed a greater premium on self-motivation to ensure productivity and profitability. These conditions have encouraged greater involvement in company decision-making processes than ever before among the dwindling core of unionized steelworkers.[11] A large international survey of working conditions in steel plants conducted in 1998 found that, while the majority of plants had moved to more flexible contracts and an increased use of subcontractors over the previous five years, the vast majority had also introduced many high-involvement work practices, including moving quality responsibility to the shop floor with problem-solving "quality circles," broadened job descriptions, self-supervision of work teams and reduced layers of management (Bacon and Blyton 2000). These findings are consistent with more general trends in organizational restructuring toward more contingent use of employees and increases in worker involvement in at least limited decision-making roles. Workers appear to be becoming more involved in more temporary jobs (see Livingstone and Scholtz 2010).

During steel's expansionary era in the West, the competitive drive to technological innovation in steel production was often muted.[12] Except for a modest mechanization spurt in the early 1900s and continuing refinements of existing machinery, the steel industry of the 1950s had experienced steady profits and relatively little technical innovation for generations. Since the 1950s, there have been two distinct stages of rapid technological change.[13] The first, under the impetus of growing international competition and continued expanding demand up to the mid-1970s, emphasized implementing technologies that increased the *quantity* of steel produced. The most important of these was the basic oxygen furnace (BOF) which — with reconstructing Japan leading the way — very rapidly replaced open-hearth furnaces (OHF) as a more productive, lower cost method of large-scale steel production (Lynn 1982). Since the global steel crisis began, much more attention has been given to implementing a variety of technologies aimed at increasing efficiency and steel quality. The prevailing mentality among Western steel industry leaders shifted during the 1980s to "only the most cost efficient, high quality producers will survive" (Kutscher 1986: 3). The "epicentre" of these innovative technologies in integrated steel plants has been continuous casting, which eliminated several steps in steelmaking and resulted in significant waste reduction, lower energy costs and greater labour productivity (see Barnett 1988; Birat 1986; Hogan 1985). Again, Japan led the way. Even more importantly, mini-mills — which fire scrap iron and steel metal in electric arc furnaces even more efficiently and without need for front-end iron ore, coal and limestone processing — spread quickly (Barnett and Crandall 1986). By the turn of the twenty-first century, mini-mills were competing with integrated mills in most steel products (Considine 2005). More generally, the rapid introduction of computers into both product design and more continuous operations scheduling led to more consistent quality and enabled the quick fabrication of a growing diversity of new steel products (McManus 1988a; Darnell et al. 1984; Hicks 1985). Other new technologies, such as developments in direct reduction systems and ladle technology, thin slab casting and mini-hot strip mills, also facilitated producing superior quality steels in low volumes at lower costs. The development of many lighter, stronger and more durable products enabled Western steelmakers both to retain traditional markets such as auto and to enter new markets such as residential housing.

The rapid implementation of continuous processing and automating technologies since the onset of the global steel crisis led to dramatic increases in productivity and reductions in operating components and costs. New equipment utilizing standardized micro-electronic design components combined with flexible labour-process restructuring dramatically reduced the number of worker hours needed to produce a ton of steel. For example, in the United States in 1953, producing a ton of steel required over sixteen hours of labour; in 1974 it required about eleven hours; in 1988 it required around six hours; in the mid-1990s, it required around three hours; by 2003 the average was around two hours per ton. The most efficient mini-mills were casting thin steel slabs from scrap steel in well under one hour per ton (see Considine 2005). As Thomas Bokland, president of Oregon Steel, observed in 1996:

> Technology is changing every day. We're in the midst of a technology revolution. We really are.... When you look back to the fifties and sixties... that was like watching the grass grow. But it's going to get better. Every day it gets better. You're using less power and fewer consumables. You're making heats quicker. You're refining them quicker. The ladle metallurgy, the whole damn thing is changing right now as we talk. Direct steelmaking — there's just all kinds of things going on.[14]

However, while technological change in the steel industry did result in many layoffs, the primary reason for job elimination in the 1980s in the North American steel industry was probably productive overcapacity:

> Though modernization itself eliminates jobs, a thorough modernization would eliminate fewer jobs than what is occurring now — a little bit of modernization and a lot of reduction in capacity (plant closings). For every one job eliminated by modernization, four are being eliminated by liquidation. (Metzgar 1984: 65)

In the wake of the early mass layoffs, collaborative training and retraining programs as well as various other government and firm-level adjustment programs for laid off steelworkers became recognized priorities in most advanced industrial countries (Auer 1992; Houseman 1991). In the context of continuing mergers of steel companies and ongoing technological innovation, the long-term decline of employment in the Western steel industry has continued. An often ignored consequence of the layoff of young workers, early retirements and minimal recruitment was the rapid aging of the steel workforce. The massive decline in apprenticeships in steel should have evoked serious questions about the development and training of the next generation of steelworkers, but these issues were largely ignored by both steel companies and governments until the new century. More recently, concerns about the polarization of older generations of steelworkers largely reliant on informal learning and younger entrants with more formal qualifications have been raised (see Fairbrother, Stroud and Coffey 2004a, 2004b).

These trends should be seen in the context of the rapid expansion of steelmaking in the developing world. By 2003, China had become the biggest global steelmaker and was producing over 20 percent of the world's steel (IISI 2004a). China alone employed well over a million steelworkers compared to just over 600,000 in the advanced market economies of the OECD, but labour productivity there was estimated to be about one-tenth of that in the developed countries (Renner, Sweeney and Kubit 2008). There is little reason to doubt that levels of steel output and labour productivity will continue to increase as China's industrialization continues and the country becomes more involved in global steel competition; after a period of massive domestic expansion, steelworker numbers will decline, probably quite rapidly in response to inter-firm competition and technological innovation. It should also be recognized that global finance capital and larger steel companies in advanced market economies have increasingly tended to invest in steel operations in developing countries, the latter having less stringent environmental regulations, cheaper labour and tax incentives, all combining for greater profits (Kamara 1983). At the same time, the availability of relatively cheap steel from developing countries has served to accentuate continuing trends toward more capital-intensive steelmaking with less workers in developed countries. Chronic overcapacity has persisted, with existing and new steel production capacity far outstripping increases in overall demand by hundreds of millions of tons throughout this period (see IISI 2004a; Bacon and Blyton 2004: 56). By the end of the 1974–2003 period, there was little doubt that the Western steel industry was in an irreversible employment decline.

The Canadian Case: Crisis Delayed

In 2003, Canada was the seventh largest steel producer among the advanced capitalist countries (behind Japan, the United States, Germany, Italy, France, and most recently passed by Spain while passing the United Kingdom). The country has become a relatively minor producer in global terms, ranking fifteenth among all countries, with a total annual tonnage around sixteen million tons, less than 2 percent of the world total (IISI 2004a). Throughout the post-war period, Canadian steel production has been highly concentrated in three Ontario-centred private companies — Stelco, Dofasco, Algoma — which together contributed about 70 percent of domestic production (Ministry of State, Science and Technology 1988). Until 1990, all three companies ranked among the top fifty steel companies in the world in terms of tonnage produced. Algoma dropped out of the top 100 companies by the early 1990s, while Stelco and Dofasco continued to rank in the top sixty until 2003 (World Steel Association 2010). As Graph 1.1 shows, the level of steel production in Canada remained fairly stable from the onset of the global steel crisis until 2003. While production levels dropped in the United States and most other developed economies, and while production levels grew significantly in developing countries (including emerging trading partner Mexico), Canadian production was virtually identical in 1980 and 2003.

In terms of the preceding general description of the Western steel industry since 1974, what is distinctive about the Canadian case is the *delayed impact* of these conditions. With regard to profitability, capacity utilization and employment stability, the Canadian steel industry outperformed most of its international competitors for over a decade.[15] Canadian integrated mills enjoyed the natural advantages of easy access to cheap raw materials and energy as well as secure major domestic markets in central Canada that were shielded from offshore competition by higher transport costs. A conserva-

Graph 1.1 Crude Steel Production, NAFTA Countries and the World, 1975–2003 (Million Metric Tons)

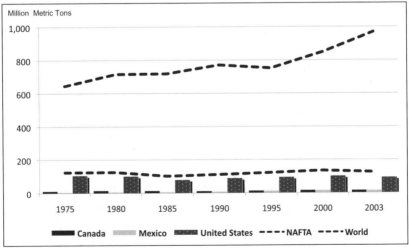

Source: Fennessy 2009

tive strategy of adding capacity to meet average rather than peak domestic demand allowed the Canadian steel industry to remain quite profitable into the 1980s.[16] Peak demand was typically met with imported steel (Clancy 2004). Capacity utilization peaked at over 95 percent in 1979 (ISTC 1992a, 1992b). Sustained profitability encouraged continual capital investment in installing equipment in order to catch up technologically with Japan and Western Europe, and enabled Canadian producers to replace declining domestic demand after 1973 with growing exports to adjacent U.S. markets. Thus, both steel shipments and employment levels continued to grow until the late 1970s.

But Canadian steelmakers could not remain insulated from global conditions for long. In the context of continued decline in domestic demand and growing competition both in Canada's relatively open home market, from cheap Third World and "dumped" European steels, and in the vital export U.S. market, from surging American mini-mills and restructured integrated producers, the continued installation of more capital-intensive equipment inevitably led to large layoffs. In the 1982 economic recession, the Canadian steel industry incurred the first major aggregate financial loss in its history. Capacity utilization fell to only 55 percent (Verma, Frost and Warrian 1995). Enterprise restructuring became imperative (see Sandberg and Bradbury 1988: 102–21; Masi 1991). Canadian steel executives started to sound like their international competition. As T.E. Dancy, vice-president of Sidbec-Dosco, declared:

> Everything we are doing is directed toward reducing costs. Unless you can really slash costs, you aren't going to be in business one of these days. You must find ways to make more efficient use of energy, more efficient use of materials, more efficient use of labour and facilities. Nobody is talking about building more facilities or more capacity these days…. The ultimate challenge is greater productivity and higher quality at lower cost. (cited in Chandler 1985: 55)

Steel imports increased from 15–20 percent in the early 1980s to around 30 percent of the Canadian market in the mid-1990s. Restructured U.S. steel firms, aided by the 1987 Canada–U.S. Free Trade Agreement, virtually erased the Canadian competitive advantage and more than doubled their share of the Canadian market to the 14–16 percent range. Canadian companies' share of the U.S. steel market was cut in half to 2 percent. An expanded continental free trade agreement added the challenge of still cheaper Mexican steel (Locker 1991; see also Daw 1991; Verma, Frost and Warrian 1995). All integrated Canadian producers experienced heavy market losses in spite of major cost reductions. The closure of small older plants, a failed merger of Dofasco with Algoma and a growing number of joint ventures with big foreign investors were all indicative of more concentrated, capital-intensive production. Increased foreign competition initially stimulated more formal collaboration among Canadian steel companies for lobbying Canadian governments to protect access to U.S. markets (see CSIA 1983, 1988; Kymlicka 1987). With the onset of free trade, large Canadian steel firms began to shift to continental market niche strategies (Verma, Frost and Warrian 1995: 8).

After the recessionary slump of the early 1980s, private Canadian steel companies intensified their capital investments in more efficient quality-enhancing technologies, greatly increasing their debt loads in the process. The capital-deficient integrated Canadian firms were forced into joint ventures with foreign capital to bring in state-of-the-art technologies. The last open-hearth furnaces were replaced by basic oxygen and electric arc furnaces, and continuous casting increased from a third to over 80 percent of Canadian production by the early 1990s (Verma, Frost and Warrian 1995: 9). Co-operative funding by Canadian steel consortia and Canadian governments for research on new "leap frog" technologies for the elimination of coke ovens and the direct casting of molten metal into thin strip coil were also initiated (Daw 1989; Van Alphen 1988). But in the early 1990s, productivity rates for the Canadian steel industry lagged behind the rates in many European countries and Japan, and were comparable to those of the restructured U.S. industry (Locker 1991; Verma, Frost and Warrian 1995). Canadian steelmakers would require substantial continuing investments in these new technologies to remain competitive.

As summarized in Graph 1.2, Canadian steel mill employment reached its peak of about 60,000 in 1980. The cutbacks which began in 1981 were marginally less than in some Western countries, but by 1992, total weekly employment in steel mills had been reduced to around 30,000, or half the 1980 level (Fennessy 2009; Shalom 1991). More gradual reductions continued over the next decade. In 2003, Canadian steel mills employed under 26,000 workers, a drop of about 57 percent from peak 1980 levels (Fennessy 2009). The decline in employment in manufacturing from purchased steel fell more modestly, from about 15,000 in 1983 to about 10,000 in 2003. In contrast, metal service centres experienced increased employment, from around 12,000 jobs in 1985 to 16,000 in 2003. According to Warrian and Mulhern, steel service centres were becoming "sophisticated and highly adaptable actors in the steel-auto supply chain" (2001: 29). Total employment for these three subsectors combined in the broader steel industry in Canada was over 52,000 in 2003. International statistical reports tend to lump these figures together (e.g., IISI 2004a) and mask the extent of reductions in steel mill employment. Over the long-term, labour displacement from Canadian steel mills is comparable to that in other Western steel countries.[17] The core of the Canadian steel industry has been and continues to be based in Hamilton, Canada's

Graph 1.2 Derived Employment for the Canadian Steel Industry, 1975–2003

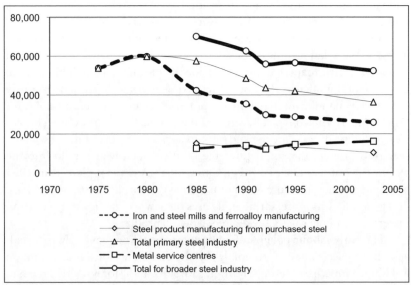

Source: Fennessy 2009

"steeltown," and the remainder of this chapter focuses on Hamilton and on Hilton Works, the plant that was, at the onset of the global steel crisis, the largest steel plant in the country.

Steeltown

Since World War II, Hamilton has been the undisputed capital of the Canadian steel industry. From the early 1900s on, the Hamilton steel industry had increasingly exploited several major locational advantages, including easy water and rail transport, cheap hydro-electricity, local government land and capital grants and tax incentives, and superior access to the country's largest steel-consuming industries in Ontario's "Golden Horseshoe." With two of the big three steel firms — Stelco and Dofasco — centred in Hamilton, the city generally produced over half of the country's post-war steel.[18] The unprecedented post-war expansion of the steel sector encouraged some observers to see Hamilton as "Canada's largest company town," with the two big steel firms dominating the economy and limiting civic politics (see, e.g., Weaver 1982; Freeman and Hewitt 1979). During the 1970s, rather than developing a more diversified manufacturing structure, Hamilton's economy became even more dependent on steel. Primary metals was the fastest growing employment sector, increasing by over 20 percent to constitute more than 40 percent of manufacturing employment and about 20 percent of total employment, while sector production increased to nearly half of the total value of shipments and value added in the Hamilton region by 1980 (Webber 1986: 204–12). Future prospects for Hamilton steel were still generally seen to be quite rosy.

Any account of the post-war Hamilton steel industry, and especially of its industrial relations, must consider the interactions between Stelco and Dofasco.[19] Their main steel works are side by side on the Hamilton harbour. Dofasco was founded in 1912 but remained a small, locally owned, narrowly specialized manufacturer reliant on purchased iron and scrap until after World War II. Stelco typically stressed the application of proven technologies, including oxygen lancing and self-fluxing sinter for blast furnaces, which served to prolong the competitive life of their open-hearth mills into the 1960s. In contrast, Dofasco became the North American pioneer in 1954 by implementing the more efficient basic oxygen furnace vessel technology, and generally was more daring in its uses of new technology to become an integrated producer with a widening array of products.[20]

The early labour policies of both companies were generally paternalistic. But Stelco's harsher version led to the emergence of a militant union at Hilton Works (see Heron, Hoffmitz, Roberts and Storey 1981; Freeman 1982). Dofasco managed to avoid unionization and to maintain a "family image." The founding Sherman family remained active in a management approach that stressed employee participation (e.g., a profit-sharing program, the "world's largest" annual Christmas party and extensive community recreational facilities) — and the matching of every wage settlement at Stelco (see Storey 1981b). Thus, Dofasco workers seemed to have it both ways, at least until mass layoffs in 1994 — as a consequence of which major organizing drives were initiated by both United Steelworkers of America (USWA) and the Canadian Auto Workers (CAW) (Storey 1996).

While these two huge integrated steel plants clearly dominated the postwar local economy, the end of a 1981 Stelco strike and the economic recession of 1982 marked a major turning point in both the history of the Hamilton steel industry and its centrality in the local economy. By 1983, the pre-strike steel labour force had been reduced by about 30 percent (from 29,000 to 21,000) (figures are from Stelco 1989; Dofasco 1990). Labour force reductions became a permanent part of the cost-cutting and restructuring efforts that continued throughout the next generation. The strategic planning by Hamilton steel leaders, like those throughout the rest of the Western steel industry, no longer assumed the eventual resumption of expanded steel production. Instead, cutting costs became an overriding survival imperative.

While Stelco and Dofasco continued to be the largest single employers, both steel companies only employed a total of about 14,000 people by 1995, or about 7 percent of the regional workforce (MacRury 1996: B3). The local economy was becoming more diversified, with major emphasis on such specific growth areas as health care, food and beverage, advanced secondary manufacturing, hospitality, telecommunications and small business sectors, and a relatively low unemployment rate of about 6 percent (Fennessy 2009). Hamilton's economic renewal was therefore becoming comparable to the industrial regeneration that had occurred in many other former "rustbelt" cities (Cooke 1995; Fennessy 2009). Most of these new jobs were much less secure and lower paid than the steel jobs they replaced.

Stelco

From its origins as an integrated steel company in a 1910 merger, the Steel Company of Canada (Stelco) grew to become by the 1950s the largest Canadian-owned industrial company in Canada (Kilbourn 1960). Stelco's 700-acre plant on the Hamilton waterfront (called "Hilton Works" for most of the post-World War II era and recently "Hamilton Works"), was always the core of the company. From the 1920s until the 1980s, Stelco was Canada's wealthiest, largest and most diversified steelmaker. It was consistently profitable until the 1980s. But, as Table 1.1 shows, Stelco was in financial decline throughout the 1980s. Its net worth dropped steadily until 1993, even in current dollars. From 1981 onward, the company experienced an extended incapacity to reinvest earnings. After its first ever losses in the 1982–83 recession, Stelco was only able to resume modest profit levels on sales in the mid-1980s through increasing its debt load to unprecedented levels (nearly 50 percent by 1990). Thus, the company was left highly vulnerable to massive financial losses in the recession that began in 1990. Stelco's labour restructuring, steel market repositioning and capital reinvestment strategies paid off briefly in the following years of upswing in North American steel markets, with profits rebounding to 1980 level in 1994–95 and debt loads falling to earlier normal levels (see Verma, Frost and Warrian 1995). But the net worth of the company never again approached the level of the early 1980s; lack of capital reinvestment became a persistent problem and profit levels again generally declined until unprecedented large losses occurred in 2003.

Changes in Stelco's general scale of production from its inception are summarized in Graph 1.3. The company employed five times as many employees in 1980 as it did in 1911 but produced over sixty times as much steel. The massive general improvements in steelmaking with new blast furnaces and continuous processing technologies are reflected in the tenfold growth in productivity between 1911 and the early 1960s, from under 20 tons to around 200 tons per employee annually. More modest increases to around 250 tons per employee by the early 1980s may be attributed mainly to replacement of more antiquated furnaces and finishing mills. A doubling of productivity to over 500 tons per employee by 2003 is largely a result of labour force reduction along with computerization and further closure of old mills.

Table 1.1 Stelco Net Worth, Debt Load, Reinvested Earnings and Return on Sales 1970–2003

Year	Net Worth (Current Millions)*	Debt/ Capital Assets**	Reinvested Earnings (Current Millions)	Return on Sales (%)***
1970	672	.14	31	9.1
1975	1010	.26	41	6.9
1980	1867	.24	49	5.9
1981	1868	.23	-14	3.8
1982	1802	.23	-117	-2.0
1983	1807	.22	-95	-0.7
1984	1783	.24	-89	-0.1
1985	1969	.24	-7.5	3.2
1986	1720	.27	-27	2.4
1987	1466	.32	-12	2.5
1988	1350	.38	33	3.6
1989	1355	.39	44	3.4
1990	920	.47	-238	-9.4
1991	998	.44	-136	-6.9
1992	821	.48	-127	-5.8
1993	798	.47	-40	-1.4
1994	1219	.32	98	3.9
1995	1341	.25	109	5.3
1996	1356	.22	66	2.7
1997	1529	.24	Not reported	4.4
1998	1477	.24	Not reported	3.8
1999	1513	.28	Not reported	3.5
2000	1499	.25	Not reported	0.1
2001	1281	.26	Not reported	-7.0
2002	1472	.22	Not reported	0.0
2003	1053	.26	Not reported	-20.6

* Estimated (Working Capital + Fixed Assets Net – Long Term Debt)
** Long Term Debt/(Working Capital + Property, Plant & Equipment [Net] + Intangible Assets) *** Net Income/Net Sales
Note: Where figures have been restated in subsequent years, the most current figures are used.
Source: Stelco Annual Reports 1960 to 2003

After Stelco achieved an annual production peak of over 6 million tons of raw steel produced in the 1978–80 period, average annual production dropped to 4.3 million tons during the 1980s, climbing to 4.6 million tons during the 1990s and 5.2 million tons a year in the early years of the new century. At the same time, Stelco reduced its total employees from over 26,000 in 1981 to about 9,000 in 2003, a drop of about two-thirds. The largest reduction, of over 4,000, occurred in 1982 following a 125-day strike in 1981 and continued with over 2,500 in 1983. Layoffs of over 1,500 followed a 106-day strike at the end of 1990. Aside from adding called-back employees in market upturns in 1984 and 1994, gradual employment reductions occurred in every year since 1981. Productivity per employee sagged with the 1981 strike and recession, then again during the 1990 strike and recession. Otherwise, tons per employee showed an upward trend since the early 1980s, to over 550 tons per employee by 2003.

The contrast between the expansionary strategy of the 1911–1980 period, in which growing numbers of steelworkers were increasingly combined with more automated machinery, and the subsequent period, in which declining numbers of steelworkers have been combined with more automated machinery, is very clear.

Graph 1.3 Stelco Production Data, 1911–2003

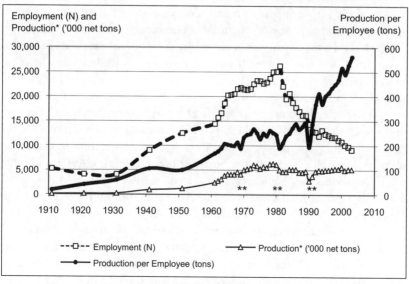

* Includes semi-finished steel and/or raw steel processed including purchases.
** Strikes occurred in 1969, 1981 and 1990.
Sources: Kilborn (1960) 1911 to 1951; Stelco Annual Reports 1960 to 2003

As Graph 1.3 indicates, Stelco's post-war history of continual growth of capital, steel production and employment came to an abrupt end during 1981. In that year, the beginning of a recession softened domestic demand for steel at the same time as Stelco's markets were being seriously threatened, especially by underpriced European and low-cost Third World steel imports. Stelco had just opened the state-of-the-art Lake Erie Works — the first "greenfield" integrated steel mill built in North America since the 1950s — which had been in process for more than a decade at a cost of over $800 million (Pegden 1980). Prior to 1981, Hilton Works was widely regarded as one of the most profitable and efficient integrated steel mills in North America. It produced 90 percent of Stelco's raw steel and was also the company's major finishing plant while employing less than 60 percent of the workforce.[21] But, in this situation of declining demand and burgeoning capacity, Stelco had to negotiate a new collective agreement with workers who had seen the company garner record profits during the period of the previous three-year contract.

The struggles of workers at Hilton Works to form a union, culminating in a historic strike in the fall of 1946, had been of pivotal importance in the consolidation of industrial unionism in Canada (Heron 1988; USWA 1005 1996: 49–51; Morton 1984: 191–3). The Steel Workers Organizing Committee (SWOC) and its successor, the United Steelworkers of America (USWA), mobilized previously fragmented and divided trades and production workers into a unitary organization that strongly contested Stelco's traditional labour policy of "firm but benevolent paternalism" (Kilbourn 1960: 153). Paternalism was replaced by a legal contract that conceded managerial prerogative over the organization of work but also answered union demands for security through the right to unionize and automatic dues check-off, standardized wage rates and job classifications, formal work rules concerning hours of work and health and safety criteria, and seniority and grievance rights (Kruger 1959). This contract became a prototype for post-war employer-employee relations and labour legislation in Canadian industry generally. Through the post-war boom period, USWA Local 1005 at Hilton Works was the largest union local in the country and a national leader in winning better wages and working conditions for workers. Hilton Works was a classic case of a capital-labour accord — workers' collective acceptance of managerial prerogative and productivity norms in exchange for increasing wages and job security. Internal political divisions had became common in Local 1005, including opposing slates for most union elections (Freeman 1982) and disaffection of the rank and file from elected leaders, as expressed most clearly in a 1966 wildcat strike (Flood 1970). But as long as both steel production and employment levels were increasing, the capital-labour accord remained secure. Relations between Stelco management and union activists over specific wage and working condition issues were often contentious and 1005 retained a reputation as one of the most militant union locals in the country. This militancy was buoyed by the fact that many steelworkers could assume they had a "job for life" if they wanted it. Prior to the 1981 strike, Stelco's Hilton Works plant had reached peaks of more than 15,000 employees (13,000 unionized and 2,000 other salaried workers) and over 4.5 million tons of shipped steel.

Under the leadership of Hilton Works Local 1005 and its president, Cec Taylor, the USWA union in 1981 struck Stelco for 125 days — the longest shutdown in Stelco's history — and eventually won a settlement in excess of 50 percent over three years (see Kervin, Gunderson and Reid 1984). This strike was centred on 1005's wage demands for a fair share of Stelco's increased profits since the 1978 collective agreement versus Stelco's anticipation of increasing competition and declining profits in the overcapacity global steel market. As Table 1.1 indicates, the 1981 strike marked the beginning of a precipitous decline from prior profit levels. This moment marked the beginning of an active search by Stelco management for different means of conducting industrial relations and regaining sustained profitability.[22] While the Hamilton steel industry had endured downturns in the past, these employment decreases were much more persistent and deeper and, in light of the even more drastic cuts experienced by most other OECD countries (Keeling 1988; Auer 1991), there were no signs that steel jobs were ever coming back. In the post-strike recessionary climate and with high wage commitments, new strategies for restoring profitability became imperative at Stelco and at Hilton Works in particular.

The rest of this chapter focuses on the restructuring efforts at Stelco and especially those associated with employment reductions at Stelco's flagship Hilton Works plant, in terms of both the local management strategies and the experiences of the unionized workforce.[23]

Restructuring the Labour Force

In the wake of the 1981 strike and the following economic recession, Stelco responded by searching for a new corporate form. It briefly reorganized itself into two companies — Stelco Steel and Stelco Enterprises — under a holding company, called itself "a materials business" and attempted to diversify beyond the steel industry (Stelco Annual Report 1987). But by the recession of the early 1990s, Stelco had decided to divest non-steel business interests and devote itself exclusively to producing "quality steel with quality people." Stelco returned its head office from Toronto to Hamilton, the "heart of the company" (Davie 1990a). Hilton Works and Stelco's other wholly owned components became stand-alone "profit centres," following the model of semi-autonomous business units pioneered by General Motors generations earlier (see Chandler 1977). In short, after the 1981 strike Stelco transformed its marketing strategy

> from being a complacent Canadian market leader to a leaner, more strategic, niche player in the North American marketplace… from Canada's one-stop steelmaker, providing any and all steel products, to being a market-driven supplier of high quality, high value-added specialty steel products. (Verma, Frost and Warrian 1995: 21–22)

By late 1984, Stelco had committed itself to the upgrading of Hilton Works to the extent of mortgaging its new Lake Erie Works continuous casting equipment in order to raise some of the cash for a $270 million installation of continuous casters at Hilton in 1987 (Mitchell 1984b).[24] Other major capital investments at Hilton involved a $100 million revamp of #1 bar mill in 1986, installation of a $172 million galvanizing "Z-Line" in 1991 and a pulverized coal injection facility in 1995, as well as various other technical improvements in operating efficiencies, computerization and waste management (see Stelco annual reports from 1985 to 1996 and Verma, Frost and Warrian 1995). Most of these improvements have been primarily to aid production of high-quality automotive speciality steels. During the 1990s, Stelco also tried to increase the efficiency of its Hilton Works facilities by reducing the great diversity of its product lines and lengthening its production runs of high value products such as galvanized steel.

Most of these new installations were joint ventures with Japanese steel interests.[25] In fact, in 1989, Stelco Steel president Fred Telmer made what amounted to a public plea for foreign takeover (Hallman 1989). Japanese steel companies demurred from full buyouts at Hilton Works and elsewhere in North America, in view of continuing market overcapacity, potential xenophobic backlash or "investment friction," and an array of "brownfield" barriers to leaner production systems — including outmoded plant facilities, large capital debts and pension liabilities, and a strong unionized workforce.[26] Consequently, in order to afford these ventures, Stelco had to close older facilities and suspend dividend payments from 1991 to 1994.

In the post-strike context of 1982, however, it was Hilton workers who would bear the immediate brunt of Stelco management's priorities "to regain market share lost during the strike, improve cost competitiveness, and restore profit and working capital positions to allow for planned expansion" (Gordon 1982: 3). The main strategies used were downsizing the core of steelworkers through layoffs of younger workers and early retirement of older ones coupled with selective use of a reserve labour force and, second, widespread reorganizing of the remaining jobs within the plant.

Downsizing the Core Steel Labour Force

The first major consequence of the 1981 strike and ensuing recession at Stelco was an unprecedented massive reduction of the labour force. As summarized in Graph 1.4, about 5,000 Local 1005 members, or 40 percent of the hourly rated workforce, were laid off in the two years following the strike. Layoffs came in several stages, culminating in a two-week shutdown of the plant in December 1982. The end of the recession in 1984 meant only a temporary reversal of long-term cutbacks in employment. More gradual reductions continued until the 1990 strike. A market downturn after this strike led to larger layoffs. By 1993, Local 1005 had lost over 60 percent of the members it had in 1980. During the mid-1990s, active membership remained at around 5,000 workers. Salaried employment also declined at Hilton Works but more gradually, so that the proportion of salaried employees increased from under 15 percent in the early 1980s to over 20 percent in the 1990s. Perhaps most significantly, in spite of all this downsizing, Hilton Works retained the majority of Stelco's employees throughout this period.

For Local 1005 members and their families, the massive layoffs and work restructuring efforts presented a major challenge to the coherence of aspects of working-class home and community life that had persisted in the industrial working-class city of Hamilton for over a century (Palmer 1979). The prospects of continuing to work in heavy industry, of being able to provide

Graph 1.4 Hilton Works Employment Levels, 1980–2004

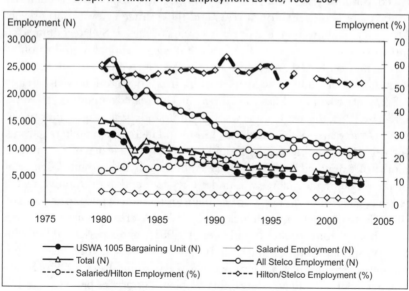

Sources: Stelco Hilton Works Personnel Reports and Stelco Annual Reports, 1980–2003

a "family wage" and of having a strong informal mutual support network of community associations based in neighbourhoods and large industrial workplaces — all traditional anchors of working-class life — were seriously undermined both for men who had worked at Stelco during most of their adult lives and the women who had married them (see Luxton and Corman 2001). Most of the men had spent most of their working lives in the Hamilton mills in secure jobs. By December 1982, nearly all steelworkers with up to five years seniority with Stelco were out on the street. In the wake of the first wave of layoffs at Hilton in early January 1982, rumours were rampant that Stelco was going to close Hilton Works and concentrate on the new Lake Erie Works. This provoked Stelco's normally reclusive chief executive, Peter Gordon, to give an extensive press interview in which he asserted that "Hilton Works, the cornerstone of the industry, will never face the wrecking ball.... Stelco planners see no end to Hilton's future. An updated plant there can continue in operation forever" (quoted in Mitchell and Wickers 1982: 19). He added that he anticipated little long-term change in the size of the Hilton workforce aside from some "gradual shrinkage" resulting from modernization. These assurances were of little solace to the thousands of Hilton workers laid off as the recession deepened and continued on layoff after it ended.

The Aging Core

In 1981, prior to the strike, Hilton Works had a generally stable and experienced workforce. As indicated in Graphs 1.5a and 1.5b, the average seniority in the plant was over thirteen years and the average age was thirty-seven. Over 40 percent were under thirty-five years of age, as Stelco continued to attract young workers who would ensure the generational reproduction of this workforce. Less than 40 percent were over forty-five years of age. The mass layoffs of younger workers starting in 1981 were followed by early retirement provisions. These measures quickly created a middle-aged workforce; by 1989, the average age was forty-four and the average seniority was twenty-one years. With virtually no hiring and increasing numbers retiring, the workforce continued to age rapidly, with an average age of fifty and seniority of twenty-eight years by 2003. At that point, only around 10 percent of the remaining workforce was under forty-five, and most of the rest were either eligible for or closing in on eligibility for retirement under provisions of the collective agreement with Stelco. The Hilton Works unionized workforce was about a third the size it had been in 1981, very experienced but with little prospect for reproducing itself. In spite of expressions of concern from union leaders and their publications (e.g., Livingstone 1997, 1999b), Stelco management did little to address this problem during this period.

The 1980s had brought diminished opportunities to leave for other jobs and mass layoffs of those with low seniority, along with the closure of the open-hearth furnace and creation of generally cleaner and safer working conditions for those who remained in the plant. The lure of relatively high wages became even more compelling for those who remained. Up to the end of the 1970s, many people who literally could not stand the heat, the dirt and the danger, particularly in the front-end coke ovens and open-hearth blast furnaces, did leave quickly for other jobs. But the lure of high wages made such conditions tolerable for many more. As one coke oven labourer put it in 1984:

> It's the money. A lot of people go in with the impression that they are only going to work here until they get their feet on the ground, a little bit of money and then they are going to go. But once you get in and you get a taste of the money, forget it. It's almost like you can't go because the money is so good.

But with the layoffs by 1984, there were very few workers under twenty-five in the plant, and by 1996 virtually no one was under thirty. In 1984, more than 90 percent of the remaining unionized workers had spent most of their working lives at Hilton Works. By 1989, the aging almost exclusively male workforce was very settled in. By the mid-1990s, the experience profile of the average worker at Hilton Works was fairly similar to that in most other integrated steel plants in the Western world, late forties with about twenty-five years' seniority (compare Albright 1995). Early retirement inducements kept the over-fifty-five cohort at around 20 percent until the late 1990s. But by 2003, two-thirds of the dwindling workforce was between forty-five and

Graph 1.5a Total Number of Workers, Age and Seniority Profile, Hilton Works Local 1005 Labour Force, 1981–2003

Sources: Stelco Active Employee Reports, 1981–2003

fifty-four — compared to 19 percent in 1981 — and there was virtually nobody to take their places, an extreme situation which other remaining integrated plants had begun to address. Young workers were still attracted by the high wages to apply to steel mills, and some steel companies had begun to recognize the need to regenerate their aging workforces (ISTC 1992a, 1992b; Kleiman 1995). But as cutbacks continued and middle-aged steelworkers continued "hanging in there for dear life," there were no new openings at Hilton Works. A *demographic crisis point* requiring an influx of more young workers as the baby boom generation retired in unprecedented proportions was rapidly approaching.

By the 1990s, the Hilton Works labour force had been reduced to an exceptionally settled core in comparison with the general mobility of waged labour in industrial market economies. Generally, jobs in the present generation have been of much shorter duration in service sector firms. Certainly these steelworkers' employed spouses have typically found jobs of much shorter tenure. The 1984 steelworker families survey found that steelworkers' employed spouses had been in their current jobs for an average of three years, a small fraction of the time their husbands had been at Hilton. Steelworkers' wives' jobs were generally low paid and frequently part-time or temporary service sector jobs with few benefits (see Luxton and Corman 2001). The central point here is that the general lack of high wages and secure jobs for either steelworkers or their wives anywhere else only served to accentuate the continuing lure of Stelco for those steelworkers who could "hang in."

Graph 1.5b Age Profile, Hilton Works Local 1005 Labour Force, 1981–2003

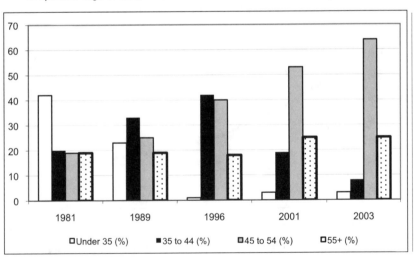

Sources: Stelco Active Employee Reports, 1981–2003

Increasing Use of Contingent Labour

The level of required employees in steel production fluctuates quite widely with business cycles. Beyond permanent hiring and layoffs, the main means steel companies have used to address these fluctuations have been layoff-recall systems, shift scheduling and overtime, and subcontracting. The development of a smaller, more contingent labour force using these strategies was a central feature of "downsizing" Hilton Works from the early 1980s on. For many years the lure of high wages and good benefit plans in large employment sites allowed steel companies to easily recruit and quickly train young workers, lay them off in downturns and expect that many of them would continue to respond to recall notices in upturns. The layoff-recall process was certainly used extensively at Hilton Works after the mass layoffs of 1981–83 (see Corman, Luxton, Livingstone and Seccombe 1993). These layoffs created a reserve pool of thousands of younger workers, many with substantial seniority and non-transferable steelmaking skills, in a labour market with few comparable employment opportunities. Stelco's vague promises of re-employment, in addition to their vested seniority, industry-specific skills and the lure of high wages, kept many of these workers waiting for permanent recall to Hilton long after there was any real likelihood. For years, hundreds of these former Hilton workers continued to subsist on a combination of summer relief or market upturn recalls, unemployment benefits and interim jobs (Luxton and Corman 2001). The temporary recalls which Stelco began in early 1983 did give many laid-off workers some hope that, with steel market upturns and older workers' retirements, they could return to well-paid, secure jobs. Even those with low seniority often continued to hope. As one of the few women steelworkers hired shortly before the 1981 strike expressed it in 1984:

> If I were fortunate to gain some seniority I don't know if I would want to give it up.... It would be a hard thing to do. Once you have worked at Stelco it's hard to work elsewhere.

But greater seniority actually offered little security to laid-off workers. A male labourer summed up the 1984 situation well:

> Anybody with less than ten years' seniority is gone if there is a cutback. You know, to me it's almost like working seasonal work at Stelco. You are there for a couple of months, and then when winter comes and things slow down, you are out.

Over the following decade, as Hilton downsizing continued and the slim chances of permanent recall became more evident, the reserve labour pool shrank accordingly. But the continuing lure of Stelco was confirmed by the fact that hundreds of those who were laid off initially in the early 1980s continued to accept recalls and further layoffs right up to the mid-1990s and beyond. In 1996, numerous Stelco workers had been on cyclical layoff for over fifteen years (Prokaska 1996d: B1). A finishing mill labourer who hung in for that long described the layoff-recall system and his frustrations about his work status in 1994:

> You get laid off a lot now over what I did ten years ago. Since the strike in [August to November] 1990 we never got recalled... until May of '91. You work twenty weeks, you get laid off. April, the following year, you get called back. You work twenty weeks, you get laid off. Now, I just got recalled again. In October I'm out again. So for four years they have just been playing stupid games with you. You know, it makes it hard... there's no future left in the job. But where do you go? If they lay me off this time I'm just going to go back for retraining somewhere.... I've got no choice. Like I've worked at Stelco fifteen years, and they just sent me a thing last week for my pension. I've only got eleven years service, because you lose every time that they lay you off.... Even though I have a start date in the 1970s, they don't recognize the start date, only company time. That's where they get you, you know, so what can you do?

Shift scheduling has been a common means of adjusting the number of hours that steelworkers get in relation to shorter term variations in required levels of steel output. Integrated steel mills require continuous operation of primary steelmaking coke ovens and blast furnaces, hence continuous presence of some workers. Many production workers and some service maintenance staff are required to work shifts beyond normal daytime hours. Traditionally, most steelworkers have worked alternating shifts and most shift schedules have included night hours. But the number of "turns" will vary and so will the number of workers needed both in primary steel and finishing mill activities. In downturns, the number of shifts worked may be reduced considerably. In upturns, shifts may be extended by use of overtime hours rather than hiring more workers. Since 1981, Stelco has relied heavily on longer shift schedules and greater overtime.

In 1984, about three-quarters of Hilton's unionized workforce were on shift work, the vast majority of these on three alternating morning, after-noon and night shifts.[27] Only a quarter of 1005 workers were on regular day shifts. With the massive downsizing since the 1981 strike, about a third of the remaining Hilton workers saw their work schedules change. But few of the remaining workers crossed the regular days/night shift divide in this period. Few Hilton workers had much good to say about shift work. A skilled trades worker who endured alternating shifts for well over a decade but left Stelco in the mid-1980s because of an injury recalled in 1994:

> I really, really hated shift work... I dreaded it. I couldn't eat properly on night shift; I couldn't sleep on afternoons. I just hated it. I hated it right from day one.... [Night shift] was just a nightmare for me. No matter how

much sleep I had… I'd still be tired because something in my body said, "It's night time. It's dark. You should be sleeping. What are you doing up?" The afternoon shifts, as far as social life goes, it's just disastrous. Like, that whole week everybody else is working, you're home. Then, as soon as everybody starts coming home, you gotta go to work. And by the time you get off work, everybody else is going to bed. And then having to work weekends, too. Like, Stelco was terrible. I've never seen a place that was worse for no weekends…. Like there is no way anybody could'a thought of a worse schedule for family life, for a social life for a young guy, there's no way anybody could'a thought of a worse schedule than that…. It was terrible.

In light of such disruptions, only a minority of Hilton workers (33 percent) expressed a preference in 1984 for the established pattern of five eight-hour shifts a week. Most workers wanted to move to a smaller number of longer shifts. A small majority (51 percent) wanted ten-hour shifts while only 16 percent preferred twelve-hour shifts (Livingstone 1996). Stelco has since opted to move to twelve-hour shifts, because they permit simpler staffing of continuous twenty-four-hour production with fewer workers. Since 1993, adoption of twelve-hour shifts has been subject to approval by 70 percent of the employees in designated departments. The best available estimates suggest that between 25 and 35 percent of the 1005 membership were working twelve-hour shifts in 1996 and the proportion increased to around 60 percent in 2003. Hilton Works' twelve-hour schedules involve a few days on a 8 a.m. to 8 p.m. shift interspersed with a few days on a 8 p.m. to 8 a.m. shift and a few days off. The introduction of twelve-hour shift schedules gave Hilton workers more consecutive time off, especially on weekends. But it also increased the proportion who had to work night shift. For steelworkers and their households, the new shift schedules often further complicated the weekly rhythms of life and did little to diminish the pull of shift work on other spheres of life, particularly its disruptive effects on household relations. As an industrial mechanic and his wife stated in 1994:

On day shift, we get up around quarter to six and I try to do some chores outside before I go to work. It's the only way to keep up because I'm working twelve-hour shifts. By the time you get home in the evening and have your supper with the family and that, it's too late to do anything, you know? You pretty well just want to flop down on the couch. You're tired. You don't feel like doing any more work. Sometimes you're forced to… especially in the spring, you know the grass is growing and you've got to cut it. In the summer, I can take advantage of the leisure time…. But twelve-hour shifts are not the greatest for social life. Put it this way, I don't have many friends because of that…. I'm off every other weekend; I'm working every other weekend. One week, the nights; one week, the days. And there's a lot of stress when I'm on nights around here, too. Like [my wife] is stressed out by the time I'm finished my stint of nights and she tries to keep [the children] quiet and she can feel that, you know?

[*Spouse:*] There's just a different feeling in the house when he's on nights. Just try and be careful. His tolerance is low, understandably, but it's just that it's low, you know. So stuff that he can normally take, he can't take it — not in night shift.

Everybody who spoke about their shift work talked mainly about night shift because it was so disruptive to the normal rhythms of daily life. The disruptions were growing as higher proportions of male Hilton workers worked some night shifts and their spouses increasingly took on paid work after the 1981 strike. Steelworkers' shift work is virtually guaranteed to diminish the quality of household life; juggling such shift work, a partner's job and other household duties creates immense strains (see Luxton and Corman 2001).

Workers at Hilton Works received fairly short notice of their upcoming work schedules. Hilton's alternating shift workers also tended to get less notice of their upcoming work schedules than their workmates with regular day hours. In 1984, over two-thirds of the workers on regular days knew their schedules at least a month in advance. But over half of alternating shift workers were receiving notice of less than a month about their shift schedules and more than a third knew less than a week ahead. After the 1981 strike, there was also a trend to less advanced notice for all steelworkers, regardless of seniority; over a quarter of steelworkers received less notice in 1984 than they got in 1981, while only about 5 percent received more notice of when they had to work (Livingstone 1996). This reduced work notice was reflective of both the downturn in the steel industry, with consequent fluctuations in the number of production runs in the mills, and the reduced workforce, which led to the bumping of some senior workers from regular days back to shift work. As a skilled worker with over a decade in the plant put it:

They have 'til 2:00 Thursday to change what you are doing three days later, and come summertime they quite often do. They have to do that for scheduling purposes. I'm not blaming them but a lot of times, especially in the nicer weather, you can't plan that far ahead because your schedule changes. (1984)

It is clear that by the mid-1980s shift work was putting heavy and increasing strains on the everyday lives of this dwindling core of steelworkers and their households. By the mid-1990s, shift work had generally become much more common in the Canadian labour force and the proportion of married women in paid jobs had increased further (Statistics Canada 2006). The "long arm of the job" (Meissner 1971) was placing immense strains on steelworker families and on many other households.

For shorter term upturns in operating divisions and major service project deadlines as well as to deal with absenteeism, Stelco became increasingly reliant after 1981 on core workers working overtime. Stelco's official position was that it only asked for voluntary overtime for rush orders and to fill in for missing co-workers. But with reduced regular workforces and budget constraints on hiring any extra workers with full benefits packages, plant-level superintendents were left with little choice but to entice and intimidate many of these workers into doing excessive overtime. Available data suggest considerable growth of overtime during the mid-1980s (Estock 1987a). In this period, those who chose to work overtime often faced the wrath of those colleagues having greater sympathy for the large number of laid-off steelworkers who still had recall rights. As a front-end production worker declared:

> As far as I'm concerned, guys that work overtime should be fined through the union. I disagree with it altogether. I had opportunities to work overtime, but I wouldn't because there are guys out on the street. I'm working but they're not and they're in the same boat as I am. There are senior guys who should be retired, working overtime like crazy. I don't buy that. I have seen fights start over it, too. We had a guy work twenty-four hours straight the other day. Sick. (1984)

Internal company documents leaked to the media in 1987 indicate that the amount of overtime became so excessive that company officials had cautioned superintendents about "breaking the law" and instructed them to reduce overtime (Hallman 1987). Nevertheless, the practice continued and there have been persistent accusations of workers regularly employed for over sixty hours a week.[28] As laid-off workers' recall rights expired, the remaining core workforce became more inclined to accept overtime to enhance their own security and earnings. As the same production worker said a decade later:

> Overtime is still running rampant in our department. It's crazy. But now I've finally started working it, after they called everybody [with recall rights] back. Other than that, I was dead set against it. Being younger with a lower wage, people looked at me and said, "What, are you nuts?" I just totally disagree because of, you know, the union. Guys were laid off, why should I be doing their jobs? It's just totally, it's outrageous actually. I know guys who are doing seventy hours in one pay. The union can't control it. Now the general attitude is if I don't do it, then somebody else is going to do it anyways. So why not grab it while I can?

This pattern — of a continuing core group of employees working longer and longer hours for higher wages, while growing numbers of people become reliant on temporary work or are chronically unemployed and increasingly impoverished — became common in the steel industry and generally across many advanced market economies in the latter part of the twentieth century (Schor 1991; Advisory Group on Working Time and the Distribution of Work 1994).

Closely related to the layoff-callback system and to the increasing incidence of longer, more varied shifts with overtime has been growing use of subcontractors. There was much celebration in the latter part of the twentieth century of the merits of leaner production systems, especially the "Japanese model," which offered lifetime security to a committed core workforce (e.g., Womack, Dabiel and Roos 1990). The underside of this labour system was typically ignored. This purportedly more efficient production model remained dependent on a contingent labour force available for occasional hire in non-routine jobs and for short-term regular hire during market upturns, that is, a highly flexible industrial reserve army of labour. The Japanese auto industry, for example, continued to rely on a wide array of poorly paid temporary workers, notably in its non-unionized supply industries (Cusumano 1985). The mass layoffs during the 1982–83 recession in Hamilton created an unprecedented pool of experienced unemployed steelworkers. Eventually, most of the early layoffs lost their eligibility for recall to Stelco. While there were fewer layoffs later in the decade, the early 1990s recession witnessed a re-intensification of the same process, involving a reserve pool of steelworkers with much greater seniority.[29] Consequently, often highly skilled people could be hired by non-unionized service contractors at a fraction of the wage they had earned from Stelco. In spite of tighter bargaining agreement language on the issue, such contractors continued to be used extensively by the company in many subsequent modernization projects as well as standard plant maintenance work which 1005 members were quite capable of performing (see Contracting Out Committee 1987).

In sum, through mass layoffs and early retirements, Stelco fundamentally recast the size and age structure of its core Hilton workforce between 1981 and 2003. At the same time, the company made extensive use of the layoff-callback system, longer, more varied shift schedules and overtime, as well growing reliance on subcontractors using former core workers without recall rights. Stelco fashioned a much more flexible labour force at Hilton Works by combining this contingent reserve with the dwindling aging core.

Job Restructuring

In the context of the massive downsizing and growing use of contingent workers, the dwindling core of aging 1005 members remaining in Hilton Works were also subject to substantial reshaping of their jobs. This involved the reorganization of the divisional and departmental structure of the plant, the amalgamation of previously separate jobs and increasing workloads with more apparent responsibility.

Departmental and Divisional Changes

The job structure of integrated steel plants has typically included a tripartite division between 1) production work in front-end units, which prepare the ingredients and make molten steel; 2) finishing mills, which roll and treat the steel into specific forms; and 3) service units, which are required to maintain, repair and modify the plant. There were many changes in the specific departmental units to which Hilton Works workers were assigned in the decade after the 1981 strike, as well as some variations in the overarching formal divisional structure. Numerous plant departments were closed and some others created. The last open-hearth steelmaking furnace was replaced in the mid-1980s by upgraded basic oxygen furnaces and new continuous casters. The functions of several old rod and bar finishing mills were taken over by new or revamped mills linked to the new casters. A large number of existing departments were amalgamated, as reflected in the 1987 contract. Hilton Work's traditional four-division structure (I Steelmaking; II Hot Rolling Mills; III Cold Mills; IV Maintenance and Services) was effectively replaced by six divisions in 1984 (I Ironmaking; II Steelmaking; III Plate and Strip; IV Cold Rolling and Coating; V Rod and Bar; VI Maintenance and Services), even though this new divisional structure was not officially recognized until the 1987 contract (interview with USWA Local 1005 officials, December 3, 1984). In the aftermath of the 1981 strike, restricted departmental seniority criteria were superseded by more flexible plant-wide seniority for job openings that were posted more widely in an entire division. With the massive cutbacks starting in 1982, a number of workers with relatively high company seniority in older departments were either "bumped" out of their departments into other jobs for which they were qualified or were out on the street, while some with less seniority in newer departments remained where they were. In 1983, at least 10 percent of the active workforce — many of whom were probably bumped from the older hot finishing mills being closed or reduced to skeletal crews with the infusion of Lake Erie caster steel — had this highly uncertain status.[30] The issue of bumped workers was a matter of persistent dispute with Stelco and dissension within Local 1005 up to 1987 (see Corman 1990: 93–4). Subsequent divisional reorganizations occurred, but they continued to recognize the basic tripartite division between front-end primary steelmaking, the finishing mills and the service and maintenance functions. Graphs 6a and 6b summarize the basic distribution of workers between these three functions during the 1972–2003 period.

As Graphs 6a and 6b show, during the turmoil of the 1981–83 period, the cuts were deeper in both absolute and relative terms in the finishing mills — which lost about half of their workers — than in the iron and steelmaking division — which continued to rely on outmoded coke ovens while suffering losses of under 15 percent of their 1981 workforce. Maintenance and

Graph 1.6a Employment by Division (N), Hilton Works, 1972–2003

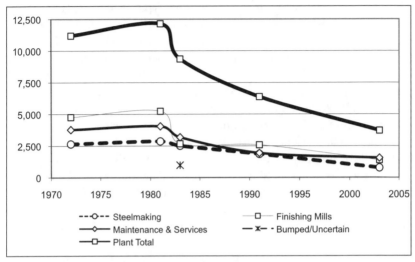

Source: USWA Local 1005 Membership Records

Graph 1.6b: Employment by Division (%), Hilton Works, 1972–2003

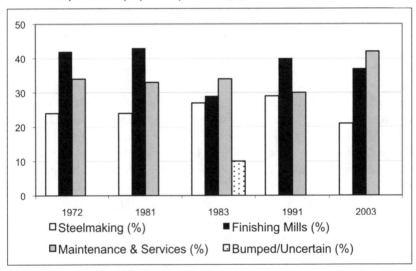

Source: USWA Local 1005 Membership Records

services division numbers were reduced by about a quarter. As downsizing continued over the 1983–2003 period, reductions in steelmaking increased so that by 2003 both steelmaking and finishing mills had lost about 70 percent of their 1981 numbers. Maintenance and services cutbacks declined less proportionately, so that after constituting about a third of the total plant employees through the 1980s, they made up around 40 percent of remaining 1005 workers in 2003. Front-end and finishing-mill production workers were diminishing both in absolute numbers and as a proportion of the Hilton Works labour force.

Job Amalgamation

Stelco management continued to close departments, reorganize divisions and seek greater flexibility to move 1005 members between them throughout the 1981–2003 period. In addition, concerted efforts were made to combine more tasks into specific jobs through amalgamation of previously separate production jobs, integrating production and maintenance work and multi-crafting of trades workers. This was a very complex process that often involved renegotiation with Local 1005 of job descriptions within the terms of the Co-operative Wage Study (CWS).

In the 1940s, steel management consultants developed the CWS to enable more effective linking of job categories and wage levels. In the early 1950s, the unionized North American steel industry ratified the CWS — one of the most elaborate specific job classification systems in the world.[31] Each type of job was supposed to be classified by the company and approved by a union committee. The ratings involved twelve different factors, including required mental and manual skills, training and experience, mental and manual effort, hazardous working conditions and especially extent of responsibility for materials, tools, operations and other workers' safety. This system was based on a sharp division between mental and manual work, job-specificity of skills and hierarchical job ladders with associated wage incentives and limited points of entry. In contrast to the nineteenth-century steel industry labour system, which was controlled by skilled trades workers, the modern system formalized in the CWS was controlled by steel employers (for a historical comparison, see Elbaum 1984: 71–107). It did, however, encourage steelworkers to develop a sense of individual "job ownership."[32] In the mid-1950s, the CWS at Hilton Works identified about 2,700 job descriptions for around 10,000 workers; by 1984, this had been reduced to around 1,200 descriptions for a comparable number of workers.[33] This downward trend continued to the point of a few dozen general job descriptions by 2003. From the 1960s, employers found the CWS to be increasingly unwieldy in relation to workplace restructuring initiatives and renegotiation of the wage-productivity deal, while workers tried to use CWS appeal mechanisms as a defence against destruction of their jobs (see, e.g., Betheil 1978). Consequently, no revision of the CWS manual was approved after 1973, in spite of the development by the USWA of a simpler, computerized job evaluation system which could also respond easily to government pay equity requirements (USWA 1992). As Petersen and Storey concluded in their study of technological change and job reclassification at Hilton Works in the 1981–86 period, "the Co-operative

Wage System has proven to be too antiquated and too inflexible to solve the problem. The result has been that job changes are negotiated piecemeal and that the resulting wage structure reflects the relative power of departments and stewards rather than the value of the jobs" (1986: 43).

Theoretically, the highest CWS job class level is 43, but such high ratings have been extremely rare throughout the steel industry. The highest class at Hilton has been 28. The most extensive North American survey found an increase of average job class from 8.5 to 10 between 1960 and 1977 (Stieber 1980). Changes in the average job class at Hilton Works between 1981 and 2003 are summarized in Table 1.2. From an average job class of 10 in 1981, there was a gradual increase to 15 in 1994 and a further increase to 17.5 by 2003. This upward trend is consistent with both the massive layoffs of junior production workers in 1981–83 and the job amalgamations that increasingly required crossover work between previously approved job classes.

The basic results of this amalgamation process have been a very significant reduction of both the types and number of jobs as well as the closer integration of production and maintenance work throughout the plant. Traditionally, maintenance tasks had relied heavily on "bull gangs" of trades workers from a separate service division. In the 1990s, many maintenance workers were reassigned from the services division to the operating divisions. In late 1992, Hilton Works management, provoked by the company's immediate financial crisis to downsize quickly, made a concerted effort to create "maintenance-operator" jobs. This entailed moving skilled trades workers from the services division into production jobs where they were expected to both operate machinery and repair it.

The leading example was the less-efficient front end, particularly the outmoded coke ovens. In the coke ovens, there were ninety-five job descriptions in 1985; this number was considerably reduced by the mid-1990s. In late 1992, the coke ovens were staffed by 308 operating employees and seventy assigned maintenance workers as well as sixty-three trades people from the

Table 1.2 Average Job Class at Hilton Works 1981–2003

Year	Average Job Class
1981	10
1984	11
1987	12
1990	12
1994	15
2003	17.5

Sources: Frost and Verma (1997) and later Stelco–USWA collective agreements

services division. By early 1993, Stelco management had reduced the coke ovens workforce to 215 maintenance operators (Frost 2000). These changes were accepted by the union president, John Martin, after significant wage increases and job security were ensured for those involved.[34] There was a backlash both from bumped coke oven operators with higher seniority and from the skilled trades workers, who found the highly supervised coke oven production work relatively unpleasant, unchallenging and physically constraining and who therefore tried to transfer out of the coke ovens as soon as they could. As a result of this backlash, union leaders began to advocate the notion of "operator-maintenance," in which production workers would be given additional training in basic maintenance to assist in minor equipment repairs and which would enable the maintenance operators to return to pure crafts positions while remaining in the operating divisions. Management agreed to this adjustment by mid–1997. But, as Terry Weaymouth, a 1005 official, stated: "People in the coke ovens are livid — still. There are [hundreds of] people out there who are really pissed" (quoted in Frost 2000: 56).

More generally, after the 1981 strike, Stelco managers proved ineffective at negotiating changes of traditional shop floor rules and job classifications. Perhaps most notably, Hilton Works was the last major holdout against multi-crafting in North America. The trades-dominated executive of Local 1005 was very animated in its opposition to this issue. As Dennis O'Brien, finishing division grievance chairperson, put it in one of the many critiques of multi-crafting to appear in 1005's monthly magazine, *Steel Shots*, during the 1980s:

> This deskilling strategy by the company is simple; increase the number of tasks a tradesman is expected to do, so it is impossible to acquire any depth of skill, create a "jack of all trades, master of none," broaden the scope of the worker's tasks and deskill his trade.... They are not interested in a worker with a complete understanding of the whole job, they want somebody who knows what relay to push, or hit a pressure switch to by-pass, even if he doesn't know why. Just get it working.... Finally, as more and more automation increases in the plants, the skilled trade work decreases, the conditions set today will be the mass conditions of tomorrow. The company clearly wants the skilled jobs to become as much like production jobs as possible with all the workers as inter-changeable as possible. In our industry, one of the main hopes for a young worker for job security and a decent work life is to get into a skilled trade. Every skilled trade job lost is one less opportunity for a quality job. (1989: 20–21)

Nevertheless, there was significant general growth of the integration of maintenance work within operating divisions. By 1989, assigned maintenance workers had increased to 20 percent of the workforce regularly working within the Hilton steelmaking and finishing plant divisions. By 2003, this figure had increased to over 30 percent (as estimated from USWA Local 1005 membership records). Either through creation of combined operator-maintenance jobs or closer embedding of trades workers within specific production areas, long-established distinctions between production and trades occupations began to dissolve.

The occupational structure of regular employees in the plant therefore also changed significantly. The main changes have been decreases in the number of production jobs requiring heavy physical labour and increases in the proportions of managerial, technical and trades employees. These shifts have been consistent with general trends in the international and Canadian steel industries (ISTC 1992a, 1992b; Ahlburg et al. 1987; Warrian 1989, CSTEC 2005). As Graphs 1.3 and 1.4 indicated, Stelco laid off a relatively small number of salaried employees after the 1981 strike, so that by the mid-1990s their proportion had increased to over 20 percent of total Hilton employment. Second, as Graph 1.4 suggests, the proportion of 1005 members in skilled trades was around 30 percent in the early 1980s. This figure increased to close to 40 percent by 2003. Increases in the proportion of non-production employees in general and maintenance workers in particular have been substantial in the North American steel industry since the late 1970s (Ahlburg et al. 1987: 231, Table 1). These proportions continued to grow into the new century (O'Grady and Warrian 2010).

Heavier Workloads, More Autonomy
The organizational and job restructuring that began seriously in 1982 at Hilton Works was aimed at expanding remaining workers' number of tasks and span of responsibility. For workers, job amalgamation translated into higher job classes with higher base wage rates as well as workload intensification. Hilton workers quickly understood the implications of the basic job structure changes that were first attempted by Stelco managers in the early 1980s. According to a 1984 survey (Corman, Luxton, Livingstone and Seccombe 1993), workers' perceptions of the changes concerning their workloads about three years after the end of the 1981 strike were predominantly in the direction of increased intensity and greater use of discretionary judgment in their jobs. Nearly half thought their workloads were heavier while less than 10 percent felt they were lighter. More than half saw no change in their use of judgment, but about a third said they were exercising more independent judgment — a tendency that was strongest among production workers. Overall, among workers who perceived heavier workloads, those who said they were exercising more independent judgment outnumbered those who felt they had less discretion by about eight to one. These tendencies are consistent with the team-oriented, leaner

production system model that Stelco had just begun to try to introduce to Hilton steelworkers.

Many survey respondents, particularly machine operators, talked extensively about both heavier workloads and an expanded range of task responsibility. In 1984, a crane operator in yard services described the changes in his area:

> There has been quite a bit of speed-up. The job now is more complicated. You haven't got enough eyes in your head to be looking so you really have to be aware of what's around you. You don't let your guard down anytime, because if you do, something will happen. Sometimes it will get strenuous.... The jobs is the same but the ways of doing it have changed. But it's more interesting now because now you are into something that, listen, you help fix this or you help put this back together.... I can see what the company is doing. They are trying to modernize the plant and they are going to run it on less people.... They pick away here and they pick away there.

Similarly, in the same year, a finishing mill press operator related the following:

> What the company is doing is combining jobs to reduce the number of people they need to operate. On this facility, they've actually combined three jobs into one... It used to be we each had a job to do. And you did that job. And somebody else had another job.... Then they started reducing the number of people operating the machines. They reduced the number of turns and what not.... But it's just to the point where you go all over the place. I understand you have to be flexible, you have to co-operate. But a person has to mentally prepare himself to go in there and do a good job and not get hurt. Instead, you're thinking of the next thing that's gonna happen. And I find it very difficult.

Hilton workers had developed a clear general sense of the job restructuring aspects of Stelco's agenda by early 1984. The major changes in the job structure of Hilton Works between 1981 and 2003 were the amalgamation of production jobs, the creation of multi-crafting among trades workers and the combination of production and maintenance functions in many jobs. Production job amalgamations generally involved a wider range of monitoring tasks and basic maintenance work for semi-skilled machine operators. Multi-crafting meant the formation of several generalist trade designations (industrial mechanic, welder fabricator and several general technician job categories) from the many traditionally certified trades, and the permanent assignment of many trades workers with multiple basic certifications to production departments where they are constantly involved in checking and repairing the more continuous and interdependent new steelmaking equipment. The crossovers between production and trades tasks as well as the intensification and expanded responsibility of individual jobs increased.

Production workers tended to stress the intensification and increased responsibility in the work as the central changes in their jobs. The following line worker's comments in 1994 were typical:

> The new line is a lot faster, it takes only a quarter of the time it used to and the time just flies by. We're working with computers now.... The responsibility actually has increased. Pay hasn't unfortunately. They seem to be putting more and more on us but not giving us an increase of money to compensate for the responsibility. At one time in my department we had over 200 people and now we're lucky if we've got 100.

Another production worker, in 1994 on the state-of-the-art Z-Line, said:

> I've moved from one line to a different line but it's the same thing. But they've amalgamated a lot of the jobs. They've cut the workforce at least in half but we still make the same product, maybe even more of the product. I'm more busy now but now we're doing it through the computer terminal. Like every job station's got its own terminal.... I guess there's more responsibility on most of the jobs because there's added work to them, so you do have more responsibility.

Crossover maintenance work remained a relatively small part of most production workers' jobs. But they were well aware of the trend. The 1993 contract item on the joint management-union work restructuring committee specified the development of the "operator-maintenance" job description, with line workers taking on more minor maintenance work. As a finishing mill operator described the job structure at Hilton Works in the mid-1990s:

> The trades people are starting to get into production. They're trying to make everybody more knowledgeable in that area anyways. That's why they want to push for us operating maintenance. They want us to fix our own machinery because they're not going to hire anybody. So they'll have to utilize the people we have to the best of our abilities.

Trades workers have tended to express more concern with job amalgamation per se, both in terms of multi-crafting and crossover into production work. A former millwright who became an industrial mechanic in a finishing mill described the main changes as follows:

> They've taken a blend of millwrights, pipefitters and machinists and they've kind of amalgamated our jobs together, multi-crafting.... Basically it's the same job except I'm working to finer tolerances. Like, the job I was on ten years ago was a lot more physical. Now it's a lot more mental and it's got a lot more finesse in it. The computers changed it a lot.... In 1990, after the contract, they upgraded all the machinists, millwrights, pipefitters — like all the multi-crafting — they upgraded them from job class 16 to job class 21. (1994)

A trades worker who remained in the service department was more sensitive to the general intensification of trades work and the crossover to production work:

> There's just less guys to do the job faster. There's also more responsibility because there's less senior guys to talk to when there's a problem.... We're running with 70 percent less men and we're still putting out the same amount of product here. So you tell me that's not efficiency! Stelco has become more trades-oriented, with the trades doing more labour work too. Trades have really crossed over and are doing more labour work than the art of the trade, because they can get rid of a janitor and you can sweep your own floor. We keep seeing the shop go down and down and down and we say, "Where's the bottom?" I think they're gonna keep cutting back until they actually get in trouble. (1994)

Simultaneously with massively reducing its core labour force and fashioning a contingent reserve "army," Stelco aimed to reorganize established work units and combine the job requirements of the remaining regular unionized workers to enable the continual change of its steel production system in order to survive in an increasingly competitive global steel industry. It is clear that the jobs of the dwindling core steel labour force at Hilton Works were beginning to take on an increasingly *abstract* character — a more general worker who could adapt to many different tasks as the need arose, and whom the employer was increasingly free to eliminate. But in light of the combative history of management-labour relations at Hilton Works and the clear sense among remaining 1005 members of the stakes they were facing, getting the support of these very experienced steelworkers was not an easy task.

"New" Industrial Relations and Core Worker Responses

Throughout the post-war expansionary era, Stelco retained a conservative authoritarian management style at Hilton Works, with no formal consultation with Local 1005 over products, prices, work organization or technology. Local 1005 remained a very tough union, negotiating trend-setting wage bargains, conducting long strikes in 1969 and 1981, and generally resisting arbitrary authority through formal grievance procedures and an active oppositional shop floor culture (for detailed accounts, see Freeman 1982; Adams and Zeytinoglu 1987: 71–99; Kervin, Gunderson and Reid 1984). Elements of the pattern of management-union interaction based on high wages, job security and fixed work rules for a core workforce — now called "the old industrial relations" — clearly persisted at Hilton Works (Adams and Zeytinoglu 1987; Adams 1988). But there were substantial changes in both management and union strategies after 1981.

Management Approaches and Union Reactions

After the 1981 strike, Stelco had no choice but to commit to refining Hilton Works' operations for the immediate future. The availability of continuously cast raw steel from Lake Erie would permit the eventual shutdown of Hilton's oldest coke ovens and the more labour intensive open-hearth furnaces. But Hilton Works still had most of Stelco's efficient steelmaking capacity in its three basic oxygen furnaces, as well as the vast majority of the company's finishing capacity in its array of plating, rolling and bar mills. So, integration of the two plants made sense, particularly as Stelco had insufficient capital to build finishing mills at Lake Erie and was now locked into a USWA collective bargaining agreement there, too.

By the end of 1982, Stelco management's orientation had shifted from a long-established "expansion at all costs" to a consolidation of existing resources. As Stelco's president, John Allan, told the Conference Board of Canada on October 8 of that year:

> The downturn that afflicts Canadian industry is not a normal cyclical slump but a protracted period of subdued growth that calls for different kinds of management and planning. At Stelco, the result has been a strategy that conserves its resources, optimizes its assets and reduces costs. (Allan 1982)

The employment costs built into the 1981 agreement became a major target of this new management strategy. Stelco appealed to workers to forget the strike and "work smarter" to help the company regain lost customers. In response, Local 1005 leadership generally stressed the inadequacy of authoritarian management and the need for greater co-operation. As union president Cec Taylor declared, in anticipation of this period of subdued growth through the 1980s:

> We acknowledge the challenges presented to companies and workers alike by these economic conditions. But we are not enthusiastic about contributing our effort to Stelco's recovery and renewed profitability on the older worker-boss basis. We want the respect from the Company, both in terms of wages and on-the-job working conditions, that is due us considering our central role in the steelmaking process. We earn Stelco's profits, surely we deserve management's respect.... I hope that from this strike Stelco has learned that the heavy-handed employee relations of the past are obsolete and will no longer work effectively. (Taylor 1982: 1)

But, as mass layoffs were coupled with unilaterally imposed experiments in reduced work crew levels for increasing productivity during 1982, union leaders quickly became less conciliatory. According to Rolf Gerstenberger, then an assistant chief steward in steelmaking:

> First they try the propaganda, the line of "working together" or "putting the strike behind us and solving our common problems," etc. If that doesn't work, then they use suspensions, disciplines, firings and their daily threats. As workers we cannot agree with any of this, whether it be the carrot or the stick. By working together, the Company means that we should take pay-cuts, or some form of concessions; we should "tighten our belts;" we should do everything that they want in order that they can make maximum profit.... They will continue to make more and more demands on workers and opposing these attacks is just as difficult a struggle as the strike struggle. (Gerstenberger 1982: 12)

In early December 1982, after laying off a small number of salaried staff and freezing the pay of the rest as well as implementing some energy-saving policies and lowering dividend payments, Stelco tried to reopen the contract with USWA. This effort was sharply rejected by 1005 president Taylor (Christmas 1982). The reality was that, despite the massive layoffs, employment costs had increased from about 30 to nearly 40 percent of sales income during 1982. Second, while Hilton Works took a disproportionate share of the initial layoffs, the Local 1005 workers required to run Hilton's steelmaking and finishing facilities still constituted nearly half of Stelco's entire workforce.[35] As the first wave of mass layoffs subsided in early 1983, Stelco initiated its direct communications campaign with Hilton workers about "market realities" and the need for increasing steel quality (Christmas 1983a). Stelco persisted throughout 1983 in its efforts to open new lines of communication with workers through letters from the chair, company magazine supplements, showing of video tapes and conducting of seminars with workers, and a continuing series of dialogues with union leaders.

By early 1984, Stelco had begun to implement a major quality improvement program focused primarily on Hilton Works (Wolman 1985). This involved an extensive reorganization of management practices. Top management was streamlined and strategic business units established. The Quality and Service Committee of senior managers, trained in Edwards Deming's total quality management (TQM) approach for constant improvement in work practices,[36] was set up to monitor performance and recommend enhanced quality measures. Training of the entire management hierarchy in this quality improvement philosophy and the associated statistical process control techniques was begun. Stelco also reduced product lines at Hilton Works and initiated modest technological upgrading of Hilton's BOF furnaces and finishing mills, with the objective of more flexible specialized production. In addition, the Interactive Management Training Program (IMTP) was set up for supervisors in order to try to improve communication and co-operation between labour and management to ensure quality, and an incentives program was established to encourage workers' suggestions to improve conditions in the plant. As John Allan, Stelco's chief executive officer, summarized:

> We're slimming down. We're going to be damned efficient.... We've been a very broadly-based corporation. As the industry has progressed and we've seen this new specialization, however, we've had to break down our whole organization to gear up to the competition. (quoted in Mitchell 1984a: B4)

While Stelco proceeded with its quality improvement program and interactive management training, the union leadership became embroiled in its own internal political struggles, which were only resolved with the ouster of Cec Taylor as president and new executive elections in mid-1985.[37] Stelco management's new initiatives and the internal preoccupations of the union, coupled with the spectre of more mass layoffs in the absence of improved Stelco market share, encouraged 1005 to agree to an early contract settlement in 1984. The contract stressed improved pension eligibility and income security, with no significant wage increase (for a detailed account of these coercive tactics at Hilton Works during the 1980s, see Corman 1990: 85–109).

By the time Local 1005 leadership had regrouped in 1985, the new works manager, Robert Milbourne, had carried out the second wave of massive layoffs, and bumping and overtime were still widespread. Union leaders pleaded for mercy. As Val Patrick, a young steward, put it in an open letter to the man who had become known throughout the plant as "Chainsaw Bob":

> It's obvious, Bob, that your role here was to shock and beat us into submission.... You have created a siege mentality that you no doubt intended would induce an effort of 150 percent per person.... You've smacked us around too much this time. We hear you haven't finished with contracting out more of our jobs. You promise only more cuts, more losses and still no commitment back to us.... You are killing Hilton Works. Your style will make the plant collapse from within. So please, no fanfare, no accolades, no kiss goodbye, just go. (Patrick 1985)

The resumption of management-labour dialogue and the implementation of interactive management techniques did encourage some union leaders to express hope for more humane relations with both the works' manager and departmental supervisors (see, e.g., Forde 1985; Martin 1986). Stelco persisted in fits and starts with its "new industrial relations" program. But management continued to rely on divisive shop floor tactics and the threat of layoffs especially around contract time, while union leaders focused on maintaining and expanding workers' contract provisions.[38] Early negotiations in 1987 resulted in a contract which gave regular workers plant-wide seniority rights to retrain for new jobs and some pension and vacation benefit improvements, but there was no wage increase beyond a cost of living allowance (Estock 1987b).

Union accusations of Stelco mismanagement, confusion and inconsistency continued into the late 1980s. Local 1005 spokespersons increasingly called for effective consultations before job changes. As Bob Mann, a chief steward in the finishing mills, expressed it in 1987:

> We are all well aware by now that jobs are rapidly disappearing and that management intends to operate with a minimum of employees. They are declaring that many of our jobs are "as required" even though they have been and are still needed.... They don't encourage input from the employees or the steward body. They impose their decision on the employees despite what the employees think.... What is sorely needed in our area is a new approach by management. This "you will do it and you will like it" mentality is not an acceptable 1980s concept. (Mann 1989: 27)

Union leaders also began to admit that the company's industrial relations strategy in the plant had undergone some substantial revisions which required a more sophisticated union response. As Val Patrick, now a chief health and safety representative, summarized:

> In most of Stelco, things have changed greatly. As the smoke cleared from the 1981 strike and the industry re-tooled for the eighties, top management switched gears. During 1982 and 1983 the Company adopted a new style and it began at the top levels of local plant management.... Over time a new game plan was even instituted in the Labour Relations department. Soon we saw in place "interaction management," or "charm school" as we called it, and all the foremen had to go. Suddenly there was a new-found willingness to meet over and resolve grievances. A spirit of co-existence if not outright co-operation was evidenced. And during the past several years the situation on the shop floor has changed tremendously.... This is not to say that there are not plenty of problems, but the change is undeniable. Where supervisors are not being able to adapt and co-operate, they are being shuffled aside.... [Front-line supervisors] have undergone a revolutionary change this decade and as we enter

49

the nineties, we as workers must ensure we are taking advantage of the changes we have seen.

There must never be any doubt that this company is in business to make not steel but money. Bad labour relations make for poor sales.... Stelco is out to cut costs at our expense in order to improve profits: this fact of economic reality has not and will not change. Simply put, the employer wants more for less. This is not new. This does not mean, however, that we cannot advance our interests while working in the changed environment.... The employer has become more sophisticated in the approach to workers and we must deal with it in new ways.... A cautious, mature approach can help make the 1990s a decade of improvement on the job and in our community. (1989: 20–21)[39]

A notable example of a new management approach was the staffing of the new continuous caster that, in 1988, replaced mould casting. With this new equipment, steel could be much more efficiently poured in a continuous ribbon and cut to manageable lengths for finishing by laser-guided automatic equipment. The caster manager negotiated a special agreement with union leaders that allowed the overriding of seniority rules, screening applicants by passing a personal interview, creating distinctive job descriptions that denied bumping rights to more senior people outside the caster and reportedly excluding anyone with a previous history of union activism. Caster crews were extensively inducted into the team concepts of the Winning in the Nineties program. These crews were told that they were special. Virtually no grievances or health and safety complaints occurred in the early years. However, by the late 1990s, arbitrary management practices led to grievances and requests for transfer from "specialness."

Throughout the 1980s, Local 1005 leaders generally took positions in strong reaction against the human impact of most of Stelco management's specific restructuring initiatives. This opposition included actions such as leading demonstrations against layoffs, contracting out, discriminatory layoffs of the few women steelworkers, and in support of unemployed workers' benefits; a long boycott of multi-crafting training programs and frequent appeals to workers to report CWS abuses; continual requests to members to refuse to work overtime; the taking of legal action against Stelco for excessive overtime; the pursuit of many previously ignored health and safety complaints; and the establishment of an independent workers' health centre. For example, on Labour Day 1988, a large delegation of steelworkers organized by Local 1005 protested in front of Stelco Tower in Hamilton against unresolved issues, including the use of contractors and overtime, multi-crafting and group benefit problems (Crone 1988; Martin 1988).

At the end of the decade, the Local 1005 executive had a deep scepticism about Stelco's early contract settlement tactics, just as they had prior to the 1981 negotiations and strike (Martin 1989). In spite of increased consultations and joint committees, the local's executive generally "kept its distance" from management.[40] Prior to the 1990 negotiations, there was another concerted management campaign involving reorganization of the labour relations department, a community advertising blitz, dinner meetings with workers for "information exchanges," more human relations courses for supervisors and worker tours of customers' facilities (Christmas 1990). But this was followed by renewed threats of layoff, increased contracting out of trades work and concerted efforts to break steelworkers' long-established model of chainwide bargaining with Stelco. As John Martin, who had been elected president of the local in 1988, declared in the lead up to the 1990 negotiations:

> Over the last two years… Stelco Steel's strategy… has attempted to lull our members into a false sense of commitment to a company that publicly states: "quality steel, quality people."… Our membership grows stronger as Stelco attempts to buy our members with chicken wings, beer, pizza and gifts. Local 1005 has been through too many battles with this company to be lured into a position of compromise just before 1990 negotiations. Stelco has attempted to break [chain-wide bargaining] by offering some of the locals the sky in return for independent bargaining with no success…. Stelco put a gun to the heads of three of our locals and attempted to literally blow away part of the chain through corporate terrorism…. Stelco has gone from one extreme to the other in an attempt to break your union down without success. (Martin 1989: 1)

The 1990 strike was in many respects a rerun of 1981. After six years of downsizing with no real wage increases and in view of Stelco's return to healthy profits in 1988–89, Local 1005 wanted some significant gains for its members. Stelco was still struggling with a very high debt burden, including substantial losses in the first half of 1990, was still strongly committed to continuing to cut its workforce especially at Hilton Works and was intent on splitting the company into a number of discrete businesses with separate union contracts (Lanthier 1990a; Godfrey 1990). Stelco built up steel inventories, laid off hundreds of workers, made separate offers to different locals in attempts to break the chain and ultimately tabled an offer to 1005 which provided minimal wage and pension increases but removed cost of living adjustments (COLA). The contract expired on July 31, and another long and bitter strike began with support from over 90 percent of the membership (Lanthier 1990b). A month and a half into the strike, Stelco slashed dividends to shareholders, cut executive salaries and threatened publicly to close some of its operations, including large parts of Hilton Works (Hallman 1990, Davie 1990b). Shortly after this, talks with the union broke down and picket lines turned violent over independent truckers carrying Stelco's warehoused steel. As John Martin exclaimed to a large membership meeting:

> This is the boiling point. How long it boils depends on how long Stelco wants to jerk people around.... The union doesn't want to turn to violence but our fuses are getting shorter by the day. We will not convene bargaining again until Stelco tables a full economic proposal to the local union office, and only if that document comes close to our economic demands will we even think of meeting with those bastards again.... It'll take at least two police officers to take me to jail and I hope to see all of you there with me. (quoted in Humphreys and Peters 1990: A1–2)

The resolution of the strike at Hilton a month later included COLA and base rate pay increases amounting to over 5 percent in each year of the three-year deal, better pension base rates and indexing, stronger limits on contracting out and permanent layoffs, an income-sharing scheme and more flexible access to training programs. These were substantial gains over Stelco's pre-strike offers and led Leo Gerard, then USWA district director, to declare the contract "one of the most socially important collective agreements negotiated in the last decade" (Lefaive and Hughes 1990c: C1). But Stelco also won its most important objective, effectively breaking chain bargaining (Lefaive and Hughes 1990a). The sense of insecurity also continued to grow among the union leadership. As union steward Fred White said when the 1990 agreement was announced, "There's a lot of good things in here, but only [a few of us] are going to get the value" (quoted in Pron and Papp 1990: A12).

Immediately after the Hilton strike, John Martin made another plea for genuine co-operation with Stelco management, much as Cec Taylor had a decade earlier:

> We have to stop fighting one another and start making this business work, or eventually it is just going to collapse underneath us. 1005 is prepared to work with the company, not to be taken advantage of by the company, but to honestly work with the company [to negotiate the next contract in 1993] without any of the pain we had to suffer in 1990. (quoted in Lefaive and Hughes 1990b: A1)

Shortly after the 1990 strike was concluded, Robert Milbourne, the same engineer who had spearheaded the massive Hilton layoffs of 1982–83, assumed the presidency of a reconsolidated Stelco. He professed greatly increased commitment to co-operation and communication between management and employees and admitted that Stelco's approach to employee relations over the past five years had been "inadequate — the institutional agenda of the union that represents our workers clashed with our model of separate businesses, leading to the failure of the collective bargaining process at the outset and a series of strikes" (Milbourne 1990: 1). With particular reference to Hilton Works, he advocated a more customer-oriented "pull through" production model of front-end standardization and back-end customization, and more cost-efficient, interconnected, team-oriented work processes. Better worker relations became imperative as business losses mounted. As he put it:

> To prosper in the nineties, I believe we have to build our organizations, and more specifically, the behaviour and attitudes of our people — the management, supervisory, technical and staff groups in particular — on the model that they are resources to the people who make and sell our steel, not simply overseers, controllers, policemen, or otherwise "directors" of other peoples' work. (Milbourne 1990: 8)

Fred Telmer, who became chair and chief executive at this point, similarly declared:

> The hard-nosed legalistic approach just doesn't work anymore. One of the underlying principles is much more open communication with our employees, to involve them in activities, discussions about what's happening in the plants themselves. Turning around the legalistic approach will take some time, well into the nineties. (quoted in Hallman 1990: 19)

Stelco executives' perceptions that their existing organizational structure had become "bureaucratic and to a great extent fossilized" and that the future of steel lay in the creation of self-sustaining semi-autonomous business units (Telmer 1994: 62) led to two specific changes in employee relations: the Winning in the Nineties management retraining program and elimination of the corporate industrial relations function. In the early 1990s, all Stelco managerial, supervisory and staff people took a two-week residential course of twelve- to fifteen-hour days in groups of twenty-four to develop more entrepreneurial and worker-responsive planning and problem-solving management practices, a much more intensive and inclusive retraining initiative than the prior Interactive Management campaign (Mitchell 1992; Telmer 1995). In 1991, most industrial relations functions were decentralized to the plant, as Stelco committed itself to find solutions to compensation and work rule problems at the local level, primarily through the joint committees established in recent contracts (Verma and Warrian 1992: 115).

In the early 1992 election of the next contract bargaining committee, the 1005 leadership also received a strong mandate from the membership to take a more co-operative approach to the company in co-ordinated rather than chain-wide bargaining. As vice-president Eric Butt said:

> Conflict resolution bargaining has to go. It's the old style of business and it doesn't work in the nineties.... We've offered Stelco the olive branch. The company is dealing in global markets, the union real-izes it must change while still protecting employees' rights.... The union now recognizes that the members' lives and Stelco's survival are at stake. (Westell 1992: B2)

A month later, in the wake of continuing financial losses, Stelco offered its own olive branch by opening its books to 1005 for the first time. In John Martin's view:

> The company's honesty in letting us look at the statements will build enormous trust and be a break from a relationship that's been hampered by turbulence and confrontation for 46 years. It will be the building base for a good relationship.... If the reality is that the performance is bad, then the union will have to deal with it. Hopefully the details will put the union in position to suggest cost-saving or profit-boosting ideas. We don't want to become managers, we just want to be able to present ideas.... Access to the financial bottom line... won't necessarily reduce our demands but it will help us focus things. (Morrison 1992: F5)

However, the immediate aftermath of the 1990 strike was also essentially a rerun of 1982–84 manoeuvres, including a very slow recall with large permanent layoffs along with circulation of closure rumours and pledges of greater co-operation (see, e.g., Lefaive and Hughes 1990b; Morrison 1991; Davie 1990a, 1990b, 1991). In the fall of 1992, as steel prices and Stelco share values continued to plummet, the company announced the layoff of over 1,000 hourly workers at Hilton Works, including over 600 permanent employees, many with more than fifteen years' seniority (Fowlie 1992). Local 1005 joined the company in calling for federal government subsidies to aid workers' early retirements and for support in fighting U.S. trade sanctions against Canadian steel, and also urged a government job creation program. As John Martin said tearfully at the joint news conference:

> We can't withstand it anymore — it's too much — No one dreamed there would be [so many jobs lost]. Hamilton is steeltown — and

steeltown is in big trouble.... Where are the issues of jobs? It's time to stand up and tell the government that we cannot withstand the devastation of the jobs in this country any further. (quoted in Papp 1992: A1, 28)

A few weeks later Stelco unilaterally announced its maintenance-operator job melding plan to cope with the layoff by blending largely unrelated operating and maintenance jobs into fewer hybrid positions in less than two months (Davie 1992a). The 1005 leadership protested that the plan was unrealistically fast and the company consented to consult the local on actual implementation of the plan (Davie 1992b). In light of Stelco's weakened market condition, local president Martin obtained a mandate both to become involved with the company in the job cutting/amalgamating process and to engage in early contract negotiations to reassure jumpy customers (Davie 1992c). A new three-year contract was approved in May 1993 after several months of intense talks. There was virtually no pay increase, and COLA became part of regular pay as Stelco had wanted in 1990 (Papp 1993). Most significantly, there was a new letter of agreement that instituted a joint work restructuring committee and training plan. This letter recognized the continuing need to restructure work in the plant and specified the committee's mandate:

> to find mutually acceptable ways and means to deal with the ongoing restructuring of work... in any of the Hilton Works businesses in order to ensure their competitive position in both the short and long term. The opportunities for stability of employment and maintenance or improvement of wage and benefit levels may be enhanced by such activity. (Stelco–USWA Local 1005 1993: 134–5)

Stelco executives and 1005 leaders maintained this consultative mode for several years after the 1993 contract, although in a much more centralized and limited form than the USWA national office advocated and Lake Erie Works implemented (Frost 2000). As John Martin said before his re-election as president in April 1994:

> The 1005 executive has developed, with the approval of the membership, a new relationship with Stelco management, a more co-operative stance that has diminished the acrimony in negotiations. We want to work with the company to make sure any future restructuring has the least impact on our members.... My fear is that, with the profitability of our industry becoming narrower and narrower, and if there is another down cycle in 1997, we have to be prepared to meet that challenge or our members will be in big trouble. (quoted in Prokaska 1994a: B1)

While the acrimony certainly diminished with more extensive man-agement-union consultations, conflicts continued to emerge. In October of 1994, Stelco announced record quarterly profits and the first-ever payout to Hilton workers from the 1990 profit sharing plan (Davie 1994). But, despite the industry upswing and widespread overtime, the company simultaneously proceeded with a planned layoff of over 200 relief workers. As Gary Howe, chairman of the adjustment committee for 1005, said:

> If the company was properly managing people, it could keep all these people working and save money by cutting overtime in half. People are frustrated because we really didn't expect there would be layoffs this time. (quoted in Prokaska 1994b: C8)

In March 1995, Stelco disclosed large executive bonuses related to the company's 1994 return to profitability, but there were no further payouts to 1005 members. Union officials reacted angrily to what they saw as a betrayal of the co-operative approach. As Bob Sutton, 1005 recording secretary, put it:

> We're very angry and dismayed. Since 1992 we have worked very hard with the company because we knew it was in a serious finan-cial condition. Now when things start to turn around, instead of something to help the people who row the ship, the people in the captain's bridge get all the benefits.... We showed them how to co-ordinate work to save money. We worked very hard at it. I would be very surprised if our members allowed us to take the same attitude [in the next contract negotiations] if the company is going to act like this. (quoted in Mitchell 1995: C8)

In spite of increasing profitability through 1995, Stelco made no further payouts to Hilton workers. Significant factional disputes re-emerged within the union, led by long-time 1005 activists who felt that the Martin regime had become too close to management or too infrequent in sharing relevant information with the membership (see, e.g., Humphreys 1995; Frost 2000).[41]

But employment remained stable as improvements in product quality, yield and energy use continued to be made "through training, job restruc-turing and automation" (Stelco 1995: 7). In early 1996, Stelco declared that Hilton Works had reinvented itself as a modern steel mill complete with an ISO 9002 certification. As Jim Alfano, Hilton general manager, asserted:

> Our ISO 9002 status gives recognition to the fact that we're shipping high quality products. And by inference, it's also recognition that we have the facilities and the highly skilled people to produce these products which meet international standards for quality.... We've

invested more than $600 million in new equipment in the past ten years.... But investment in training people is the most essential element in Hilton Works' evolution into a modern steelmaking plant. Our strategy is to continue identifying and correcting weaknesses on an incremental basis so that we can make the best possible use of our people and our asset base. (Davie 1996: D10)

A high point of mutual accommodation between Stelco management and the union leadership occurred around the time of this declaration. The largest labour demonstration in Hamilton's history occurred on February 23–24, 1996, when as many as 100,000 people marched downtown to protest the anti-union policies of the Conservative provincial government of Ontario (Herron 1996; Phillips 1996). Local 1005 publicly supported these days of protest but agreed not to picket the plant (Prokaska 1996a). The many Hilton workers who wanted to participate were given holiday time to do so, while the plant remained open and functioning with reduced staff (Poling 1996).

During the early bargaining round of spring 1996, the new era of management-union relations at Hilton Works culminated in the longest ever proposed contract in the Canadian steel industry — six years. The first contract recommended by the executive in March included better pensions, improvements to health benefits and income sharing, and an end to cyclical layoffs for eligible workers who had been on layoff-callback for many years (Holt 1996). But there was no wage increase beyond COLA (Prokaska 1996b). This contract was narrowly rejected by the membership, at least partly because younger workers would not accept such a long term without a wage increase (Prokaska 1996c). A month later, a revised six-year contract with a lump sum payment of $500 up front and wage increases in the last three years was accepted by a two-thirds majority (Stelco–USWA Local 1005 1996). Jim Alfano celebrated workers' support for Hilton Works:

This agreement provides long-term stability for our employees, customers, suppliers and the community of Hamilton. It will allow Hilton Works to continue its improvement process with renewed focus and vigour. (Prokaska 1996e: A1)

However, the following six-year period of industrial relations was characterized by more harmonious talk but more unstable, harsher management actions. The Hilton Works managers and Industrial Relations managers were changed several times. The Industrial Relations Department was renamed "Human Resources" and management did have more joint consultations with the union as specified by the new contract. This approach could be termed "soft talk but hard measures" — asking for union input, then doing something contrary. Simultaneous with the 1997 election of a new 1005 president, Warren Smith, two of the most prominent union leaders in the plant were fired. There were persistent disputes over cutting members and dependents off health benefits. Arbitrary restrictions were put on access to vacation time. There were attempts to reduce wage rates for temporary workers. Stronger discipline was imposed after accident investigations. The Income Sharing Plan in the new contract paid well at Lake Erie Works but not at Hilton, creating deep resentment within Local 1005. Early in Smith's presidency, a very large deficiency in funding the pension plan was documented and a complaint to the Ontario Labour Relations Board (OLRB) over bad-faith bargaining dragged on throughout this period. Management-union relations did vary quite widely throughout the plant. For example, there were generally more relaxed relations in the profitable cold mill and more bitter ones in the less dependable plate and strip mill, which also had one of the more activist rank-and-file memberships in the plant. But overall, the stability promised by this long-term contract was not translated into much fuller sharing of knowledge and co-operation in the new joint committees or on the shop floor.

Rank-and-File Worker Responses
The rank-and-file membership of USWA Local 1005 had a well-earned reputation for both trade union activism and union democracy (see Freeman 1982). A practical solidarity of the diminishing core workforce was further forged through the long strikes of 1981 and 1990. The 1984 steelworker families survey (Corman, Livingstone, Luxton and Seccombe 1985; Corman, Luxton, Livingstone and Seccombe 1993) found that a very large proportion of the rank-and-file membership, over two-thirds, had actively participated in some union-sponsored industrial or political actions, and about 40 percent had filed a grievance against Stelco.[42] In spite of closer consultations between management and union leaders after the 1990 contract, rank-and-file militancy on the shop floor in defence of their bargaining rights showed few signs of diminishing. The rate of grievances filed according to the formal grievance procedure at step 2 in the 1990s was even greater than the rate after the 1981 strike, averaging over 1,700 grievances a year in the 1990–93 period (Frost and Verma 1997). Grievance rates in the 1970s had averaged around 100 per year, much lower than the post-1981 rates (Adams and Zeytinoglu 1987: 91). Grievance complaints continued to include employee discipline and increasingly involved seniority system disputes. What did change significantly after the 1990 strike was the diminishing number of grievances the union leadership decided to proceed with beyond step 3 to arbitration; the arbitration rate declined to lower than it was in the expansionary, more tranquil 1970s (Frost and Verma 1997). There may have been many motives on the part of the responsible union officials, including the union's increased financial constraints for engaging in costly legal proceedings and their growing

awareness of management's financial problems. But the reduced arbitration rate was not a sign of the mellowing of 1005's oppositional shop floor culture. In 1997, when Warren Smith was elected president of 1005, there was a huge backlog of over 1,900 filings on the list; the majority awaited third step grievance meetings or were scheduled for arbitration, and some were as much as four years old. While many grievances historically had been resolved in contract bargaining, the only grievances resolved in 1996 bargaining were related to the recall of workers after the 1990 strike. By 1999, grievances were being settled in groups and the total had been cut to 900. By the middle of 2001, the backlog had again swollen to 1,500. But by the next early bargaining round in 2002, the backlog was down to about 100 cases, all referred to arbitration. During the 1997 to 2003 period, under Smith's leadership, Local 1005 filed policy grievances and negotiated with Stelco management over the lack of payments from the profit-sharing program, abandoning the concept of progressive discipline, erosion of prime vacation time access and arbitrary layoff of disabled workers. But the rate of individual grievances filed continued to be high, involving mainly discipline, forced overtime and layoff irregularities.

There was no sign in 1984 interviews with rank-and-file workers that Stelco's recent experiments in interactive management had moved any in the declining core 1005 workforce to repress their memories of previous bitter struggles and to consider the reformed Stelco as a compassionate employer. A service division trades worker reflected the general sentiment:

> There's no incentive there to really try and improve or anything. The company always come out with these propaganda films. They're always saying how we want to work together. Well, they don't try to work with us, they don't try to make things better for us…. You're just a number at Stelco. It's just that there's always a threat that you don't know what's going to happen tomorrow. That's basically it. You're always on edge there.

As Stelco's downsizing and interactive management efforts continued, growing proportions of the remaining workforce did engage in more regular consultations with managers and supervisors. But the 1990 strike evoked more violent worker responses than the longer one in 1981. These sentiments were at least partly related to Hilton workers' sense of betrayal by Stelco management, a feeling that consultation had not been serious or fair and that the company had lost opportunities for improvement while continuing to lay off large numbers of workers. As a service department worker stated at the time of the 1990 strike:

> If Stelco management *really* listened to the guy on the floor, many production problems would be gone. But they're not gonna do that. They see that as an admission that they don't know what the hell they're doing…. Why

let them pick your brain, because you're just gonna get screwed around tomorrow. Why bother? Eventually they're gonna screw you one way or the other. If it's not you, it's your kids. We've got a plant that's lost 6,000 people. Maybe your kid would have liked the opportunity to work there. They've taken that away. Through being inept, they've lost much of their market share. The company almost went belly up in the eighties. They've screwed the whole community.

However, after the 1990 strike, more and more of the dwindling core of steelworkers came to see management-worker co-operation as necessary for survival of both. In the words of a veteran trades worker now retired from Hilton:

Workers now realize in order for the company to survive and them to survive, they gotta get along. There's an awful lot of head butting in the past. That's common knowledge — the head butting that went on between 1005 and Stelco. Now they seem to be getting along which, as I say, became a necessity for either one to survive.... Everyone's got to be flexible, whether it's a company, school board, a government, a union, a federation. In this particular day and age, you've got to be flexible. 1005 used to be hard line. In order to survive, we've got to be flexible. (1994)

Among this greatly reduced core of steelworkers, there was by the mid-1990s a general recognition that Stelco management had made some significant efforts to involve the remaining workers in company affairs. In 1994, an industrial mechanic observed:

The company cut the whole place to pieces. They cut the workforce in half. [But] they don't want to shut the place down. You still keep your distance with supervisors, but generally the company is treatin' us pretty good.... There's no job security guarantees. We don't get the orders, there's gonna be big problems. But we're given briefings every day. There's a paper circulated across the plant. You know, they don't keep the employees in the dark anymore like they used to. Before, a lot of people used to feel negative about the company, now it's a little more positive. Stelco, Dofasco, everybody's struggling to stay alive.

But Hilton workers also generally remained aware of serious limits to more co-operative management approaches, in the wake of sometimes unco-operative or misleading supervisors, shoddy company treatment of pensioners, subcontracting of departed workmates' jobs and company claims that did not square with their own experiences. A service department trades worker provided a good summary of these concerns:

In some ways supervisors seem very incompetent. Now they just sit in the office and hand out work. It's not as efficient as lead hands. They don't seem to listen to you. You suggest something, they do it their way, whether it's right or wrong.... Stelco has changed, but I think they've had to because there are so few people. Now they more or less have to kiss up to people to get them to do it. A little more co-operation works better than what they did before. But I still think there's a problem. Like when you see all those people that were supposed to go on pension and their widows. Like our foreman will tell us something and tell us it's gospel, right. But when you go outside the shop and you find out what's really going on, then you find out he's really lying to you. And I think upper management is pretty much the same way.... And they'll just keep bringing in more and more contractors and not hire anybody... there's no pension for them at the end. (1994)

Production workers tended to be even less impressed with management's more conciliatory approach than the skilled trades, both because they continued to experience less direct consultation in their jobs and because it was their straight production jobs that continued to disappear most quickly. In all manufacturing industries, alienation from both the work itself and the employer has always tended to be greater among production workers because of their greater expendability (Ollman 1976). As a young finishing mill labourer put it in 1984:

You punch in and then hate it for the next eight hours. You never know where you are working when you go in really.... Let's face it. We can spend thirty years working for them. And if they can eliminate your job, you're nothing. You're just a piece of meat. They couldn't care less.

A decade later, this same labourer was in a different mill with considerably more training and knowledge. But he had even less job stability and a more intense dislike for what he saw as profound hypocrisy in Stelco's new appeals for teamwork:

It's the same monotonous garbage day after day after day. Our foreman wants to be able to use us to do this job this day and that job that day, and then he'll send you to do this job the next day.... You just get so frustrated you don't even care. Everybody feels the same way.... And they just screw you somewhere down the line. The company doesn't care [about mistakes made by overtime workers], so you get so damn frustrated you don't care yourself. So you either do it so that nobody bothers you, or you get an ulcer. And I'm not getting no ulcer for them. I don't care. Stelco's not worth an ulcer. Their employee relations are bloody awful. This "quality people, quality steel" [i.e., the Stelco motto], they should be sued for false advertising, the bastards.... We finish the steel, the company shows a profit, but we get no bonus. You wonder why guys are saying, well, stick your "quality" job up your ass! It's totally terrible. Look at what they are doing to these widows of these guys that died in the plant. They're spending big bucks on legal appeals so they don't have to pay the widows' pensions. And then they say, well, be happy guys, get on the team. Help us out here. What the hell for? There's no future down there anymore. Well, to hell with the team.

But, even if they saw interactive management as largely rhetoric, most production workers increasingly took a more pragmatic approach to both relations with direct supervisors and the persistent threat of layoff. Another finishing mill labourer expressed fairly common sentiments of the mid-1990s when he said:

> [There are] the usual personality clashes with supervisors, but everybody seems to get along now. But the guys up the ladder still like to give us the shaft. Profit sharing for six years and we're still getting nothing.... I expect each time I get up in the morning the gate is going to be closed at Stelco. But it doesn't bother me. I consider it part of life. You've got to have some realism in the world and Stelco is about as real as you can get. So if that happens, there is nothing that I can do about it.

Overall, the basic responses to Stelco's revised management strategies among Hilton's dwindling workforce became more and more reactive defences of their remaining entitlements. A service department trades worker offers the best summary of rank-and-file worker responses to plant conditions in the mid-1990s:

> The company is putting more and more pressure on. I recently had to do a very hard labour job even though I had just had a serious injury, because we couldn't get anybody from the labour department and we had to get the job done. I have no idea what this company is going to do in the future. I just hope to get my 30 [i.e., thirty years pension].... Everything's going for a dive. You're more pessimistic and concerned about the future. One day at a time, that's all you can really do.

The six-year contract agreed to in 1996 did not significantly diminish the rate of grievances filed by 1005 members. But it did decrease the amount of leverage the diminishing numbers of workers and their union had to complain about workplace conditions during much of this period and the collective agreement also formally established joint committees for consultation on most of these issues. In sum, improvements in management-union co-operation in terms of the reliability of a long-term labour contract may have helped to recast Hilton Works into one of the more viable of the old integrated steel plants in North America during the late 1990s. In steel firms as in all other capitalist enterprises, the major objective of industrial relations systems is to maintain a reliable, attentive and loyal labour supply. Various combinations of carrot-and-stick tactics may prove effective. The collective experience of the dwindling core of Hilton steelworkers probably made them more likely both to understand and to resist this underlying agenda than many other working people, even as there was more co-operation to ensure the survival of their jobs. An earlier critical assessment of experiments with co-operative management strategies in U.S. auto and steel plants concluded:

> While effective in eliminating traditional shop floor rules, threats will not be sufficient in eliciting co-operation in the long run. The willingness to co-operate needs to be nurtured by guarantees of employment. But so far management has shown little consistency in implementing trust-enhancing measures. Partly because of height-ened competition... or because of the dominance of capital markets with their short-term outlook, management has shifted frequently between the carrot and the stick in its dealings with workers.... It is therefore not surprising that the introduction of the team concept has not gone smoothly and is far from being a success. (Scherrer 1991: 112)

In the late 1990s, Hilton Works still contained the vast majority of Stelco's finishing capacity to produce high value-added products for its intended con-tinental niche markets. Hilton Works still produced the majority of the steel with a majority of the Stelco workforce. But semi-finished steel productivity at Lake Erie continued to increase faster. Continental market pressures to reduce person hours per ton to competitive U.S. levels also grew. The relative stability of employment at Hilton Works in the late 1990s and Stelco's return to modest profitability during these years may have increased core workers' sense of optimism somewhat. But the industrial relations system at Hilton Works remained highly centralized with little real worker involvement. As Frost concluded her assessment of the Hilton industrial relations system:

> Stewards and other representatives have gained no added role in workplace decision-making. The local union continues to represent the interests of its members in a traditional manner, with the local union president negotiating tightly worded contract language and the steward network policing that language through the grievance process. (Frost 2000: 569)

With further downturns in the steel cycle, coercive management tactics may be more prevalent, including further downsizing demands and unilateral workplace restructuring. But through steel cycles, one aspect of worker in-volvement has become a constant issue in Hilton Works as in all steel plants: involvement in training and retraining.

Steelworker Training and Retraining

Early in the 1980s, a report of the International Labour Organization (ILO) Metal Trades Committee concluded:

> The heavy social consequences of the failure of an enterprise or an industry... to adjust the organization and skills of the people constituting it, makes the task of providing adequate training and retraining... in the metal trades a *joint concern* of society, of employers and of workers. All have a share in ensuring that the training systems respond in time and adequately. (1983: 59)

There was an emerging general consensus that current technological changes, most notably in computerization and electronics, called for massive retraining programs for the skilled trades as well as other workers in steel and other manufacturing industries. In the steel industry, this concern was coupled with a recognized need for retraining the large numbers of laid-off workers.

In Canada by 1985, concern over layoffs provoked national trade union leaders to propose a new joint labour-management institution for the steel sector. Recognizing the growing centrality of the allegiance of their diminishing numbers of employees for sustained profitability, the steel companies agreed to establish the Canadian Steel Trade and Employment Conference (CSTEC) (see Allan 1985; Warrian 1990), with the aid of subsidies from the federal government. In its early years, CSTEC focused mainly on providing "downside" employment adjustment services, especially retraining opportunities, for laid-off steelworkers to enable them to find jobs in other areas. But, as a consequence of the downsizing of workers with low seniority since 1981, the Canadian steel industry faced an older, *relatively* low formally educated workforce in the context of a more competitive steel market (Verma, Frost and Warrian 1995). Employers became concerned to confirm that employees' had adequate working knowledge to run their increasingly capital-intensive, computerized plants.[43] "Upside" formal retraining of experienced steelworkers expanded after the mid-1980s. According to a CSTEC-sponsored survey (Human Resources Development Canada 1994), Canadian steel companies were spending about 2 percent of their wage bill or $800 per employee on training in 1990. The main methods were supervised on-the-job training and in-house courses. This amounted to over forty hours of funded training for each employee. More than 40 percent of this training was for health and safety purposes in response to the introduction of the Workplace Hazardous Materials Information System (WHMIS) throughout Canada. Apprenticeship training accounted for about 30 percent of the total training hours. Provision of other technical and computer training increased quite rapidly. However, from the vantage point of national union leaders, there was little spillover of the co-operation in the early downside adjustment program into labour relations within the enterprise. Gerard Docquier, Canadian director of USWA, stated:

In some relationships, I think it is fair to say that we understand each other better…. In others, however, the objective appears to be to keep the CSTEC relationship in a watertight compartment. Co-operation and communication on CSTEC issues; the law of the jungle at the bargaining table and the shop floor. (1989)

So by the early 1990s, there was a consensus among management and union representatives that a new, more responsive industry-wide training program had to be developed. CSTEC (1996) developed the Steel Industry Training Program (SITP) in conjunction with Canada's community colleges. The active co-operation of plant-level management and union representatives in joint training committees was required for these programs to be viable. The working knowledge of steelworkers traditionally had been understood to be comprised of quite specialized skills grounded in localized apprenticeships and on-the-job training practices (Bowen 1976). Traditional apprenticeships involving four or five years working with a master crafts person, in a system extensively controlled by trade unions were still regarded as the best means of qualifying for many steel trades in the early 1980s. Production operatives were still exclusively reliant on on-the-job training as well. Consistent with a general trend toward shorter formalized modular training in manufacturing industries, CSTEC developed such courses as Steel Industry Trades Replacement, Computer Based Training and General Manufacturing Techniques in conjunction with community colleges located in steel regions (MacPherson 2002). Training time for job entrants became more focused on generic standardized processes learned off the job; the necessity for substantial experience in real job situations for novice workers to become competent tended to be depreciated. Steel companies' growing concern with more formal certification of workers' knowledge may have served to undermine the tacit knowledge and "know-how" received from more experienced workers.

In 1984, about half of the steelworkers at Hilton Works had not finished high school and less than 20 percent had any postsecondary education (Corman, Luxton, Livingstone and Seccombe 1993). It is likely that little formal schooling was needed to do many steel or other manufacturing jobs in earlier generations (see Blackburn and Mann 1979). In any case, by the late 1960s, Stelco was using a grade twelve diploma as a hiring screen. Trades certification was not correlated with higher educational attainment among older Hilton workers; but younger trades workers required high school completion for trades entry. However, the insistence on a high school diploma for production jobs at that point was at least partially in response to the fact that the Canadian labour force had one of the highest educational attainments in the world (Statistics Canada 2006). According to the 2001 Canada census, around 90 percent of all steelworkers between twenty-five and thirty-four had at least completed high school (CSTEC 2005: 32). The use of formal education credentials as a hiring screen for the small number of jobs available in the wake of the massive layoffs had probably increased entry level requirements in the Canadian steel industry somewhat arbitrarily. The older workforce at Hilton Works, with virtually no new hiring, still had less formal education than either steelworkers generally or the overall Canadian labour force. But the relevant question was whether they had sufficient knowledge to perform their jobs well.

A large body of research over the past generation on work and learning has demonstrated several relevant points (see Livingstone 2009 for an overview):

1) self-reported participation in informal learning activities by adults is much more extensive than participation in formal schooling and further education courses;

2) those with less formal schooling are generally no less actively engaged in informal learning in relation to paid employment;

3) economic classes (most notably large employers, managers and professional employees versus industrial and service workers) remain highly differentiated by formal educational attainments, less so by further education participation and very little by incidence of job-related informal learning;

4) job requirements have increased since the 1980s in terms of formal education levels required for entry or performance, as well as training time to learn the job, but increases in the educational attainments of the employed labour force exceed increases in job requirements;

5) the general rate of underutilization or underemployment (i.e., formal educational attainments greater than the formal education required for jobs) has been estimated recently to be around 30 percent; the trend has been toward increasing underemployment on most dimensions and industrial workers have exhibited among the highest rates of underemployment; and

6) the proportion of workers who use a computer in their paid work more than doubled between the late 1980s and 2003, but a majority of workers continued to have higher computer skills than their jobs require. (Livingstone and Scholtz 2010: 39–40)

Hilton Works had a very experienced, aging workforce by the late 1990s, with an average age in the late forties and with over twenty-five years' average seniority. Mainly through extensive informal learning on the job and in their working-class communities, this workforce had a deep collective knowledge about working in steel that could have been coupled effectively with formal training in new techniques.

Whatever the officially recognized training requirements of their jobs, virtually all Hilton workers had benefitted from this extensive and often subtle informal learning culture (see Chapter 2 for a detailed discussion of changes in this learning process). The informal training provided by more experienced operators remained essential to any novice wanting to perform the job. For example, in 2004 a young mill operator described his experience from the mid-1990s, after computerized controls had become widespread on the machinery he operated:

> Reading the tolerances in molten steel is *all* eyeball because we burn wood against it, it makes an impression, and each mark on the impression dictates what you need to do. That was the hardest part about the job, learning how to read that wood. The first time I saw this guy stick a piece of wood against the bar flying by him I thought: "He's just doing that for the hell of it." [Laughs.] But that's the learning process, figuring out what the steel is doing, or what grade, or what your tolerances are, and how it reacts with different types of wood…. The guy who trained me is *absolutely* a super guy…. He told me that *sound* would save my life there one day. And I wear earmuffs, and I wear earplugs. And when I was there for the first couple of weeks, I just looked at him like he was from outer space, because I had no idea what he was talking about. I hear things now that I shouldn't hear…. That mill, when it changes speed, I know. I know where it changed speed, if the bar is loose somewhere I can hear it, if it breaks out somewhere — the sound plays that much of a role…. Basically I learned the job like he did… a senior guy said, "Come with me, shut up, sit down, watch what I do."… I think I'm probably a year away from proficiency, to the point where I'll never be questioned ever again [by supervisors] on what I do.

Similarly, experienced trades workers had earlier stressed the importance of other workers' tacit knowledge for doing their own jobs. In 1984 a repair electrician observed that:

> We fix anything that's electrical…. We've learned from experience that if you want to find out what's wrong with a machine, you listen to the operator. 'Cuz it's like your wife looking at you. She sees you everyday, if something changes, she notices. The operators know the sounds.

Like other steel companies in the context of computerization and heightened competition, Stelco became much less willing to rely on gradual informal workplace learning to ensure adequate knowledge among its employees. Formal joint management-union training programs increased greatly in the

1990s. Hilton Works employees received an average of about four days of CSTEC-assisted training each year (CSTEC 1993). Virtually all Local 1005 members were involved in an extensive health and safety training program. The maintenance-operator and operator-maintenance training programs entailed several weeks of formal training. Multi-craft training and other technical skill upgrading programs were regularly provided, as were computer literacy and quality improvement courses (Warrian 1989; CSTEC 1993).

The actual practice of multi-craft training typically involved veteran trades workers in one area learning the rudiments of another and drawing on the knowledge of experienced workers in these other trades when they actually needed to crossover. As a certified electrician in the service department described it in the mid-1990s:

> We had some Mohawk College training of a week and we had two days down at the welding services and then we had some in-house training.... The hard part is trying to remember some of it because you don't use it as often 'cuz we're kind of specialized in different areas and you basically stay in your own specialty. You don't crossover too much, but when you do, you gotta start thinking. But there's still enough guys around in the other trade. You're usually working with them. So it's not too bad.... But there's less and less senior guys to talk to when there's a problem.

Experienced trades workers assigned to newer production departments had more extensive retraining. In 1994 a construction mechanic who became an industrial mechanic on the continuous caster noted:

> They still keep separate lists of each craft. At first, they tried to amalgamate everything and it just didn't work out. So they're teaching us all the same principles and everything. After being in my trade for such a long time, in 1990 they came to an agreement and Stelco put us on a five-year training program right after the strike. So we're going back to Mohawk College once a year for upgrading.... They gave us extensive training before this place started up. When we came to the caster, it was like going back to school. They made us get our gas tickets and then we had eighty hours in hydraulics upgrading, right? Like forty hours in class and forty hours on the job.

For the few younger workers who have been able to enter these new combined trades jobs without prior certification, the required training time has been modularized and reduced to about one-sixth of the prior apprenticeships, with attendant losses in the extent of the tacit knowledge conveyed to trainees (see Petersen and Storey 1986; Sanger 1988). The general emphasis has been on obtaining generic "bits and pieces" of basic trades knowledge through short courses. This diversity appealed to some new entrants, including the following industrial mechanic:

We're in an ongoing training process.... You're assuming bits and pieces of different trades. So instead of having four or five separate trades, now they're concentrating on just having one person do the duties of the other five. So that's the ongoing training program. It's more efficient for the company and it's more interesting for us. I mean, you can never learn too much. If they want to send you back to school, I'm all for it. (1994)

However, in spite of the increases in the proportions of trades and general maintenance workers, as well as the upward movement of the average job class level compared to earlier decades, it is debatable whether there has been a general upgrading of the skill levels needed to perform the work that retained and retrained Hilton steelworkers actually do.[44] Certainly workers are increasingly expected to perform a wider array of tasks and to co-operate among themselves in executing them. But the individual worker's depth of formal and informal knowledge and job control of work design often have been undermined (see Villa 1987). Many Hilton workers recognized that there had been little actual upgrading of the knowledge base of their work. As a younger mill labourer put it in 1994:

There's no future left in the job.... If they lay me off this time, I'm just going to go back for retraining somewhere, probably through CSTEC. My options are open really, electronics maybe.... The job hasn't really changed over the past ten years, it's basically the same deal, same job, everything's identical. The skill requirements are just the same as it was when I started here.

A veteran construction electrician, who became a general industrial technician in assigned maintenance, offers one of the most explicit accounts of the gap between acquisition and application of working knowledge in the plant:

Now that we're in maintenance, they don't know how a construction department really runs. They figure you can just go in and do the job, be given the job that morning and have it done that day. It doesn't work that way.... Now one day we come in, we could be on maintenance, or could be doing something else. It's more disruptive now. If we stuck to construction jobs, they haven't changed, but now we are industrial electrician technicians general, so that with multi-crafting (we call it "multi-shafting"), we can be put anywhere. Really, the way it is now, all we are, is numbers to fill in for maintenance guys, because as far as multi-crafting is concerned all we have ever done is maintenance work. I have not done instrumentation, I have not done electronics, etc. So they're giving the good old government a run for their training money.... Being in electrical construction, you've always basically troubleshot things. So, yes, we should know more about instrumentation. Well, we've taken the training. You go to the training at Mohawk [College], you come back and don't use it, so you lose it. Really, that's it, so really, as far as I'm concerned, the training is a washout. They're training you, but they're not using your knowledge. It's now happening in all departments. (1994)

In spite of a pervasive public rhetoric about a necessity for skill upgrading in response to global competition and technological change, an increased span of job tasks and intensification of work should not be confused with genuine upgrading of job requirements. Most in-depth studies of workplaces have offered little evidence of a greater increase in the cognitive skills and substantive knowledge actually required to perform the work than in the skill and knowledge of workers themselves. A tendency toward increasing underemployment has been evident both in Canada and elsewhere in the advanced industrial countries (see Livingstone 1999a, Livingstone and Sawchuk 2004b). These Hilton workers, along with growing numbers of working-class, underclass and professional/managerial workers, recognize that they are generally quite well qualified to perform most of the available jobs, that there is underemployment of both formal credentials and existing tacit knowledge in their paid workplaces, and that the primary problem is not a lack of suitable training but a lack of suitable jobs.[45] The veteran construction electrician again says it well:

> The company wants us to be subservient, different from salaried workers. The company wants to see us differently. But we're not, we all have our talents and individual priorities.... If I was laid off, there are skills I could fall back on. I've taken some courses and I have my own computer, for example. I'd have to do something, because your sense of self-worth would really drop off. But I would want to support my family, so I would do anything I could to do that. But it's difficult now because there just aren't many jobs out there. The only jobs there are part-time employment, you'd have to take two or three crummy jobs. (1994)

Indeed, the discovery by Stelco and other steel employers of the merits of formal retraining programs may well be driven less by a genuine need to enhance most workers' required knowledge and more by the desire to use "credentialism" to recreate and streamline job ladders (also known as "reconversion plans") in the plant as a means to reorganize and control an already highly experienced and practically knowledgeable workforce along more flexible lines (see Kelley 1988; and compare Stone 1974 on the origins of job ladders in steel). In any event, many formal work skill retraining programs seem to have ignored or disrupted steelworkers' existing skills and knowledge rather than more fully engaging them. In contrast to the old job ladders, the new ones have been largely devoid of any sense of "job ownership" (Storey 1994). A production labourer's complaint about not being able to apply his increased formal training to a specific job became fairly widespread in the plant by the mid-1990s:

They don't want us to do the job that we've been trained for, they want to use us as floaters. You go, "Wait a minute," you got a letter signed by everybody that says the job is mine. [The supervisor] says, "Well, we're not honouring that."

The bottom line is that both at Hilton Works and in labour markets generally the basic problem has become not a lack of skills and knowledge but a lack of decent jobs in which to apply them. As a service department trades worker said in 1994:

We have such a big work area and so few people. [Laughs.] It's like some- times you look around and wonder if anybody's in the shop…. They aren't hiring anybody at Stelco but you really have to be qualified to get any job. Actually there are so many people looking for jobs, everybody is over qualified and it's more or less personality or if they like you or whatever.

In order to realize the joint concern of society, employers and workers — as declared at the outset of this section — to provide adequate formal training and retraining to aid in sustaining steel and other manufacturing enterprises, such formal programs will have to build more effectively on the deep practical knowledge of experienced workers like those remaining in Hilton Works. These steelworkers may be less formally schooled than corporate executives, managers and professional employees, but they are just as likely to devote time and energy to both informal job-related learn- ing, ranging from computer literacy to health and safety, as well as to other kinds of informal learning (Livingstone 2002). While much of this general work knowledge may be irrelevant from the immediate employer's objective of increasing productivity in jobs as currently designed, much of it could be directly applicable in other socially useful work and, potentially, in jobs redesigned to more fully use workers' actual repertoire of skills. We return to this point in Chapter 3.

Concluding Remarks

In 1981, steelworkers and their households constituted the relatively stable core of the Hamilton industrial working class. The bargain of high wages for secure steel work was then rapidly broken for most of this core group. By the turn of the century, the core group of aging steelworkers in Hilton Works was still diminishing and increasingly insecure. Some former members found steady work in lighter manufacturing and service industries, typically for lower wages and benefits. Many became part of a growing contingent labour force available for temporary work in the steel plant or elsewhere.

Up until 1981, Hilton steelworkers' relatively high wages and job security enabled these men to support dependent wives and children as the primary and often exclusive breadwinner. Steeltown consistently had among the lowest rates of women's employment in Canada (Webber 1986). Steel plants had always been male work preserves. Some women were hired at Hilton Works during World War II, to replace male workers who had joined the army, but after the war almost all those women were let go and few were hired later. Between 1961 and 1978, the company hired no women, although about 30,000 women applied for jobs (Luxton and Corman 1991). In the 1979–80 period, a union-supported campaign to get women back into Stelco resulted in the hiring of 200 women, most of whom were promptly laid off after the 1981 strike. In the aftermath of the strike, the wives of many of the previously stable male core of the industrial working class were compelled to seek paid employment to make ends meet (see Luxton and Corman 2001).

In retrospect, the 1982–83 period of mass layoffs can be seen as a transformative moment in the lives of Hilton steelworkers and their families. The job for life if they wanted it, which virtually all steelworkers with more than a few years' seniority had been able to assume, was suddenly revoked for junior workers and increasingly for more senior workers as well. Steelworkers' male breadwinner mindset was also undermined, first by the experience of the Women Back into Stelco campaign, then by the necessity of many of their wives having to go out to paid work in order for the household to continue to make ends meet. As large areas of Hilton Works became human deserts — to the extent that workers often "wondered whether there was anybody else in the shop" — the plant-based networks of community life also began to disintegrate. These tendencies only became widely evident over the following decade, and the affected steelworkers and their wives almost immediately began to reconstitute the employment, household and community spheres of their lives (see Luxton and Corman 2001 and the in-depth discussion in the next chapter in this book). But the downsizing and reorganization of the heart of Hamilton's steel industry irrevocably changed a way of life not just for steelworkers and their wives but for the entire community.

The dwindling core of aging Hilton workers responded to the drastic restructuring of their industry by sticking with their employer and adapting as best they could. The effects on their spouses' employment and on the domestic and community lives of both partners were often even more disruptive. The effects on those who left Hilton Works and the rest of steeltown were also disruptive. But there is not much evidence that these people became dispirited or debilitated for very long. A machine operator who took early retirement speaks for many former steelworkers when in the mid-1990s he said:

> When I was part of that 14,000 workforce, I was part of a very large family. There were always a lot of things going on. Being on my own now, you don't get the big family feeling that you had when you were part of the

steel company.... But there is life after Stelco.... It's unbelievable but a number of people plan their whole life around the steel company, and when it's ended they found out that, hey, there are other things to do. And they are just as interesting, and there is life, there is life after Stelco. The steel company is never going to be the dominant force in life that it was. Like it's not coming back.

A machine operator with about twenty years' seniority sounded much the same:

I've got a lot of responsibility now and I'm getting fair compensation.... But I still work shifts and it's getting a little rougher on me, because when I'm on dayshift, I live on about six hours of sleep a week. But now I take it in stride. It's something I got to do... all I have is another ten years to be eligible to get out of there. We're making a pretty decent wage down there and we got a little bit of security. (1994)

There was little mystery to the continuing lure of Stelco jobs for Hilton workers remaining in the plant in 2003. The wages and benefits offered "a little bit of security" in an increasingly uncertain labour market. Whether they remained in Hilton Works or moved on, the will and capacity of the former core of the Hamilton industrial working class to create the best lives they could for themselves and their families in times of pervasive challenge to a long-established way of life provided hope for a sustainable future community in steeltown. Steel will remain one of the most essential materials to sustain twenty-first century societies. But in terms of Stelco's sustainability, as Graph 1.5b shows, only 3 percent of this dwindling core of Hilton steelworkers was under thirty-five in 2003. The most pertinent questions, to which the following case studies turn, are "what are the barriers in everyday life to the transmission of the deep working knowledge of these very experienced steelworkers to younger workers" and "where is the next generation of Hilton steelworkers?"

Notes

1. Unless otherwise indicated, all quotes used in this chapter are drawn from interviews with USWA members at Stelco's Hamilton Works. These interviews were conducted in 1984, 1994 and 2004, as indicated in the text or at the end of the quote.
2. Portions of this chapter are derived from Livingstone (1993 and 1996).
3. This plant was known as Hilton Works until the takeover by U.S. Steel in 2007, after which it was renamed Hamilton Works. The two terms are used interchangeably in this text.
4. The data source for all international trends referred to in this section, unless otherwise specified, is the International Iron and Steel Institute (IISI) (2004 and earlier years).

5. For detailed accounts of state activities in post-1974 steel restructuring, see Howell et al. (1988); Mény and Wright (1985); Scheuerman (1986); Jones (1986); and M. Donaldson (1982).

6. The social impacts of steel job losses have been most fully documented, predictably, in the United Kingdom, France and the United States. On the United Kingdom, see Morgan (1983); Harris, Lee and Morris (1985); Westergard, Noble and Walker (1989); and Hudson and Sadler (1989). On France, see Noirel (1980) and Villeval (1988). On the United States, see Buss and Redburn (1983a, 1983b); Cunningham and Martz (1986); and Bensman and Lynch (1987).

7. For summary accounts of steel companies' industrial relations approaches in advanced capitalist economies after the onset of the global crisis, see Aylen (1986); Rhodes and Wright (1988); Villeval (1988); Villa (1987); Ahlburg et al. (1987); Clark (1987); Haughton (1989) and Klein and Paul (1986).

8. See, e.g., the papers presented at the International Conference on Workplace Change: Human Resources and Rationalization in the Global Steel Industry, June 5–6, 1995, Toronto (Verma, Frost and Warrian 1995).

9. For an insightful account of the historical development of capitalist strategies in these terms, with particular attention to the steel industry, see Lazonick (1983).

10. From this perspective, Henry Ford's introduction of the mechanical assembly line and the five dollar day in 1914 is merely one highly influential effort in a wide array of production strategies. Discussions of Fordist and post-Fordist production eras tend to exaggerate both the pervasiveness and distinctiveness of Fordist features. For a critical discussion, see Foster (1988). On more recent neo-Taylorist adaptations of the labour process and potential challenges to neo-Taylorism with computerization, see Palloix (1978) and Lojkine (1986). For suggestive arguments about a broader cultural tendency of "Social Taylorism," see Robins and Webster (1988).

11. See, e.g., the "New Directions Bargaining Program," adopted by the United Steelworkers of America (USWA) in early 1993 (Kleiman 1995).

12. Fairly detailed accounts appear in McGannon (1971).

13. A similar distinction is made by Darnell, Miles and Morrison (1984). Useful descriptions and evaluations of most of the technical innovations cited here may be found in Office of Technology Assessment (OTA) (1980).

14. Thomas Boklund, chairman, president and CEO of Oregon Steel Mills, as quoted in New Steel Roundtable (1996: 68).

15. For general accounts of the comparative performance of the Canadian steel industry after 1974, see Litvak and Moule (1986); Cheung, Krinsky and Lynn (1985); Ontario Premier's Council (1988); Ministry of State, Science and Technology (1988); Masi (1991); Verma and Warrian (1992); Verma, Frost and Warrian (1995).

16. This conservative capacity strategy on the part of Canadian steel firms has been widely noted in the literature, along with a related tendency among the largest firms to intensify vertical integration during market downturns rather than diversifying into other industrial sectors. According to one estimate, the profit rate of the Canadian steel industry remained over 20 percent during the 1974–1980 period. See Webber (1986: 219); see also Masi (1991).

17. See Fennessy (2009) for a detailed account of employment estimates for the Canadian steel industry.

18. For general historical accounts of the development of the Hamilton steel companies, see Kilbourn (1960). For post-war production share data, see Woods, Gordon and Co. (1977).

19. Relevant historical accounts dealing primarily with the period up to 1946 may be found in Heron (1982, 1988) and Storey (1981a, 1981b).

20. On technological developments in the Canadian steel industry with a special focus on Hamilton's mills, see Williams (1986); Storey and Petersen (1987); McMulkin (1964); Chandler (1985); Sandberg and Bradbury (1988).

21. Percentages are estimated from data in Stelco annual reports.

22. For a detailed account of Stelco management's search for changes in the post-war industrial relations model and Local 1005's responses, see Corman, Luxton, Livingstone and Seccombe (1993).

23. For a comparable overview of Stelco's restructuring, based on interviews with Stelco executives, Hilton Works managers and 1005 officials and including a comparative case study of workplace restructuring at Hilton Works and Lake Erie Works, see Frost and Verma (1997) and Frost (2000).

24. For a detailed account of the completion of this $350 million modernization program, see Samways (1988).

25. During the 1980s, most major steel modernization projects in North America involved joint ventures with Japanese or German companies and were supervised by their engineers; see Scherrer (1991). In Hamilton, Mitsui Corporation loaned Stelco $300 million to build the Hilton casters and later loaned $300 million to Dofasco to build a new cold rolling mill. Mitsubishi Corporation assumed joint ownership and control of Hilton's Z-Line galvanizing facility, and Sanyo Steel Company was involved in the design of the new Hilton bar line; see, e.g., Davie (1989). These ventures increasingly included Japanese steel firms training Hilton workers; see Stinson (1991).

26. For an accessible account of the Japanese-designed "lean production system" as well as the greater Japanese penetration of the North American auto industry, see Womack, Daniel and Roos (1990: esp. 223–75). On international joint ventures, see Mangum, Kim and Tallman (1996).

27. A 1984 Hamilton-wide survey found that among the industrial working class, generally about half worked regular days while 40 percent had shift schedules that included nights. In contrast, large majorities of the workforce in all other occupational classes worked regular daytime hours. Over 80 percent of managers and professionals worked regular days, and nearly 70 percent of supervisors did. Hamilton industrial workers kept production going largely on their own after dark (Livingstone 1996; Luxton and Corman 2001).

28. For the most prominent case pursued by the Ontario Ministry of Labour, see Papp 1991: A10.

29. For earlier comparative analyses of the operation of layoff-recall systems in mature unionized industries, see Berg (1981).

30. In the December 1984 interview just mentioned, Local 1005 officials estimated that on the basis of changes in their members' clock numbers, up to 15 percent may have been bumped.

31. *Co-operative Wage Study Manual for Job Description, Classification and Wage Administration* (1973). For an insightful account of the historical construction of this system, see Stone (1974: 61–97).

32. On the application of the notions of individual and collective job ownership in the steel industry and the associated struggles between management and labour, see Storey (1994).

33. Interview with A. Gillis, USWA Local 1005, December 3, 1984.

34. In contrast to Hilton Works, a similar restructuring process at Lake Erie Works led to greater worker job choice, semi-autonomous crews and sustained productivity gains. At Hilton, there was little direct worker consultation about job redesign and no job rotation or cross-training to develop competencies with the entire coking process (Frost 2000).

35. Percentages are calculated from Stelco annual reports for the period 1989–2003 and also personnel reports (Stelco 1989, 1996). Employment costs were again reduced to about 30 percent of sales income by 1988 and fluctuated around that level until 1996. Local 1005 remained over 46 percent of the total Stelco workforce in 1995.

36. For a detailed account of this management strategy, see Edwards Deming (1982: esp. 18–96 on the principles for transformation of Western management).

37. Cec Taylor was narrowly voted out of the Local 1005 presidency on August 9, 1983, over accusations of financial irregularities during the 1981 strike. The dispute over these accusations and an underlying concern among many activists about Taylor's allegedly arrogant style continued to seriously divide and distract the union's leadership until the April 1985 executive election. See, e.g., Pettapiece (1983) and Christmas (1983a and 1983b).

38. For both historical and current analyses of management and union initiatives around these issues in Canadian steel, with particular attention to Hilton Works, see R. Storey (1981a).

39. For a similar union account of Stelco's implementation of the new industrial relations model, see Groom (1990).

40. For insightful accounts of the development of Hilton's shop floor culture, see Heron (1982), Heron and Storey (1989), Storey (1981a) and the union magazine's special issue on the fortieth anniversary of the 1946 strike and the associated regular issue on its current relevance in *Steel Shots* (July 1986).

41. With regard to the flow of information from the union hall to the membership, *Steel Shots*, 1005's award-winning monthly magazine, ceased publication in June 1990, and very few information leaflets besides those related to contract bargaining rounds were distributed in the plant between late 1990 and late 1996. Some of our 1994 interview respondents complained about the difficulty in raising their concerns at general membership meetings; similar complaints were expressed by many respondents with regard to Cec Taylor's regime in 1983–84 (see Corman, Luxton, Livingstone and Seccombe 1993).

42. For a general comparative review of research on union participation, see Leicht (1989: 331–62).

43. For a representative international overview, see ILO (1983). For an in-depth account of the reorganization of training programs at Hilton Works during the 1980s, see Sanger (1988).

44. The post-Braverman debate about labour process deskilling or upgrading has been plagued with numerous conceptual and empirical confusions. For critical overviews, see Spenner (1983); Wood (1989), Livingstone (1999a); as well as Chapter 2 in this book.

45. Documentation of the increasing extent of awareness of underemployment among different occupational class groups in Ontario is presented in Livingstone (1999a) and Livingstone, Hart and Davie (1997).

Chapter 2

Storing and Transmitting Skills
The Expropriation of Working-class Control

Dorothy E. Smith and Stephan Dobson

The research for this chapter was conducted for the most part between 1998 and 2002 at a time when Stelco, and indeed the steel industry in Canada, could still be seen to have a historical continuity with its past. Since then, there have been radical changes, including a change in ownership and a radical reduction in the workforce employed from the local community in Hamilton at Hilton Works. The working-class community that is explored here and that had, over time and intergenerationally, stored, transmitted and perpetuated the manual skills that underpinned the industrial labour force in North America has now been undermined and depleted by the reductions in the industrial workforce in the region. What is described in this chapter no longer exists as it did.

The material herein is now a historical observation to be evaluated in relation to a historical trajectory in the making of a skilled labour force, a trajectory that moves from the centrality of the working-class community in storing and transmitting manual skills to an increasingly direct management of skill development and transmission by government and corporations. Our interest is in bringing into view what working-class communities have contributed to the growth of industrial capitalism. Our account speaks out of the past into a present that has displaced much of what our inter-views had to tell us. It draws attention to the changing institutional and organizational contexts implicit in what those we talked with had to tell us. These are the changes that project into the future the virtual destruction of the social relations and organization reproducing manual skills among (mostly) men in working-class communities supplying the labour force for major industrial complexes such as those of the steel industry in Hamilton, Ontario.

The Study

This chapter emerges from a study that explored the relationships between the great working-class communities and the industries that they both sustained and were sustained by in terms of the production, storage and transmission of skills. Among men, so-called "manual skills" were learned in part experientially, on-the-job, but they were also learned intergenerationally, both in the community and in the workplace. The last forty years of economic reorganization has radically undermined the processes of skills storage and transmission vested in a social organization among working-class men — and sometimes women — intersecting workplace and community. This chapter is based in part on the ethnographic literature on industrial workplaces and the working-class communities associated with them and in part on interviews with eight steelworkers employed at Stelco in Hamilton, Ontario. All but two of these started work at Stelco's Hilton Works in the 1970s (the exceptions started in the late 1960s); all were employed at the plant; three were also on the staff of Local 1005 of the United Steelworkers.[1] In our interviews, we talked in an unstructured fashion with these workers about how they learned their jobs at various points in their working lives and from whom and how they acquired the manual/mechanical skills they brought into their work in the plant. The working lives of those we interviewed have been a local experience of the radical restructuring of the steel industry in North America that was taking place during the 1980s and early 1990s.

What these people had to tell us has been our major resource, and we have tried to draw on these interviews in such a way that their voices are heard and are not dominated by ours. Indeed, much that is written here is in a sense "dictated" by what we learned from the interviews. The general approach adopted in our investigation has been influenced by a sociology known as institutional ethnography (Smith 2006). Institutional ethnography takes up people's everyday experiences as they tell them and explores the relations beyond the local that enter into and organize them. Other than the manner in which we oriented our interviews by asking respondents to tell us about learning on the job, we did not work with specific questions. Rather, we ourselves were learning and discovering much that we could not have known before our conversations. It was when we were reading through our transcribed interviews and bringing them together in another kind of conversation that we came to recognize traces of the historical trajectory from the early 1980s through the time of our interviews (2000–1) shifting the locus of what had been on-the-job learning to community college courses and programs designed for specific corporations.

In addition to interviewing people at that time employed at Stelco, we also drew on the ethnographic literature on working-class communities and the industrial workplace. Learning and training are not generally a focus in this literature so that material on these topics was on the whole sparse and indirect. Nonetheless, there has been much to learn from these sources and it is introduced here as it becomes relevant. In addition, we made use of some of the research that George Smith and Dorothy Smith undertook in the late

1980s on issues of training in the plastics processing industry (Smith 1988; Smith and Smith 1990).

Our interest in the interview part of the work was in learning processes and on being able to describe these as people experienced them. Of course, our number of interviewees is small and we make no claims to a representative sample. Rather, our focus is on what we can learn about *processes* of learning and of transmitting that which was learned outside formalized learning in classrooms or other situations of formalized instruction in the plant and in the community. We talked with our respondents at length, sometimes on more than one occasion. They were people who had trained as technicians and production workers. We were interested primarily in how people learned their jobs and particularly in experiential learning (the topic of the third section of this chapter). Formulations of "skill" as these are recognized in personnel files or as credentials are a barrier to our learning more about the social organization within which skills — as people's actual know-how — have been learned and transmitted within the working class.

Looking back through the prism of our transcribed interviews, it seems that our questions and the responses we were given focused on the "how" of informal learning rather than the content of learning; what would be understood as "learning" was defined by those we interviewed. We did not work from a formalized definition of learning, thereby restricting questions to definitional parameters. We took "learning" in its everyday senses, taking advantage of the ordinary way in which everyday terms become expanded and specified in the course of talk (see Campbell and Gregor 2002: 69, 77–79; Smith 2005: Ch. 6). Focusing on the "how" of learning allowed those with whom we talked to take it up as active, as something they did rather than as an abstract process. As such, learning did not become defined on analogy with formalized learning, which differentiates a period of learning from its result in a competence, generally represented in formal educational settings by a credential. Though that kind of formalized structure was represented in some accounts, the people we talked to described learning as taking place in many settings and as part of their everyday working and community lives. Asking about learning focused attention on what could count as learning in everyday work settings.

A good deal is known about the formal processes of storing and transmitting skills and very little about the social *forms* that organize the storing and transmitting of skills that are defined as informal, in part because they have not been "recognized" by formal educational processes and do not result, for those who exercise them, in definite qualifications.[2] The topic of this chapter is precisely that of the social organization storing and transmitting informal skills in the community and in the workplace, as well as the significance of the industrial restructuring of the 1980s and 1990s for their social organization.

Ethnographic and historical studies of workplace and working-class communities give clues to the character of relations that reproduced skills among working-class men across generations. Historically, the intergenerational storing and transmitting of skills has generally been identified with apprenticeships into guilds, crafts and trades. Forms of collective organization establishing a monopoly of specialized skills and formalizing relationships in which the next generation learned from the earlier one as apprenticeships has a very long history. In late nineteenth-century North America they became established as an aspect of the operation of craft and trade unions (in contrast to industrial union forms of organization). Since that time, apprenticeships and the associated formalized credentials have been increasingly incorporated into college systems. Such visible and formalized forms of transmitting skills are not the only ones; rather, they are the institutional surface of a largely hidden history of the social organization of skills transmission in the North American working class.

Our interest in this study is twofold: first, in identifying the traces of a past when access to workplace skills (for the most part among men) was largely controlled by working-class men, and second, in the former dependence of industrial production on systems of storing and transmitting skills that were buried in the relations between so-called "stable" working-class communities and large-scale industrial enterprises. These systems of storing and transmitting informal skills have been disrupted in processes of technological and managerial restructuring that have radically reduced the numbers of a workforce in a given industry and hence that workforce's ability to sustain a stable working-class community over several generations.[3] As we shall see, the process outlined here can be traced in the lives of the steelworkers we interviewed.

"Downsizing," "restructuring," "quality" initiatives, "efficiency" efforts and so on refer to the contemporary reorganization of capitalist enterprise. New technologies and, in particular, the computer have been transforming not only technologies of production but also technologies of management. These new technologies of management have standardized procedures and introduced systems of accountability and supervision that radically reduce the agentic role of labour in large-scale manufacturing (and indeed in other sectors). Such changes are not only oriented to reducing the cost of labour to the corporation. They are also part of the continuing project of subjecting the workplace to an increasingly pervasive managerial control (see, e.g., Noble 1984; Waring 1991).[4] Work processes have been increasingly intimately articulated to the managerial and financial accounting systems that, eventually, tie the enterprise as a whole into global financial markets. Workers, in turn, develop strategies aimed to shape the labour process from their own standpoint. While the outcomes of management efforts to shape the workplace for increased capital accumulation are not always as intended, an aspect of that increased managerial control that is of special interest here is the development of skills training technologies and managerial and corporate strategies that are aimed at breaking workers' monopoly of skills training vested in workplace hierarchies and in stable working-class communities.

The first part of this chapter focuses on skill as a social relation — on the storage and transmission of skills within the everyday sites of workers' lives and how the intergenerational transmission of skills is disrupted by processes usually labelled as "restructuring." The second section, arising from interviews with steelworkers, examines the distinctive role of informal skills in the plant and how they have been learned and transmitted among workers. The third section analyzes how worker-controlled skills training has been displaced, expropriated and worked up into textual devices such that management could further the project of control over the labour process. The final section, on experiential learning, examines just what it is that is being disrupted through such managerial devices.

The notion of "skill" in this context has no special theoretical weight. It differentiates among individuals with respect to their capacities and competencies to perform in definite work settings and in definite tasks or types of tasks. *Formal* skills are differentiated from *informal* ones by institutional processes of training. The former are "produced" as qualifications based on courses of instruction that are standardized across institutional settings. The resulting qualifications have recognized status in the labour market (Gaskell 1992: Ch. 6) and in job classifications specifying definite skills (such as the Co-operative Wage Study [CWS]) in the steel industry.[5] Informal skills are those that are learned outside definite institutionalized processes of training and do not result in definite qualifications that as a result are institutionally actionable (see Chapter 1). The kinds of housewifely skills that women may learn from other women in the course of growing are classic examples of informal skills (Griffith and Smith 2005; Eichler 2005). Early apprenticeships were purely on-the-job learning; as manufacturing technologies advanced, such learning through working with someone already knowledgeable was supplemented by programs in community colleges, usually staffed by instructors who were themselves certified in particular crafts or trades. Certification criteria were established by craft or trade associations and validated by provincial governments. As we later hear from Steve, who was apprenticed as an instrument technician while employed at Stelco, while the company might pay for certain college courses while he was employed at the steel plant, the courses themselves were not designed specifically for the corporation. Indeed, the form of apprenticeship combining on-the-job learning with supplemental college courses meant that the company was contributing indirectly to skills that were identifiable with a government-certified qualification and were hence marketable elsewhere.

While there are definite processes of transmitting informal skills, they are not institutionally recognized, though they may be valued informally within the paid workforce. The double focus on skills storage and transmission in working-class communities and on the acquisition and transmission of skills in the paid workplace illuminates the nature of the skills resources created by workers in both community and industrial settings. The concern here in general is with informal skills that have been traditionally sustained, both in the community and in the plant, by workers among themselves. The conditions and circumstances that generated these skills resources and enabled their transmission are undermined in the management and governmental processes of restructuring. The social organization of skills storage and transmission, both in the plant and in the community, is at risk in the combination of the downsizing that dismantles the great working-class communities, the technological and managerial restructuring of an industry and the increasing substitution of formalized and institutionally controlled forms of training for the informal modes among working-class women and men.

The Contingent Destruction of the Worker-Controlled System of Storing and Transmitting Skills

As skill becomes increasingly taken up within relations of formalized instruction, as in colleges and non-craft apprenticeship programs, skill becomes a property of institutional knowledge and is alienated from worker control. When the issue of loss of control over skills and of the degradation of labour is examined in terms of intersecting social relations, we suggest that what comes into view is the progressive destruction of a "system" of storing, producing and reproducing the skills of hand, eye and brain which was lodged in the intersection of industrial enterprise and working-class community, and largely organized and reproduced by working-class men outside the formal educational processes instituted by the state. The great industrial engine of capitalism that we know as "Fordism" depended on these systems of storing and transmitting skills at the same time as these systems were being progressively appropriated by management in efforts to wrest control of the production process from labour in the cause of capital accumulation.[6]

We do not view our line of argument and investigation as conflicting with the emphasis on either skills as they are operative in the workplace or on the changing nature of controls in the workplace (Burawoy 1978, 1979). Rather, we are concerned to examine the storage and transmission of skills as a social organization internal to the working class in both workplace and community and how this organization has been undermined, if not destroyed, by the changes popularly called "restructuring." The very existence of large working-class communities in the previously established industrial centres of the northeastern United States and of southeastern Canada has been undermined by the "flight" of industrial production to the southern United States and to Mexico, as well as offshore. This relocation of industrial production was undertaken as a deliberate and conscious strategy on the part of absentee[7] capitalists to lower costs, in part through establishing greenfield production in areas either of low union density or in so-called "right to work" states.[8]

That technological innovations, job task reorganization and other forms of restructuring aim at reducing labour costs is scarcely news. The costs for working people's lives is another matter entirely, as succinctly stated by Livingstone:

> The major human consequence of this cost-cutting logic in steel has been the most massive single-industry job losses in the history of capitalist manufacturing, with widespread disruption of the communities that had grown up around these large integrated steel plants. By 1990 the steel industries of the advanced capitalist economies had eliminated more than a million jobs and more than half their 1974 work force, with the vast majority of these reductions occurring prior to 1983. Whether in the form of plant closures or chronic layoffs, destroying the long-established wage-earning relationship in steel has meant that many workers have faced early retirement, prolonged unemployment, or the prospect of much lower paid jobs, often far afield. Their household partners have increasingly been impelled to seek generally low-paying, often temporary jobs in an attempt to reconstitute the "family wage." Young men can no longer expect to follow their fathers into secure jobs at the local steel mill. (1993: 19)

Intergenerational transmission and peer exchange of skills that have been integral aspects of the social relations of working-class communities and the industrial settings of the past have been disrupted. An incidental effect has been the destruction of the social organization reproducing skills and masculine values across generations:

> In Hamilton, as elsewhere, the new jobs in the 1980s were being furnished by small firms operating mostly in the service sector. The steel industry, while still central to the city's economy, had ceased to be a source of employment for working-class male youths graduating from the city's high schools, whose fathers, in many cases, were steelworkers.... Increasingly, steelworkers were older men nearing retirement age: the average employee at Hilton Works has now worked for Stelco for more than twenty-five years. "Global restruc-

turing" has produced a deep generational split in the working class. (Corman et al. 1993: 10)

The great working-class communities of the past and the industries on which they depended, and which in turn depended on them, can be imagined as engines reproducing manual/mechanical competency skills, with both industry and community creating a generalized level of manual accomplishment in the male working class. This included an increasing knowledge of mechanical systems and the uses of manual tools of considerable technological sophistication. This was a culture according respect to men who excelled in manual and mechanical skills and knowledge, both those relevant to non-workplace activities, such as home renovation and repair, automotive repair and reconstructions, and those produced and reproduced in the workplace. The former activities, we are suggesting, were foundational to the latter and created a reservoir of "human capital" that was certainly deployed in the interests of working-class communities and individuals but were also surely of direct and indirect — though largely invisible — benefit to capital.

A second dimension of these changes, extrapolating from the work of Harry Braverman (1974, 1982), who had been a craft metalworker, is what can be described as a phase of class struggle in which capital in new managerial forms has been constantly and restlessly in search of more effective means of expropriating — or displacing the need for — that which Marx called the knowledge, judgment and will of workers (1954: 341). Braverman's study, *Labor and Monopoly Capital* (1974), developed a thesis of the progressive degradation of labour as a consequence of the introduction of forms of "scientific" management, coupled with technological change. Mechanical and electronic technologies tend to displace the role in production of workers' thinking, the scope for making autonomous decisions and experientially elaborated know-how; managerial technologies exercise increasingly intimate control over the production process. In this study, we explore how the long struggle between capital and labour over the control of skills appears in the social relations in which skills are stored and through which they are transmitted. The research reported in this chapter explores a particular historical juncture in this struggle.

Braverman's study initiated a major debate: one side put in the foreground the technological changes that were represented as giving workers greater control over their work situation, freeing them from the constraints and stress of automated work processes (Blauner 1964; Hirschhorn 1984; Zuboff 1984). Rather than "degradation," these writers saw technological change as contributing to an *upgrading* of workers' skills, particularly their conceptual skills.[9] In contention with them are those who built on Braverman by emphasizing the "deskilling"[10] effects of the new forms of automation and managerial strategies, together resulting in an increasingly effective subordination of workers to the changing regime of accumulation (Thompson 1989; Wood 1989; Crompton and Jones 1984; Vallas and Beck 1996).[11]

In this chapter, Braverman's account of the emergence of managerial technologies and their expropriation of workers' skills and knowledge is seen as registering part of a larger development. From the late nineteenth century onward, objectified and trans-local forms of organization have been emerging and expanding their scope in tandem with the development of the joint-stock company and the corporation. The ruling relations — the complex of objectified social relations that organize and regulate our lives in contemporary society — progressively absorb or displace forms of social organization that arise directly among people in local settings of their lives, displacing the perspectives and concerns of individuals. Objectifications, as locally achieved *practices*, require individuals to subordinate personal and local perspectives to those that can be expressed in formalized discourses determining not so much what individuals think as what they can speak or write of in the settings of their work (Smith 1999), and hence what can be recognized and taken into account and so made institutionally actionable; indeed, it is these objectifications that make large-scale, trans-local organization possible. In the industrial setting, these objectified formalized discourses include systems of accounting and of organizational design, new managerial ideologies and specific managerial devices such as procedural pathways, quality control manuals, job classification books, job descriptions and the many other textual devices through which management brings work at the level of the shop floor and the overall activity of a corporation into line with its status on the financial markets.

Our notion of skill builds upon but goes further than Braverman's. He analyzes the *social* aspect of the notion of "skill" by arguing that it is a function of job and census classifications: "Classifications of workers, however, are neither 'natural' nor self-evident, nor is the degree of skill a self-evident quality which can simply be read from the labels given to various such classifications" (1974: 428). To this, we add that classifications of "skill" — that is, so-called "formal skill" — are a product of *textual processes of accounting* which standardize across multiple local settings of work; as such, they are the product of the classifier's "method of assessment" (see Smith 1988: 3),[12] which ascribes "skill" to an individual *as an ontological property of that person* rather than as a social relation. In her critique of a concept of skill that excludes many of the skills that women acquire in school or in their traditional roles in the family, Gaskell (1992) suggested that skills should be understood as a property of the organization of a labour market. She is concerned with the contrast between skills that have some recognized value versus others that may be "skills" in terms of the actual competencies of individuals but are not recognized or marketable as such; similarly, within a large industrial organization, skills may be recognized or marketable in an internal labour market in more or less clearly defined ways (1992: 113, 119). Though Gaskell's formulation is not explicitly in terms of social relations, her proposal to see "skills" as a property of a labour market is fully compatible with such an approach.

Defining skill in terms of what is recognized and has significance in the social relations of a market or of the social organization of large-scale industrial organization is a significant difference from Braverman's use of the term. He is talking about skills as properties of individuals, their know-how. His account of what he calls the "degradation" of work focuses on the managerial expropriation of the knowledge and decision-making capacities that were a defining attribute of skills in the past.[13] Control of the work and work process is progressively transferred to management (itself subject to downsizing), in part through technological innovations designed to reduce workers' control over the production process rather than to complement workers' skills (e.g., Noble 1984), and in part through the elaboration of the textual technologies of managerial accounting, including more recently computerization (in a sense, Braverman's story ends too soon). However, his study collapses the complexities of managerial and technological changes into the concept of "scientific management," thereby bypassing the social organization of the "degradation of skilled work" at the level of people's everyday lives. The latter is the object of inquiry in this chapter. "Skill" in the sense that we are getting at does not exist *in potentia*, as a possibility accounted for by systems of classification, but rather as it has been learned and used in concrete contexts within the labour process; as such, "skill" is a feature of *organization*, and it is the "hidden," "informal" aspects of workers' knowledge and competency as expropriated that is the focus of inquiry and analysis here.

At the turn of the twentieth century in North America and other "developed" countries, rapid innovations were being made that have permanently transformed the way in which the social is organized at the level of the society at large (Beniger 1986). Developments in the bureaucratization of the state, familiar in sociological literature from the writings of Max Weber (1978) and Thorstein Veblen (1954), were accompanied by radical innovations in the management of business enterprises (Waring 1991) and, associated with the rise of corporations, a move away from the identification of business with individual owner/managers (Braverman 1974: 258; Chandler 1977; Noble 1977; Roy 1997). The governance of cities began to be transformed from forms of patronage to bureaucratic administrations. Public schooling came to be organized through the administrative apparatus of school districts and a professional educational staff of college- or university-trained teachers.

Generally speaking, professions came into new prominence as a method of guaranteeing training, credentials and standards in the widely dispersed settings of professional practice (Larson 1977; Noble 1977; Collins 1979), a development of special importance given the geography of North America.

The trajectory of the ruling relations since the late nineteenth century, at least in North America, has been one that progressively expropriates locally developed forms of social organization embedded in particularized relationships. In his major studies of the emergence of what he calls "the visible hand," Chandler (1977) directed attention to the progressive *incorporation* of the local organization of economic functions and their *co-ordination* through networks of market relations into the large-scale corporation. The unregulated processes of the market became integrated with the administration of the corporation. Problems of financing and of credit that dogged systems of exchange based on sequences of transactions among small local businesses came to be regulated under the administrative umbrella of a corporation's managerial and accounting systems. Uncertainties in sources of supplies were resolved by vertical integration with manufacturing (Galbraith 1985: 25, 29). For example, General Motors (Sloan 1964) first expanded in a process of vertical integration of independent craft firms that were suppliers of parts. The objective was to secure a co-ordination of supplies with expanding production. A second kind of acquisition was of firms making automobiles occupying different market segments from General Motors, but potentially in competition with it. Similarly, the expansion of mail order retailing and of department stores appropriated and displaced the local organization of jobbers, incorporating their functions into a single administrative system (Mills 1951: 25–6; Braverman 1974: 371 and 371n; Chandler 1977).

Complementing Chandler's account was Thorstein Veblen's earlier observation of the transformation of the country town with the expansion of what he calls "Big Business." He described the country town as a "retail trading-station" in which towns people competed for the product of farms or to sell to farmers the means of production (Veblen 1954: 144). The coming of "Big Business" transformed this. Smaller retail and wholesale businesses were subordinated to the new large-scale forms of organizing business:

> Increased facilities of transport and communication; increased size and combination of the business concerns engaged in the wholesale trade, as packers, jobbers, warehouse-concerns handling farm products; increased resort to package-goods, brands, and trademarks, advertised on a liberal plan which runs over the heads of the retailers; increased employment of chain-store methods and agencies; increased dependence of local bankers on the greater credit establishments of the financial centers. (Veblen 1954: 154)

"The country town," he wrote, "is no longer what it once was," a local habitation in which a man might "bear his share in the control of affairs without being accountable to any master-concern 'higher up' in the hierarchy of business" (Veblen 1954: 155; see also Mills 1951).

Braverman's account of how managerial technologies have displaced the forms of skills and judgment that were the property of workers is thus, we argue, to be seen as a part of a more general process of the expanding ruling relations,[14] an expansion that has accelerated rapidly in the last twenty years or so with the advances of computer technologies and that, viewed from the perspective of a new century, can be seen as an expansion of capital's penetration of the organization of people's everyday lives, whether in the workplace or community. What we call "restructuring" is more than change in the technologies of production; it involves changes in the technologies of ruling or governance that go significantly beyond the industrial setting itself. Restructuring links the industrial setting to technological initiatives (originating in engineering) that hook up, via the refinement of systems of accounting, the managerial system of control of production to the market dynamics of financial capital. At the level of production, skills have been both "degraded" and displaced by new kinds of skills. The latter, however, are not skills that can be learned informally in the traditional pattern of transmission, of which apprenticeship was the ideal type, and various authors have pointed out that under lean production these "new" skills are hardly "upgraded" in any meaningful sense from the perspective of workers (Livingstone 1996: 48–49; Rinehart, Huxley and Robertson 1997: 37–38, 46; T. Smith 2000: Ch. 2; Braverman 1974: Ch. 20). Training functions are progressively transferred from relationships among workers in a given plant to the local community college (such as Mohawk College, in Hamilton, Ontario) and to government funded or subsidized programs delivered by both private and public training institutions. In addition to apprenticeship programs — themselves increasingly involving formal learning that participates in the same technical and intellectual discourses as engineering — community colleges provide courses and "modules" for production workers tailormade for the specific needs of companies. The transfer of knowledge, judgment and skills is not only from workers as individuals to management, but from the workplace and relationships among workers to formalized educational institutions integrated with the technical and scientific knowledge systems that directly or indirectly serve the main business of capital, namely capital accumulation.

Increasingly, skills training involves formal training in the classroom as well as on-the-job training. Formalized learning is located in scientific and technical discourses that are standardized not just for a particular plant or region but as technical and scientific knowledge that is developed and is transmitted discursively. When skills were passed on directly from individual to individual at work, traditions varied — depending on the individuals through whom it was transmitted, their experience, discoveries and abilities. By contrast, in formalized learning situations, teaching materials, such as textbooks, the formal training and credentialing of instructors and the like, standardize at least the formal dimensions of skills across local settings and draw upon a scientifically generated knowledge base in engineering and the natural sciences.

These changes in the organization of skills storage and transmission invite us to go beyond Harry Braverman's account of how the development and expansion of the managerial technologies associated with the work of Taylor have resulted in the "degradation" of work. He argues that as these technologies advance, they expropriate the knowledge and judgment of workers. Progressively the dimensions of skill that have been essential to industrial labour are displaced by transformations of machine technologies and the transfer of forms of co-operation from interrelations among people on the shop floor to machines. Increasingly, computers directly integrate the co-ordination of industrial processes with the managerial system. The kinds of changes that have been occurring with increased rapidity in the last thirty years call for an expanded conception that goes beyond management to attend to wider transformations of the ruling relations (Smith 1999).

What has subsequently been emphasized in studies stemming from Braverman is the effect of changing and increasingly engrossing technologies of management on the deskilling of jobs and workers. Studies that focus on deskilling, however, drop an important dimension of Braverman's study. For Braverman, the degradation of work is an integral part of class struggle, not in the sense of a social movement, but as Marx originally conceptualized it, particularly in his account of so-called primitive accumulation in the first volume of *Capital* (1954). There, Marx described the active role of the rising bourgeoisie in establishing a working class. He showed the complementary relation between owners of the means of production and those lacking such means that constitutes capital as a social relation (1954: 667–715). Braverman, having described modes of control used by capitalists in the early days of industrialization in the United States, goes on to note the interests of capital in expanding control over workers. Braverman extended his argument into the contemporary forms of class struggle that he observed and analyzed:

> In those early efforts, the capitalists were groping toward a theory and practice of management. Having created new social relations of production, and having begun to transform the mode of produc-tion, they found themselves confronted by problems of management which were different not only in scope but also in kind from those characteristic of earlier production processes. Under the special

and new relations of capitalism, which presupposed a "free labour contract," they had to extract from their employees that daily conduct which would best serve their interests, to impose their will upon their workers while operating a labor process on a voluntary contractual basis. (1974: 67)

The major managerial innovation responding to this problem, inherent in capitalism, was that of scientific management, associated in particular with the name of Frederick Winslow Taylor, and developed in the late nineteenth and early twentieth centuries:

> The essential element is the systematic pre-planning and pre-calcula-tion of all elements of the labor process, which now no longer exists as a process in the imagination of the worker but only as a process in the imagination of a special management staff. Thus, if the first principle is the gathering and development of knowledge of labor processes, and the second is the concentration of this knowledge as the exclusive province of management — together with its essential converse, the absence of such knowledge among workers — then the third is the *use of this monopoly over knowledge to control each step of the labor process and its mode of execution*. (Braverman 1974: 119, emphasis in the original)

Braverman's analysis was confined to industry, particularly manufacturing, with some attention to service and clerical jobs (1974: Part IV) and the role of education in creating a "manageable" and socialized labour force (1974: 287–88; 436). The concept of "ruling relations" (Smith 1999, 2005) locates these changes in a more general framework of the development of objectified forms of social organization and relations that include, as described earlier, not only management but also the variety of institutional forms including formal education institutions (schools, community colleges and universities). The ruling relations are represented as a trajectory of increasing transfer of control and organization from individuals and local settings and relationships, to objectified and abstracted forms. Veblen's account of the radical change in the social relations of local cities as multiple small businesses, individually owned, are displaced by corporations no longer identified with particular individual owners is an example of this trajectory.

The expansion of the ruling relations is not just internal to industry. Radical changes in the educational system shift significant dimensions of skills learning from the internal organization of industry and from relationships within the working class to formalized training in definite institutional settings. Developments in science and engineering stemming from research, changes in the professional education of engineers, reworking of government regulation of qualifications and credentials, and the redesign of courses and programs in community colleges (Dennison and Gallagher 1986; Smith 1990; Hull 1998; Hull 2003: 66), among others, are no less part of the overall transformation that we call "restructuring" than are the reorganization of industry and of the relations of capital itself.[15] The conceptualization of these as part of the expanding trajectory of the ruling relations draws attention to the following three dimensions:

1) the co-ordination of people's activities in multiple local sites through social relations organized outside those local settings, connecting people and co-ordinating their work in modes that do not depend on particularized relationships between people;

2) the progressive standardization and generalization of specific forms, procedures, files, criteria, technologies, knowledges and so on and so on, across such local sites; and finally,

3) the ways in which the expanding trajectory of these relations expropriate forms of organization, knowledge and skills that are vested in local settings, localized relationships and particular individuals. (see Smith 1999)

The remainder of this chapter is organized as three sections: the first focuses on the storing and transmission of informal skills as these have been embedded in relationships in the working-class community. We are concerned to trace the relational contexts in which the manual/mechanical skills by which industries drew on the manpower — and we use the term advisedly; the vast majority were men — of a given community could be taken for granted. The second topic is that of the changing organization of training from those forms largely under working-class control. In the interviews with people working at Stelco from the 1970s to the period of the research (i.e., 1998 to 2003), we discovered learning that was still embedded in localized relationships and had not yet been displaced by formalized training in the company or drawn into the formalizations and regulated relations of colleges and universities. This experiential learning is explored in the third section. Those interviewed were mostly individuals who had learned their jobs within the plant, although there were two whose learning on the job had been supplemented with courses at local community colleges. Since our interest was not strictly about, or not only in, issues of management "control" but rather in the extent to which learning had been incorporated into the systems of regulation, here called ruling relations, we did not explore the more formalized modes in which skills have been transmitted in the working class, namely apprenticeship in trades and crafts. For some time, such apprenticeships were linked to general vocational programs within high schools and required completion of secondary education (LeMaster 1975: 112); they have now been brought within the institutional system of training in community colleges and of state-regulated credentials.

The focus in this chapter is on the kinds of informal learning that took place on the job and in association with other workers or from operating and observing machine processes, or both. In a sense our study captures a particular historical moment of the longer trajectory that Braverman explicated. The very notion of "informal" skills itself attests to the ways in which the formalizations of training and credentials have increasingly encroached on learning that was formerly largely internal to the working class, whether in the community or in the workplace. In a sense, informal learning and skills are the fundamentals of people's everyday doings. The notion of learning isolates a normal process in which people's activities respond to, anticipate and transform our everyday lives. Such processes become defined in contrast to the ongoing appropriation of skills and skills learning into formally defined training processes that are specifically tied into scientific and technical knowledges generated by scientific, engineering and related institutions.

The general institutional account developed above is thus complemented by a picture, drawn from interviews that we conducted, of the changes as experienced by the Stelco workers we talked to. The account that follows weaves together the topic of change and restructuring with these experiential accounts. It draws on stories of the informal skills learning that was part of our respondents' leisure time activities, of the informal networks of skills learning among workers on the job and of the learning of the machine processes and of properties of the plant and its organization outside of those learnings that are formally recognized. The interest here is not just in uncovering the distinctive character of this form of learning, but also in indicating how, over time, the transmission of informal skills became increasingly uncertain under the changing industrial regime at Stelco.

Mechanical/Manual Skills and Working-Class Community Social Organization

The ethnographic literature has given little attention to the strictly informal learning among men of working-class communities. We can get clues about such learning from ethnographies and descriptions of these communities (e.g., Kusterer 1978; Halle 1984; Dunk 1991; Nash 1989, Harper 1987; Orr 1996; Hamper 1986; LeMasters 1975; Freeman 1982; and the ethnographic material in Livingstone and Sawchuk 2004b) and from remarkable studies of earlier periods (e.g., Rose 2001). In the community context, we are interested in informal skills that may not generally be recognized and that consist of a familiarity with certain kinds of tools and their uses (a mitre-box for example), with particular geographies and patterns of traffic, with what is inside the walls and underneath the floor, with what connects the gas cooker to the mains, the electric light switch to the lights, the spark plugs (in an older car) to the carburetor, the workings of transmission and clutch, and so on — the kind of knowledge that is prior to and presupposed in the learning of more specialized skills and in the kind of work that working-class men have traditionally undertaken and been assigned to in the industrial enterprise (see, e.g., Dunk 1991: 149).

Such "familiarities" became visible as skills, for example, for women when they first began to take vocational courses in preparation for entering trades. Dorothy remembers in the 1970s being told about shop courses in which women participated; the courses took for granted extensive prior experience in the names and uses of a variety of tools and practices associated with them. Alison, one of our Stelco interviewees, experienced this firsthand when she took a course around 1985:

> Okay. They used to talk about bearings, okay. I, being a woman, had no idea what a bearing was. Okay, so they used to say bearing, bearing, bearing, right? And I'd be there and I'd just regurgitate it, just say "It's a bearing and it does this, blah-blah-blah" but I didn't really understand it. Then you go into the plant and you see exactly what a bearing is, right?[16]

Similarly, in the workplace, informal knowledges of the particular local histories and geographies of plants, machines and people have been maintained and transmitted in gender-specific hierarchies of learning. This is knowledge that is prior to and taken for granted in knowledge at more "visible" levels. Michael Polanyi (1966) used the concept of "tacit knowledge" to locate that which people know that is not explicit, not named and not inculcated through a formalized process of instruction. He used as an example the spelling of a railway station in Wales with the longest name. It is one thing, he said, to know how to read it. But to know that it is a name and the name of a station on the railway line is presupposed in reading it as such. It is a knowledge on which knowing how to pronounce the name relies; such knowledges are tacit. In an analogous way, being able to do a particular kind of job depends on tacit knowledges which, at least in the past, have largely been learned experientially by doing, by watching and by being "shown" by someone who knows how and in informal relationships among people, relatives, friends, peers or workmates in workplace, community or household settings. This kind of learning goes on among people who do not occupy institutionalized positions designating them as responsible for transmitting formalized systems of knowledge and skill. It has gone on in working-class communities between kinfolk of senior generations and their juniors — fathers, grandfathers and uncles teaching boys and young men; mothers, grandmothers and aunts teaching girls and young women — by tacit example, by encouraging and criticizing attempts and by occasional instruction or intervention.

According to David Halle (1984: 35), the informal skill learning of leisure hours were strikingly "sex segregated," involving many of the married men and most of the single ones. LeMaster's study of a working-class community described deliberate strategies on the part of some men of the senior generation designed to prevent the "feminization" of boys and young men:

> These men share the belief of the British upper class that boys should never be reared by their mothers or other women, since they will make a "goddam sissy" of him. Since these men do not have the English boarding school system to rear their sons, they have to improvise. In the past, one of their strategies was to get the boy out of school as early as possible and get him on the job with other men, but this has become increasingly difficult as the craft unions have begun to require a high school diploma for entering apprentice programs. (1975: 112)

His study suggests that the senior generation of that time often consciously sought to wean boys from the influence of school, identified with feminization, stressing the importance of a toughening that would prepare a boy for what he could expect to confront in the future. Male workers favoured weaning boys from school to get them away from women teachers. Here is the view of a sheet-metal worker LeMaster talked to:

> If you can't get the boy out of the school system and away from the "goddam women teachers," then the next best bet is to get him into school athletics, especially football. One man, a sheet metal worker, put it this way: "I'll say one thing for that football coach up at the high school — he makes those guys get down in the mud and go at each other. By God, that's what they need to get along in this world." (1975: 112)

Glimpses such as this suggest that Paul Willis's (1988) exclusive focus on the class dynamics of the school may miss the process of learning masculinity from a senior generation consciously concerned to discourage boys from an educational exposure that would undermine it.[17]

Some of the workers we interviewed in Hamilton described learning the use of tools from their fathers. In our interviews with Stelco workers, transmission of skills with tools from father to son was a reoccurring theme, for example as with Steve, an instrument technician:

> My dad did a lot of woodworking and construction work around the house as well, did electrical work and stuff like that. So probably by the time I was

ten or twelve, if I wanted to add an electrical circuit in my bedroom to plug something in, I knew how to do that. I knew that it had to be in a box and… I had to use clamps every three feet for the wire. So when I took electrical in high school, they weren't teaching me anything I didn't already know. And a lot of that came from because my dad did that. He would also do it at my aunt's house and everywhere else where somebody asked him, you know, "Would you help me do this?" or "Would you help me to do that?"

Alison, an electrical utilities worker and the only woman in the group of workers we talked to at Stelco, described learning skills with tools from her father:

My father, as far as tools and everything, he always allowed me to help him. Like I could always repair my own bicycles and things like that. I didn't realize until later on that that was unusual for a girl at that time, to be able to do that, right? But he was always, like you know, if he was working on the car, he would always ask me and I'd help out or that kind of thing.

Notice that Alison attended to how her learning experiences differed from those of other girls in the community. The gendered transmission of skills appeared at a number of points in the interviews. In this example, the topic is not gender; rather, gender emerges in the interview process itself.

Learning informal skills at home was associated by many with "fooling around" with automobiles. This is a distinctly gendered leisure activity. In describing how he goes about working with an apprentice technician, Steve talked with pleasure about showing him the way he liked to work:

Steve: Occasionally we would take an instrument completely apart, and re-paint the case and clean each and every piece, and I enjoyed showing him the way that I like to work by rolling out a piece of paper towel and cleaning each and every part, polishing it up, and putting it in order, and then going back and reassembling it all.

Dorothy: You'd arrange it in like the assembly order, the order in which — Yeah.

Steve: Yeah. But I always liked to have the idea that you put it on a piece of paper towel, you'd roll out three or four pieces of paper towel, and each and every piece, when you put it on the paper towel, there was no rust on it, it was clean and shiny like a brand new part.

Stephan: You probably did that with automobiles.

Steve: Yeah.

Stephan: It's an automobile technique.

Dorothy: Oh yeah?

Stephan and Steve shared a knowledge of an "automobile technique," a method of organizing disassembly and reassembly of parts applicable to mechanical and electronic devices, that Dorothy did not share.

Various mechanical devices — automobiles, motorcycles, dune buggies, model boats — referred to in our interviews suggest the existence of a mechanical culture in the community. Here's Steve again:

> When I was in grade eleven, I bought a Hillman car and my buddy had a Morris Minor and we used to go to the car races every Friday and Saturday. So we were always under the hood of somebody's car.

Alison can be seen to participate in this culture when she described being able to share problems she encounters at work with her husband:

> My husband used to be... he used to work in a garage. I used his knowledge that way mechanically when I started there, very much so. So I used to go home and go "I've got this problem" and then I would explain it to him and he would say "Well, you could try this," you know.

Learning automobile techniques seemed, in our interviews, to involve peers rather than relationships between father and son or daughter. Bill, for example, had no special interest in cars, but he described helping friends out with theirs or hanging around with friends who made dune buggies:

> *Interviewer:* In your 20s, yeah so you were in the mill. Would you sometimes help friends out when their machines needed fixing, their cars, or their motorcycles or whatever or would you...?

> *Bill:* Whenever somebody asked me, I'd help them with something. I'd probably tell them if I didn't know anything about it, "well, I don't really know anything about it but I'll do what I can."

> *Interviewer:* Yeah, because like one of the things that I sometimes see, you know, that... a kid will have a car or a motorcycle and there may be a couple of guys kind of hanging around, you know, kind of talking about it.

> *Bill:* If that was your interest, if cars were your interest, like people hanging around and gravitate towards the people who have same interest as you and discuss cars and engines and whatever, and help each other working on them. I knew a couple of guys that built dune buggies. I used to hang around with them quite a bit, like for hours, just taking them apart and putting them back together again and welding a frame together.

Bill had rebuilt a carburetor just because he had never done it before: "So I just bought a kit, a carburetor rebuild kit, took everything apart, tried to put it back together and get it to run."

Other steelworkers we interviewed had similar interests in vehicles. Alex, a production worker at Stelco, had an antique car and belonged to a car club that included others working at Stelco; Steve, in addition to his interest in cars, raced motorcycles in his youth. Jim, also a production worker at Stelco, provided us with this account of his involvement with cars:

> *Interviewer:* Okay. So your cars, you talked about, one of the first things you did as soon as you were earning some decent money was buy two cars. Two cars. Did you fix them yourself?
>
> *Jim:* No, I bought a — I did. I fixed part of it. I bought a '67 Mustang, I've always liked the Mustang GT. Had a '67 and that was going to be my cruise car. And then I was going to buy — bought a junker to go back and forth to Stelco. So I bought two cars.
>
> *Interviewer:* And did you do the mechanical work on them yourself?
>
> *Jim:* No. My brother is into cars. Yeah. My brother plays with cars. [*Interviewer:* Older? Younger?] Younger. He likes playing with the cars. And a friend of mine who works at Stelco, we all had Mustangs, six of us all had Mustangs. So we all had Mustangs, and we all tried to outdo each other with our Mustangs and stuff like that. But my brother and my friend from Stelco were the guys that built my car. Built my 289. I mean, I paid them to do it and stuff like that, I bought the parts. My brother didn't charge me but this guy over here, yeah, he did. He does — the guy at work — builds engines and everything. He's smart.

Alex thought that his experience of working with cars made it easier for him to learn jobs at Stelco:

> I think when you're mechanically inclined, it makes that type of stuff come easier to you. It does. And you're not intimidated by it.

A common ground in a mechanically oriented community culture is evident in Steve's story of how two of his friends got jobs at Stelco:

> Interestingly enough, one of my closest friends — they [Stelco] had a bus come down from West Hill High School and took most of the electronics class during what was the Easter break then... and showed us movies, gave us demonstrations of their electrical maintenance program. A close friend of mine, there was two of them, they decided, "No, we're not interested in the electrical maintenance program," decided "We're going to sneak out for a cigarette." And they were going out the door for a cigarette and they ran into somebody from Utilities... who was the training supervisor for instrument repair, which they were interested in. He said, "Where are you guys going?" They said, "We're not interested in this program, so we're going to go for a cigarette." He said, "Well, come on with me, you can smoke in

my office." They talked about model boats for an hour, and they were both offered jobs in instruments. [laughter]

Presumably the instrument-repair training supervisor could recognize from the discussion of their shared interests the kinds of mechanical abilities and background these young men would bring to their training in addition to the shared interest in boats. Analogously, Alison is able to draw on the same common ground in a mechanically oriented community culture when she consults with her husband about problems at work. As we saw, though his skills are primarily in woodworking, he had earlier experience as an auto mechanic.

We asked Bill whether the skills he was learning building a carburetor or hanging around with guys constructing a dune buggy helped in the work he does now. His reply illustrates how learning specific skills may be generalized to a wider application:

> I think the more you play with something you learn how to think or you develop problem-solving skills. And they can apply to all kinds of things. Just the way you think. You notice a lot of people don't want to think at all; they'll take something instead of trying to fix it themselves, [instead of] taking a few minutes and learn it yourself. I'll take something apart and — What I did when I first started this finisher's job was to [take it] completely apart, see. Just saw how it worked, you know, put it back together. "Okay, now I know how it works."

The manual/mechanical culture among the men of the working-class community also contributed directly to the community's wealth. Several of those we talked to described an informal exchange of skills that enriched the local community's domestic life. The storing and transmitting of skills with tools and manual skills in general, whether among women or men, have enriched working-class communities, particularly since the success of struggles to limit the working day has meant that substantial time is available for use in and around the home, and help was often available:

> Whenever possible they avoid the market place, especially when it comes to constructing homes, refinishing interiors, making car and small equipment repairs, and so on. There is a flourishing "informal" labour exchange between individuals with different skills and different kinds of equipment. (Dunk 1991: 146–47)

Jim is particularly aware of the value of the varieties of complementary skills available in his group of friends:

> Like me, I was more into the physical. I'm not afraid to do any lifting or shovelling or moving people or stuff like that. And like some of my friends

were opposite, they loved the mechanical end of it, the intellectual end of it, eh? We all... did our own thing, but I mean like we all did everything, helped every — Like me, like when it came to moving each other, helping moving the house, we all were there for each other and stuff like that. So I mean, it's funny how we're all different in ways, but we all are so close. But it's nice to help out each other. Like I'd do anything for them, and they would do that [for me].

Jim, who does not think of himself as particularly skilled with tools, built his own basement with the help of a friend and his father:

I built my basement. Yes, I did, with a friend. I used a jackhammer. He helped me do my bathroom. I did the physical work, he put the — I dig the hole, he put the pipe in. I do all the physical work and he did all the, he knew how to — My dad helped too, when I did my bathroom, but he did, like, the hook-up of the toilet, and the shower, and the sink and everything. But the manual work, it's me.

Andy, an electrician at Stelco, described informal exchanges among neighbours in the community he lives:

Andy: Yes, I'm an electrician and I'm able to wire homes and I have done various homes in this subdivision and from the outset. And of course, then the problem [comes up] in life, that the circuit does not work, the light does not work, why? Then you have to go down and figure out why...

Interviewer: Yeah. So would you do that, would people pay you? Would you do it for free, or do they sometimes do things for you?

Andy: Well, usually people want to, I will do something for them, they will do something back, pay me back some other way. So this guy could be a mechanic and of course, my car needs to be tuned up and instead of paying me, he could just tune up my car.

Resources such as tools may be shared. Jim told us that he doesn't need to keep a lot of tools because he can borrow tools from others:

I haven't a lot of tools. My dad has tools so if I have to borrow anything I can borrow — Or my friend Al, like my good friend, he's got everything, every tool you need, he's got. He's got a wall like this [gestures spreading his arms], he's got all the toys. Mind, him and his wife make good money, and that's his hobby. He loves tools and everything. Like he's not afraid to try anything. So any time I need any, like he's an electrician by trade, but he's a handy man too. So I mean, I got people that anything I need to do. Like, I'll help them, I'll rip everything apart and dig it out, and I'll watch him and hand him the tools he wants. But I've never really had to do a lot of fixing little gadgets and stuff like that.

Jim's friends or family, with the skills he needs to supplement his own, are a major resource.

Though these descriptions are only sketchy, they tap into a hidden cultural life among men in working-class communities[18] that represents a real source of wealth outside the economic relations strictly defined in terms of the interchange of money and commodities. It is a form of "human capital" that is generated within the working-class community itself and is built into and gives substance to relationships among neighbours, friends and kin. Though it contributes wealth of various kinds to the community, it does not, as it should according to "human capital" theory, translate directly into workers' earnings, even though it contributes to the industries that have relied on and continue to take it for granted (see Livingstone and Sawchuk 2004a).

We know little about what happens when the processes of restructuring and, in some instances, of de-industrialization, undermine the economic bases of the informal friendship and/or familial networks transmitting such skills. For sure, much of the intergenerational transmission of skills would be at least attenuated (see Livingstone 1999a) and the kinds of local relationships of support and exchange of skills contributing to the local standard of living would also be disrupted, relying as they clearly did in the examples cited here on a pre-existing texture of relationships, some of them originating in the community and others in an intersection of workplace and community. Further, the gains in leisure time that were made by workers' struggles to limit the working day are being eroded by the overall restructuring of industry and, along with that, the increased reliance by workers on multiple part-time employment or self-employment, or both.

The Displacement of Worker-Controlled Skills Training in Industry and Resource Extraction

The field studies undertaken by George Smith and Dorothy Smith of skills training in the Ontario plastics industry in the 1980s provided us with several accounts of manufacturing plants where skills training was exclusively worker to worker and on the shop floor (Smith 1988). These studies provide a model against which the training transformations that accompany restructuring, as in the case of the steel industry, can be examined. The Canadian plastics industry was then relatively new. There were no traditional forms of skills acquisition such as were represented by trades. Promoting the expansion of the plastics industry required government intervention in the creation of a skilled labour force that did not pre-exist. In many companies, the knowledge stored in the workforce and even in management was largely a product of experiential learning passed on by precept and example and learned hands-on. The following account of the Compton Company (about twenty-five years old at the time George and Dorothy did their research)[19] is an almost pure example of a plant in which training and advancement were organized in this way. This provides a model against which the training transformations that accompany restructuring can be examined.

The Compton Company was unusual in that management as well as supervisory staff had come up through the shop floor process of skills acquisition, so there was no disjuncture between the supervisory and managerial levels of the organization so far as knowledge of production processes at the shop floor level:

> The Compton Company produces a range of standardized products using automated and computerized machinery. All training at the Compton Company is hands-on (with the exception of short courses in health and safety). With the exception of two people in maintenance who have European training, supervisors, department heads and the general manager himself have all learned the business of plastic processing through experience and learning from others with experience. The replication of its skills-through-experience workforce is a routine aspect of how the company operates and is integrated into the supervisory hierarchy. People come into the plant at the labouring level. Not much training is involved at this level: "In most cases it's on-the-job training for two or three days and after that any other training besides that would be to move up the ladder." Hands-on or on-the-job training is integrated into the production hierarchy.[20]

On-the-job training at the Compton Company was integrated with the internal shop floor hierarchy. A lead-hand (a level below foreman[21]) or foreman trained the "labour-type people" as they were hired. Training for production workers was exclusively on-the-job and by demonstration:

> [The foreman] just shows him. In most cases he shows him. We have internal books with specifications — our own company specification for the different products. Some time is spent in that. Basically most of the training is done right on the floor where they actually see what he's talking about.

Training involved in moving up the ladder was initiated by the foreman of a shift:

> A lot of the shifts the foreman will kind of take somebody in hand and advance them. There is also a foreman who specializes in training, going from shift to shift working with these people that seem to show an eagerness to learn and advance. He spends most of his time with them, showing them different jobs.

The foremen themselves had learned their skills on the job. They were, in the view of the personnel manager we interviewed, knowledgeable but, as he phrased it, they had no "theoretical" knowledge of plastics processing. Foremen themselves were recruited internally.

> We hire a few people from outside [who have had previous experience working in plastics]... but most of the rest of the people we have now are being trained on the premises by ourselves. We haven't found a place where you can go and hire a foreman that could come in and work in our plant. [It takes] a lot of development to learn the process. There just doesn't seem to be any training facility that we're aware of.

Training and advancement in set-up and quality control departments also drew on the pool of plant-trained people. The senior set-up man, who ran the Set-Up Department and had "probably been doin' it for twenty years," trained the others. Most of the people in Quality Control came from production. The manager we interviewed described the selection procedure:

> The Quality Control people go around and they talk to all these operators that operate the machine and they see that, "Oh yeah, this chap knows how to measure the plate. And he's very interested in quality," and this and that. So suppose you have a requirement, that's the first place we try.

Thus, in the Compton Company the entire cycle of learning, including evaluation of performance (apart from the monitoring of performance through productivity) was internal to the shop floor and among workers. The company relied for the reproduction of skills on the experiential learning of workers on the shop floor. Foremen have learned experientially and from others before them the know-how they deploy in supervision and in training. They selected who to assign to more senior workers for training; they allocated workers to jobs in which more advanced skills could be acquired. They selected men to act as lead-hands. Advancement into jobs requiring more skills and greater earnings were entirely through men who had learned the work from others like themselves, and experientially. The processes of transmission and storage of skills was internal to the Compton worker-centred shop floor training, and management played no direct part in it. Indeed, the management in the company came out of the same skills-learning background as the workers.

In the factory described by Michael Burawoy (1979), learning the skills of a turret lathe operator (a good deal more demanding than anything at the plastics moulding plant referred to above) was also internal to the shop floor. Skills were the basis of informal hierarchies among workers. At the Compton Company, continuous processing was automated in such a way that production could not be identified with particular individuals, so such differentials in skills and informal status would not have been so marked. At the factory described by Burawoy, training other workers was a cost in lost production to the worker who did the training; hence, workers who trained others received modest compensation for lost time on the lathe:

The most frequent arrangement was for operators to break in new employees and to receive setup-man pay (the highest pay scale) for the period if they did not make out after adding the new employee's pieces to their own. In other arrangements, those breaking in were to receive a fixed number of hours, say four, at setup-man pay. But training is still the subject of bargaining and negotiation between operator and foreman. Part of the reason for this lies in the ambiguity of the trainer's obligations to the trainee. As the shop euphemism puts it, one doesn't have to "show everything" to the new employee. (Burawoy 1979: 102)

Though accountable to management, it is clear that management could not exercise direct control over the process by which skills were transmitted from more experienced workers to trainees. Experienced workers maintained the value of their specialized knowledges and upheld the "natural" monopoly that the course of learning experientially creates, fending off potential competitors and consolidating the value of a knowledge appropriated by particular individuals. Internal hierarchies among workers were organized to a significant extent around skills. Skills were "owned" by the more experienced, and it gave them advantages in competitive situations over other workers — the trainer did not have "to show them everything." It also gave them a valuable resource that could be shared sparingly in the interests of its "owner." Joy Parr described how experienced workers protected their advantage in the skills hierarchy in a furniture factory in southwestern Ontario in the 1920s and 1930s:

A young man could not learn enough to run a machine merely by being present in the room and observing; older men were frugal with their knowledge, their only job security, willing to train only a successor who would acknowledge the teaching as a personal favour and not betray the trust by displaying precocious mastery of the work.... Karl Ruhl [one of the men interviewed] was candid about the process. Although he benefitted by his kin connections, he saw the highly personalized barriers to knowledge about the machines as "one of the big faults" at Knechtel. He recalled as a tailor asking the router operator for whom he worked how to read the design drawing for their machine and being told, "Go ask your Dad." (Parr 1990: 170)

Decades later, Steven Vallas and John Beck (1996) described the carefully guarded black books of older workers in pulp and paper mills, books containing notes of what workers had learned over a lifetime of smelling, tasting, watching and testing the state of pulp and paper on the rolls. Skills were a source of status, whether or not the worker who possessed them was incorporated into the formalized hierarchy of lead-hand, foreman, etc. The processes of reproducing skills among workers gave rise to informal hierarchies and loyalties among workers that presented a barrier to management's ability to control the workplace.

Joy Parr also described the hierarchy of experience and skill in the furniture factory as follows:

> Progressing through the hierarchy in the machine room was a schooling in patriarchal relations, which young men learned and later reproduced. As boys got their jobs through the interventions of male kin, so later they gained the experience and knowledge they would need to succeed to a machine of their own through their personal relationships with older men in the room. Even after Knechtel tried in the 1920s to install a scientific management regime in the plant, machine operators in practice retained the right to choose their successors. (Parr 1990: 169–70)

Her study is particularly interesting as it is the only one we have located that described an intersection of relationships in the community with the skills hierarchy in the workplace. She commented that the "best-placed men were sons with fathers working in the room" and that:

> Among relatives the passing on of knowledge was a legacy and in practicality a loan. Male kin kept some joint entitlement to whatever earnings the bequeathed information might command. (1990: 170)

Where managers (unlike the situation at the Compton Company) had not participated in the skills-based system of status, their perceived lack of skills could undermine their authority. At a plant studied by Kenneth Kusterer:

> Workers had only a very vague idea of the various responsibilities of these men (managers directly responsible for production in their area), and were generally convinced that [they] didn't do much of anything:

>> (He) doesn't do nothing. Take it from me, he doesn't know nothing from nothing about this department.... A good thing he doesn't do nothing because every time he does come in and do something, it just fucks somebody up. (1978: 39–40)

Workers under older industrial regimes maintained considerable control over who learned and what they learned and over knowledge of the work and technical processes of production. Shop floor social organization of this kind would have been relatively impenetrable to anyone who had not themselves been part of it.

Wallace Clement's study of hardrock mining records how foremen and management used competition in attempts to undermine the hierarchies and loyalties among workers that arose because of miners' ability to monopolize skills training:

> The use of existing mining crews to teach novices the necessary skills — because they certainly do not learn them in one week's class — has a disruptive effect on the crews themselves. A Thompson miner commented: "We've got to train these guys. When a new guy gets in the stope you have to take your time to train him. It costs us money. You train somebody and they up and leave." Not only is their bonus affected, but people are seldom allowed to work together for long periods of time. As a Sudbury miner said: "When a couple of fellows got together and they became pretty well experienced and good miners, then one would be the leader and the other the driller. Afterward the bosses would get the other fellow [the driller] to either bid on a leader's job or they would appoint him to a leader's job anyway, so they could put a couple of new men with these two fellows. As a rule, if two fellows worked together for two or three years, well, that was long." (1981: 284)

Attempts of this kind to get control of skills passed from worker to worker accounts in part for the reluctance of senior workers to pass on knowledge to others. Instances of this kind occurred in the logging industry as it transitioned from informal on-the-job transmission of skills to more formalized routines (Radforth 1987) and were reported by some of those we talked to at Stelco.

The incorporation of skills into written texts of some kind was an alternative approach to the expropriation of skills. An early version of this is described by Joy Parr. At the turn-of-the-century furniture factory in southwestern Ontario she describes, the owner sought to undermine "the craft knowledge and craft autonomy his father had honoured":

> J.S. Knechtel wanted craft knowledge sceptically scrutinized and scientifically systematized, what worthy remnants survived the test secured in the "hands and handbooks" of managers and engineers. (1990: 134)

This is an early example of a systematic project of expropriating the workplace-developed skills of workers through the development of technical methods of recording their how-to knowledge and making it available to engineers and managers. Such attempts have accelerated rapidly over the past forty years and have become increasingly sophisticated. Both capital and the state have been at work in the development of technological (Noble 1984) and textual devices enabling management to appropriate and control workers' skills and experience acquired on the job and to take over and displace the skills training functions formerly internal to intergenerational and peer relationships among working-class men.

In 1973, the Task Force on Industrial Training set up by the Manpower Training Branch of Ontario's Ministry of Colleges and Universities recommended "modular training" as a means of meeting training needs identified by "industry":

> In the 1950s and early 1960s changing labour market conditions together with public opinion caused the nature of the industrial manpower training problems facing Ontario to be altered greatly. During the late fifties public pressure was placed on government to support training-in-industry in addition to the traditional regulated apprenticeship. It was felt that apprenticeship did not adequately meet industry's needs, particularly in manufacturing, and that it was not appropriate for retraining, upgrading, and skill maintenance programs. Systems of industrial training less rigid than those typically available under apprenticeship legislation were required. Concern was focussed on the way in which industrial training had been organized around specific occupations rather than in relation to actual functions of workers on the job. It was argued that workers often became locked into specific occupations and were unable, because of the specialization of their training, to adapt to differences in skill requirements resulting from technological change. (Ontario Ministry of Colleges and Universities 1974: 174)

This passage raises issues about the extent to which the organization of training in community colleges was still outside the control of corporate management. While contributing to the skills of a labour force in the region, community colleges were not co-ordinating the skills training provided to the needs of particular manufacturing corporations. Further, the introduction of modular methods of analyzing skills and training objectives was aimed at breaking up certified trades through multi-tasking and at securing managerial control over precisely those processes of skills acquisition that had been controlled largely by workers on the shop floor or down the mine. Not surprisingly, it was the Canadian Manufacturers Association (CMA) that was pushing for the introduction of a modular approach to skills training (Ontario 1963), and these initiatives were related to the amalgamation of production jobs and the multi-crafting of trades.

In the early 1980s in Ontario, the plastics industry was the focus of a combined industry-provincial government initiative making use of a procedure that drew on the experience of workers in the industry to construct detailed explications of the steps involved in the performance of given tasks. These explications could then be used as the training objectives of formally designed training programs. The program was instituted because the expanding industry was experiencing a shortage of skilled/experienced operatives (the plastic industry lacked the continuities of traditional working-class skills available to other industries). The then-Ministry of Skills Development was called on to develop systematically formulated modules specifying in detail the tasks making up the skills required for a given job or position and within each task, and the steps needed to complete it. George Smith and Dorothy were observers of the process. The procedure brought together a group of experienced workers who, under the guidance of a community college instructor familiar with the technique, explicated their own, largely tacit knowledge in the formalized task descriptions required by the Designing a Curriculum (DACUM) method; each job was broken down into a set of tasks and then the sequential steps involved in each task were described. This made it possible to isolate a particular task for training or to break down a whole job into component parts which could be reassigned. Analysis of tasks of this kind could then be used to set up training modules, with performance objectives already defined by the specification of what was involved in each task.[22]

What George and Dorothy were observing was a transfer of the informal knowledges stored and transmitted among workers on the shop floor of plastics processing companies into a textual system controlled by government education institutions and/or directly or indirectly by corporations in the business of plastics processing.[23] In the ongoing efforts of capital to reduce the labour-cost component of production, the problem of production's dependence on skills reproduced outside the formal educational and training system and controlled by workers themselves has had two solutions: first, the technological transformations are implemented in such a way that the dependence of the production process on workers' informal skills is radically reduced (Noble 1984: 21–41; Vallas and Beck 1996); and second, and generally less well understood, "technologies" of training and management enabling the extraction of informal skills and knowledge-bases in the working class have been developed and incorporated into formalized training processes.

Some twenty years ago Dorothy was witness (on the union side) at the hearing of a grievance brought by the then-Mine, Mill and Smelter Workers Union (MMSW) local against Falconbridge Mines. The issue was control of access to the position of repair crew helper. According to the collective agreement, access to this position was through bidding on the basis of seniority.

The position had been traditionally one to which older men, no longer up to the physical demands of drilling and shift work, could bring their extensive experientially based knowledge of the mine, its people and its workings. The issue being arbitrated at the hearing was the company's introduction of a test as a condition of access. A miner had bid for the job, but had been turned down because he failed the test. He was, incidentally, French-speaking, and the language of the test was English (this was made an issue at the hearings).

In the course of the arbitration hearing, it became clear that the company was not concerned about the qualifications of this particular candidate for the position. Rather, they had been concerned more generally with establishing the right to substitute formalized tests for seniority as a criterion for the position. In the motel room where we stayed in Sudbury, we talked with a Falconbridge worker who was one of the witnesses brought by the union. He was ambivalent about the change. The introduction of a formalized test would diminish the union's control over access to this class of positions. On the other hand, foremen were members of the working-class community. Because of their power in the mine to assign people to jobs, they had to be courted, with gifts of game killed in hunting or bottles of spirits given at Thanksgiving and Christmas. If you wanted to get or keep a good job, you had to be in with the foremen.[24] Under the new system, the arbitrary power of the foremen would be broken. Formalized tests were a means through which control of the internal labour market of the mine would pass to management. The insertion of a formal, textual process meant bypassing the informal reciprocities between foremen and workers who belonged to the same local community. Management wanted selection procedures wholly controlled by management and regulated in ways fully accountable within its bureaucratic regime and system of accounting.[25]

The issue is more than one of management control; it is also one of the articulation of controls into an overall system of technical managerial organization. For a period some ten years earlier than the Mine Mill example, Wallace Clement described the introduction of similar managerial technologies at Inco:

> In 1970 Inco undertook a pilot experiment in "functional modular training." Called the Instrumentation Training Program, it instructed forty instrument mechanics in the maintenance of instrument control systems for use in all its automated plants. First all processes and instrument equipment had to be surveyed and modules designed to teach the mechanics how to test and repair the equipment. The fact that this was necessary reflects the increased use of instrumentation in Inco surface operations. Traditionally the training for this work was a four-year apprenticeship, but when new

techniques were introduced at the Copper Cliff Nickel Refinery and elsewhere, a shorter training period had to be devised. According to a senior Inco official involved in implementing the system, "the increased needs were imposed by new technology; traditional training couldn't respond." The use of the modular system shortened the qualification time from four to two years, obviously an advantage to the company. This modular training programme is a registered trade in Ontario, but it is a non-regulated trade, which means that the government does not supervise the course content. This is different from the apprenticeship program, where the government specifies the content and provides a broader training package. Here was the basis for Inco's objection to apprenticeships: they contained much training not needed for specific work at Inco plants. Management wanted something tailormade. (Clement 1981: 286–87)

Not only was the time taken to train workers shortened, such training could also be taken out of the hands of trades and the jurisdiction of government and incorporated into the corporation's managerial regime. It is also worth pointing out that a company's interests in training for internal needs does not necessarily coincide with government's interests in the creation of a skilled labour force.[26]

Modular treatment of skills enables the shop floor knowledge of workers to be analyzed as detailed sequences that can be produced as units of formalized training. Course units can then be tailored to the specific requirements of the company. The evolution of internal hierarchies among workers in the plant is bypassed; the "surplus" of skills and experience embodied in older workers can be resolved into standardized and reproducible training units; technological changes can be prepared for by designing appropriate modules; and the internal labour market of plant or corporation can be fully regulated by using formalized tests, training objectives and products. In one of the plastics processing plants George and Dorothy visited — what was left after the main tire-manufacturing plant had been transferred to the southern United States — the personnel manager complained to them about senior workers who refused to participate in an effort to draw on their knowledge in the making of training modules for the parent company, headquartered in Ohio. It was clear that the company's interests were less in controlling the skills resources of this small plastic processing plant than in being able to transfer skills that had been created and reproduced among workers in the original and much larger manufacturing plant into a form that could be reproduced within the corporation at large.

Learning Steel at Stelco

Major technological changes were introduced into the steel industry in Ontario starting in the 1980s and accelerating in the 1990s (Livingstone 1993; Frost and Verma 1997). However, changes in approaches to training were already apparent during the 1970s. In particular, Stelco began to get out of the business of training internally, for which it had formerly been renowned; in a sense, Stelco had been training for the industry in general (see, e.g., Sanger 1988: 101–02). This, of course, was costly and was gradually phased out during the period covered by the interviews that we undertook.

Changes in the industry at large were complemented by government initiatives to create a labour force that could sustain both technological and managerial aspects of restructuring. In the 1980s, restructuring confronted the federal and provincial governments with the need to recast the labour force. In 1985, George and Dorothy interviewed a federal government official who, in providing a rationale for government policies, cited Peter Drucker as an authority:

> [Drucker] makes some very distressing statements about the fortunes of any country's industry and he goes on to say that an industry that fails to sacrifice blue collar employment in favour of higher skilled training for a new manufacturing environment will not only lose those blue collar jobs they weren't prepared to sacrifice but they will lose other employment as well.

Both federally and provincially, government funds became available to support the training needs of industry. Community colleges began to redesign their classic focus on training in skilled trades and crafts and to find ways of responding to the requirements of the local skilled labour market and to the specific needs of industries (Smith and Smith 1990; McCoy 1999). By way of example, Mohawk Community College, which serves the Hamilton area, has changed its training programs significantly over the past thirty years. There have been curriculum changes in apprenticeship and technician programs to keep up with the rapidly changing technologies of the period. In the area of engineering technology, the major change, however, has been the introduction of courses tailored to the Hamilton big steel companies such as Stelco and Dofasco (McCoy 1999).[27] Henry, an instrument technician at Stelco interviewed by Livingstone and Stephan Dobson in 2003, described the transition period in this way:

> We [Henry's cohort] were virtually the first or second group [leaving Mohawk and entering a Stelco in-house apprenticeship].... Before that they did have apprenticeships, but there was a different level to them, because they were basically people that came out of the plant, or they hired them at grade twelve. But then Stelco, the instrument people there got together and they started, well basically it was a group called ISA, the Instrument Society

of America, and through this group with other companies [they] got together and they developed a program at Mohawk College. And at that time they had two feeders. Mohawk College was theirs, they also had an input at Sir Winston Churchill High School, so they were actually setting up a two-year program at Sir Winston Churchill, so they were obligated to hire so many people out of Churchill. So you know my class was three out of Churchill and three out of Mohawk. And then the others they got out of Mohawk. But [19]71, I would say, was the first year it became really put together. Mohawk was built in 1970, so the first group that graduated was [19]71.

Because the work design changed to one that required a *systems* overview, Henry believed that new apprentices would have at a minimum a college education:

The next group of people that would be coming in, assuming that there will be new apprentices, will all be absolutely minimum two if not three years out of Mohawk. I do not believe that you will see anybody in the different trades that will come in with less than grade twelve. That's my opinion. Because there's enough people at colleges that will work in a company like Stelco, even in mechanical, be it pipe fitter, mill wrights.[28]

Though courses may be designed to add up to government certification, they have been tailored to the specific needs of the companies and taught by instructors from the companies, whose pay is covered by the provincial government in a kind of hidden subsidy to industry. Some courses are designed according to task analyses of the kind described above to meet very specific training needs. The Canadian Steel Trades and Employment Congress (CSTEC), a joint management-union initiative that began in the mid-1980s, is one example of this; CSTEC was involved in the development of a basic steelworker training program at Sault College in Sault Ste. Marie.

As a group, the work-life experience of those we talked to spanned a period of twenty-five years or more. Their experience of learning and of teaching on-the-job was part of those widespread processes of change described in the previous section as well as of major technological changes in steel manufacture. Between 1950 and 1956 an elaborate system of grading of jobs based on a number of skill factors combined with working conditions and hazards had been negotiated between company and union. This agreement, the Co-operative Wage Study (CWS), despite its becoming a focus for resistance by Local 1005, survived the technological changes and the massive layoffs of the 1980s and the company's moves towards contracting out and multi-crafting. The system of job classifications that had been established by the CWS had, as Livingstone points out, encouraged workers to have a sense of ownership in their jobs and a sense of entitlement, which come up in the course of the interviews (1993: 38–39).

Those we talked to had started at Stelco in the late 1960s or 1970s. Restructuring began in the late 1970s and accelerated through the 1980s and early 1990s. Accounts of the experience of learning before restructuring accelerated showed considerably greater reliance on the transmission of skills and experience among workers than reports describing a later period. Later experiences of learning the job, among those we talked to, were, of course, of building upon a considerable depth of experience even if they were moved to a new job. However, for later periods, we also have accounts of how workers went about training or otherwise passing on their experientially acquired knowledge to others.

From the earlier period, those we talked to described for us three or four different types of training settings, depending on the type of job. The job Jim started with called for minimal training. It amounted to scarcely more than being shown where to work and told what to do:

> Well, I first started off as a labourer. So labour, we just did heavy lifting, sweeping, painting, you know, cleaning rubble, moving things over here where they need them. It was just dirty jobs. Like... shovelling grease up and everything else. That stuff. They used to have a gang leader, he'd go down there and he'd show you what to do, pick up this, pick up the bands and throw it here. So it wasn't really anything that was hard to learn, from being a labourer.

Later he worked in a blast furnace:

> There was four or five of us, we all worked together. It was scary going in there when I first started. Believe me, it's like, you go inside a furnace and you're sitting there drilling all the slags, okay?

Bill started in a production department in which there were a number of distinct processes:

> They used to do a whole bunch of — in our department we had maybe six or seven different processes. I can't really say they were related. We had a straightening machine. The coils came from the rod mill. We had a machine that took scale off steel and put an anti-rust agent on it. The bars came from the bar mill. The washer department — that was all just scrap steel. We stored a lot of reinforcing bar for other companies that come from the bar mill again — we'd store it for the customer until they needed it and then it was gone... there used to be a spike mill down beside [inaudible].... It's not like you get a bar billet come in the door and then go out the other door and there's coils and everything in between is connected. It wasn't like that.

Bill described learning as a helper by doing work that complemented the operator's:

> Well, on different machines it would be a two-man job, so you'd have an operator and a helper. Well, when you just start out you'd be the helper, so you'd just assist the operator. If you were on... there's a shear there that cut plate... there'd be pieces of pipe maybe the size of this tape or bigger and different widths for each... each washer machine was [a] different size. Like one was 250 ton per square inch that'd punch out washers, the other one was sixty tons. So they were different sizes. So, on a shear you would cut plate down the width for each individual machine.... So the operator would be in charge of size and getting the steel and making sure he had the right gauge and whatnot and the helper he'd just help with the sheets, putting them in the machine and then after that bundle was cut he'd hook it up to the crane and the crane would take it away and... that's all you'd do or if you were working on, say, this 250-ton press again you'd just assist the operator. He's in charge.

Bill showed us in this account a form of learning which is embedded in a co-ordinated work organization. It's in fact a tripartite organization: operator, machine and helper. The helper is not doing the same work as the operator. He's learning the operator's job by doing its reciprocal, feeding the machine operated by the operator and dealing with its product. But — if he's Bill — he's also watching the operator:

> Well, you're with the person all the time, you're seeing what they're doing, you're — sometimes he would explain what he was doing and why, but just being around.... You might be stuck on a particular job for months, so after that period of time you learn pretty well everything the operator knows.

Alison trained as a serviceman [sic] in an operator-helper relationship. Though in her experience the training period was designated as such and the person she worked with was more actively engaged in the training process than the situation Jim and Bill described, she too was learning on the job:

> What they start you off as, is they have a three month probationary period and you're what they call a labour trainee. And then you were assigned to somebody and they would teach you a little bit about the job and they would give you basic things to do, very simple things to do. And that's just so that they, whether or not they get to know you because they can lay you off after, before the three months is up, that type of thing. Then after that, I went to what they call Job Class 9, which is a Serviceman and a Serviceman is like the helper of an Operator and then you learn from the Operators.

The organization of training as Jim, Bill and Alison described it still took the same general character as that of the Compton Company in the 1980s. The newly hired work with a gang boss or with an operator and learn by doing the job or doing a job complementary to the operator. However, when those we talked to started work at Stelco, unlike the Compton Company and the plastics industry in general at that time, the steel industry had a long history and a developed reservoir of skills. Alex's experience of training to be a crane operator shows the degree of reliance on the store of workers' skills laid down in previous work experience:

Interviewer. Could you tell me, like when you're talking about being trained… were you just doing the job and learning as you go or really did they try to show you?

Alex. They tried to show you. You had to, well, on the safety factor, working with the cranes, they showed you the no-noes of the job, they'll say "Don't do this, don't do that."… As far as a crane operator, being a crane operator, that's just some people are crane operators, some people aren't crane operators. So that was, you had it or you didn't have it.

Interviewer. Was it because of the way in which you sort of tune in to a particular kind of machine?

Alex. Well cranes, because they're overhead cranes, the height, the perspective, you know, your depth perception, your ability to catch swings, you know, as far as using the levers, your eyes, your mind and your hands, telling you what to do. And some people are better at it than others, some didn't qualify for the cranes, so they stayed on those jobs.

Interviewer. Yeah. So how would you go from being a helper on a crane to actually operating it? Or how would you go from, how would they let you loose on the crane, as it were, when you were just…?

Alex. There was a training period, at that time [late 1960s, early 1970s], there was a training period of six weeks. You trained, the first couple of days, you watched, some operators would let you operate, the first day even, just to run the crane, to get the feel of the crane, the levers and whatever. You know, within a couple of days, you were making lifts, you know, like certain lifts you wouldn't make because they were too delicate. But they'd make you make, like unloading a truck or something like that, they'd allow you to do that. And then it was just the procedure, repetition, repetition, repetition. And you know, you either got better at it or you got worse at it, one or the other.

Interviewer. Yeah. So, when you say you were qualified, what would that mean? Was that anything in writing, did it go on the company's books?

Alex. No. At the time I started, they used to have a crew that came around that they actually tested you.… Because there were certain, at that time, safety procedures as far as pulling switches, you had to do an inspection of the crane before you boarded the crane and that type of thing. They would ask you those questions, then they would ask you questions as far as lifts, like the capacity of the bale and that type of thing. And then they would actually watch you make a couple of lifts. And then they would say "Okay, you passed your crane lift" or "No, you didn't pass, you need some more time." And they would come back and test you, and if you didn't get any better than that, usually they wouldn't use you up there.... Then, at that time. Now it's a different thing altogether, like no, supervisors just pass you. You know, they look at you and say "you can drive a crane."...

Interviewer: So... would these be people who were themselves crane operators [*Alex:* Yeah, they were] so they were actually pulled off the job?

Alex: No, they were a crew that... [*Interviewer:* That was their job?] Yes, they were specific. That was their job, to test cranes, to check cranes. They were a crane crew, you know, their job was specifically... but after that... that wasn't in place very long from when I started. After that it was up to the supervisor to check if the gentleman involved was qualified to run the crane. And in most cases, they didn't care. They qualified everybody.

Similarly, Tony, at the time of the interview a utility worker in the cold mill, described the late 1970s process of being qualified on the crane. There was no longer a crew to test the beginning crane operator and check his performance. Rather, Tony learned from a qualified operator who would also be responsible for deciding if he was ready:

Like the cranes, you needed to learn the job off of a qualified crane man. And a lot of time, he would sit behind you and watch you operate the frame. And then, in the end, if he felt that you were... ready, then they called in the crane foreman and he would sit up there and watch you operate, and say "yes, you're qualified" or "No, you're not. You need another month's training."

Steve described for us the training of an apprentice instrument techni- cian from his experience of starting at Stelco in the late 1960s:

Steve: I started in Stelco in the 1960s... it was about a four and a half year apprenticeship.... They had the apprenticeships role strictly in the plant. We also took night school... there was an instrument course that they sent us for at Hamilton Institute of Technology, which was the pre-Mohawk College.... So they paid us our hourly wage to go to night school, three hours a week. I also took Math 1 and Math 2 at Mohawk, that they paid for, that wasn't really very related to the apprenticeship. But they were willing to pay, so I took two years of math.... What we did, at that time in the six- ties, there was actually about one apprentice for each technician. And we would have, in a six-month period, we would start at Job Class 1, which was the lowest rate of pay in the plant, and we would progress one job class every six months. During the six-month period, you would have five pieces of equipment that you would demonstrate, we called it a bench test, we'd have to demonstrate that we can repair a certain piece of equipment. In the first six months, it wasn't spelled out it had to be this five pieces, but it was five pieces out of, say, thirty. So at the end of the apprenticeship, you would have done all the bench tests.

Interviewer: So how did you learn from a technician or how did a technician teach?

Steve: We would take off in the morning. I was at that time in ironmaking, which was the coke ovens, the blast furnace, the big boiler station. We'd be assigned a work area. First thing in the morning, we would walk through that area, check most of the recorders. Basically we'd look at them, we'd look at the ink on the pen, make sure that the pens were leaving ink on the chart, so we could see what happened during the night. If there was a controller that was not functioning properly, we would usually, if it was something that wasn't critical, we'd continue our tour, and then go for coffee, come back to that piece of equipment later and clean it and do whatever was required.

Interviewer: So was it your responsibility or the technician's responsibility to see that you covered, you know, the equipment you needed to learn for that particular period?

Steve: Basically, it was our responsibility, really. The technician, depending who they were, some people were helpful, some people would say "Oh, this is what we're going to do today." Generally, it wasn't a high work load. You know, we'd have a fair amount of time to shoot the breeze, sometimes we'd talk about cars or boats or what we were doing the night before. Other times, you'd ask them. It depends on how interested you were. Most of the guys, if you asked them questions, they'd answer them. A lot of times you might grab a manual and just read it. But it was, when you learned the most was when something was broken and you had to fix it. And lots of times it would be a mixture of yourself and the technician. If it was a temperature control, it was steam heating, it probably could be either the controller or at the valve, or if it's temperature, there would be a thermal-coupler or a temperature sensor, it would go to the controller, then to the valve. So sometimes you change the temperature element or you check it first. The technician would be turning the controller up and down, most of it worked on pneumatics, compressed air. So he would turn the controller up and down, and you'd be down at the valve watching to see how smooth the valve ran. So you'd kind of break the job up, a lot of it.

Interviewer: So in breaking the job up, you're also in a sense kind of learning how the thing is put together.

Steve: Yeah. If he's turning the controller up and down and you're watching to see if the valve is sticky, and it is, of course, then he'd go and say to him "I think the valve is sticking" and you'd switch jobs so he could see himself as well. Then if it was a sticky valve, we'd either get the pipe fitter to change it, or if it was a packing line problem or something, the two of you would repair it.

Training as an instrument technician was internal, with supplemental night schooling; qualification did not have government recognition and hence no formal status on the labour market. Though supplemented by a few night courses, training was otherwise exclusively with technicians already qualified within the plant.

Critiques of the Traditional Training Method

It would be a mistake to idealize the earlier forms of training preceding the period of restructuring. Those we talked to described them as uneven in terms of their outcome. Not every operator took care to inform the person assigned to him to train; opportunities for interchange among workers were also uncertain. Here is Bill's appraisal:

> What you learn depends on how good the guy is that teaches you. What I learn, I'm most likely going to keep for as long as I'm on that job. The majority of people are like that, once they've learned something, that's it, that's the way it's done, that's the way they'll always do it, even though it might have been taught to them wrong or incompletely or it wasn't explained to them properly, so they can reason when something goes wrong — "oh he told me that if I see this, most likely it was a problem right here." If that doesn't happen, these guys are just on the job and they'll do something wrong for as long as they're on that job. Won't do it properly or completely.

The kinds of situations that Steve described, where apprentice technicians could consult with senior men, no longer existed. But even for Steve, the training situation was somewhat haphazard and seems to have depended on the initiative of the learners. He described the on-the-job aspect of training as uncertain. Some trainers were helpful; others not (compare Sennett 2008: 181). Responsibility for training devolved to the trainee. If they were interested, they could learn either by asking questions or by reading the manuals. Later, when Steve was a shop steward, he took up with the supervisor the lackadaisical approach of some of the technicians assigned a trainee:

> One of the new [guys] really got in trouble for reading a pocket book and sitting dozing off or whatever. And I'd say to the supervisor, "Why are you blaming him? You know, you send him to work with worker A, who you know goes for coffee, likes to have a snooze for half an hour. Why don't you send him to somebody that's going to teach him something? Don't blame the apprentice because he only does what the technician tells him to."

Dan was highly critical of traditional training practices, which he called "grandfathering." The traditional training practices as they were managed in the plant did not give the trainee sufficient time to gain "proficiency." In our interview, we had been talking about when Dan started at Stelco. He described the experience in this way:

> *Dan:* It was overwhelming. It was overwhelming. And what happens is, at that time, they made the same mistake that they had made for years, as far as I was concerned, as an instructor and as a trainer. They'd give you an overview of how everything works —
>
> *Interviewer:* So this may be the supervisor?...
>
> *Dan:* The operator... He would take you around and tell you how everything works. You'd follow him around, you'd be totally overwhelmed with what was going on. And eventually you'd be given a task to do and you'd learn how to do that task. And then you'd be given another task to do and you learn how to do that task. And eventually, over the span of months and months, you would end up knowing all the tasks in there, but not at any proficient level because it was just too much. It took you quite some time. Grandfathering causes a lot of problems in trying to minimize the time for proficiency.

Bill was also critical. In his view, the company failed to make sure that operators set a good standard of work for trainees. The standard set varied with the operator. "If he's good at his job, well, there's a good chance you might be good at it." Tony also described considerable variations in the kind of training operators provided.

> The odd person, yeah, was different. There was the guy that took advantage of the trainee and says, "Well, you go ahead and do what you can do. I'm going to lay down for an hour." And I had to learn the job on my own.

Stories of withholding knowledge of a given process — the private black books that Vallas and Beck (1996) described — and similar practices were not often mentioned by those we talked to. It had, we were told, existed earlier. Withholding knowledge protected the senior man on the job since, once trained, the newcomer, paid at a lower rate, could be used to replace the operator. It was in the operator's interest not to pass on his experientially acquired methods. The union's intervention had eliminated the practice of substituting the junior for the senior man on the job.[29] Nonetheless, training was not systematized and seems to have varied with the interest and sense of responsibility of the trainer. When good practices were innovated, their perpetuation as a tradition was fragile. Occasionally we heard of the emergence of a mini-tradition in a particular worksite, as in the case of Jim when he was a hooker — a person who bundles slabs of steel with chains for transport by crane:

You learned by being there, telling you, then you got better [at] learning. And I used to train other guys when they got hired, that's where most of the junior people came in as hookers and that. I even stayed there, I was senior and I stayed there for a long time. They really liked me when I left there. My foreman wanted me to move up. The general foreman liked me as a hooker because I used to work. I'd clean up the area, like it made it easier for everybody else. I wasn't afraid to have the area cleaned. I had a pretty — I had it set up the way that other guy would show me, okay, the way he was, there was probably only two other guys like him — the guy that trained him, and him who trained me. Us three were the same way, our area, you had to see it to believe it. But he taught you that.

He was a whiz kid, like I mean he was an older guy but he loved his job. And like I mean he was different than I was but I mean, you wanted to learn, you learned... we used to have a book over there and it would tell you the locations where to put all the steel and everything.... What he said [was] that they had certain areas, [where] different types of steel had to be loaded, because we had different doors and they had different sections where they had to be put, so assistant loaders would know where the steel was. We had to put it there. Different customers had different locations. So when a guy went looking for the steel to load it on a truck or a rail car, that's where they would look, in that area, to find this piece of steel. And back then, it wasn't hard to learn. I mean, when you got better, you didn't have to open up that book. He never opened up the book. He knew this customer was section 43, this customer like this. I'm saying to myself, "How long did it take you to learn that?" But it didn't take long, you know what I mean? You always carried that book. Most hookers never have to carry it, most good hookers would never have to open up that book. And like I mean, he knew that mill. And he said to me "By the time I finish training you kid, you'll know this place inside out." And it was fun. He was a nice guy, he was quiet, eh. Always ate his lunch on the job. And he was sort of the guy that wasn't too personal but that's fine. You know, me, I'm more outspoken, I like to have a guy talk. But he wasn't that way.... And he got trained by somebody else, and he trains. But then I stayed there for maybe four years. And the foreman asked me to go on this job, which was more money.... I didn't really want to go, but he says "Can you go and try and do this job?" and stuff like that, eh. Hey, my foreman was a pretty good guy, and I said "Okay, I'll go and try it."

The chain of skills, from Jim's whiz kid mentor, to Jim, who became a senior in the department and then trained others, was broken when, after Jim left, the department was reorganized. When those who had reproduced it moved on to other jobs, there was no mechanism, no social relation, for transferring their knowledge to those who took over. Jim commented on the state of the shop floor, which had been so thoughtfully organized in the past:

You take a look at the shop floor over there, it's a mess now. I take a look at it sometimes, "oh God."... They changed a lot of areas because they restructured. So the building is a little bit smaller, but it doesn't look like it's organized properly. And I take a look and it's "Ughh." I said to the foreman, I tease him, I said "Chuck, maybe I've got to come back hooking." He says "We'd love to have you back here, Jim. We can't find half the steel."... I had no problem, my shift, my guys liked it because they knew I'd have it organized. I wouldn't pile the — some of the new people would pile the new steel on top of old steel. [That] doubled the work. This guy taught you to make it easier and the guys would like you better. Even if I sometimes had to move a couple of piles and clean a couple of pallets off. But you're trying to keep it, you know, organized. You learn that from experience.

Restructuring

Restructuring at Stelco did not appear in the accounts of those we talked to as a single coherent process. Some changes were largely ad hoc reorganization; some were clearly a systematic reorganization of managerial policies; others were major technological innovations. The earlier changes were not dramatic. For example, Bill described a reorganization of production that reduced the variety of products and did away with the variety of work and learning situations that had been characteristic of his job when he first started at Stelco:

> Actually, the mill at that time, it did a lot of things. We did storage, we made washers, metal washers for nuts and bolts, they had a straightening machine for straightening coils and cutting bars in length, and another machine that cleaned scale off steel. It was a whole bunch of things in one building. And after a while, they just started getting out of certain things. The washer department, we ran on scrap steel from other departments, then that pretty well dried up for whatever reason, I don't really understand. Then we were using prime steel, then it became not cost effective any more, so they got rid of the washer department.... There was another machine there that used to bend bars for carrying ingots and whatnot, and that went out.

Alex worked in one of the mills where machines that would be considered "archaic" (his term) in North America were still being operated. But no one was being trained on these and at least part of what used to be done in the mill was being contracted out, presumably as a way to avoid recapitalization. Alex described the kinds of changes that have taken place:

> *Interviewer:* I know the changes over time, like the range of different things that were done at the Stelco plant here in Hamilton, I know some of them were cut out here and continued in Montreal or whatever it might be. Is that...?

> *Alex:* Well, they shut some of the mills down, okay. But those jobs weren't there. The training methods and the expectations of my supervision in my department are a lot less than they were in the sixties and seventies. So

a lot of the operators couldn't even grind these rolls any more, like the old rolls. So what they did with them, because it became sort of cost prohibitive in the sense that if they wanted them done they couldn't get them done, so they had to wait until maybe this operator came in or whatever it is, to do it. So they started shipping it out. So we don't even see that work any more.

Interviewer: I see. So it is contracted out?

Alex: Some of it is contracted out, some of it is like redundant, the mills aren't there any more so we don't do it. So now basically all we do is flat roll products, that's all we do.

Interviewer: Was it an operation that could be computerized in any way?

Alex: The machines we operate are archaic compared to the modern machinery doing the same job. So most of our machines are manual machines, whereas the machines they have out there, if you bought a brand new one, I mean, they're self-loading machines, they're computerized, etc.

Interviewer: So people are still being trained to do this, now?

Alex: Not for a long time, only because of the cut-backs. And as I say, a lot of our future in those shops I don't think is long-term. I think eventually that will be contracted out to others, you know. I think it will, personally, that's only a personal opinion. But most of it, I think will be contracted out eventually.

Contracting out is a complex phenomenon in heavy industries like Stelco. Aside from avoiding the recapitalization of heavy machinery, cost savings in benefits and pensions are also at play. And as the union points out, Stelco hires contractors, some of whom actually worked in the plant previously; however, the *crews* of these contractors are often inexperienced and in some cases must be shepherded around by employees. Liability is also an issue: work that is contracted out means that the contractor is liable for breakdowns in production. Liability issues, while having an old pedigree within industry, have a new twist within the era of restructuring and contracting out, as Warren Smith identified:

I think, there's a number of things that are happening here that only make sense if you consider what the lawyer and the risk manager are telling the guy who's actually running the department down in the mill. One, they know they are cutting out a lot of protections, Health and Safety stuff and.... It's been a huge battle, they've slashed it terribly. At the same time, they're insisting on more certificates hanging on the wall for the people that are employed there, right? I read that as a conscious attempt to shift liability to the worker, if you are insisting people come into the workplace with some certificate that says "I am a fill-in-the-blank." I think that comes directly out of risk management in an industry that knows it's slashing right to the safety margin. I looked at the news from Algoma this morning [chuckles], I know they've done as much serious slashing as Stelco has done…. But the same stuff happens up there. It's not that the opportunities don't exist for the older guy to show somebody else his skills, ah, the company doesn't even want to waste that time. (interview with Warren Smith and Bob Sutton by Livingstone, Smith, and Dobson, May 15, 2002)

As an added bonus, accounting calculations of person-hours per ton of steel produced *do not* factor in the contractors' hours worked. Thus, contracting out as a strategy of restructuring becomes hooked into accounting and liability practices within the ruling relations.[30]

More major changes involved the introduction of new technologies, particularly forms of continuous processing. Unlike in other accounts of technological restructuring (e.g., Vallas and Beck 1996; Zuboff 1984), the controls were not fully mediated by computers. The kind of learning that Jim described in the following passage is clearly very different from that characteristic of production at an earlier stage:

Jim: When we restructured the mill, I got involved in the restructuring of the mill and negotiated big money for that, and they paid Job Class 15. So I went from Job Class 7 to 15. Even though I loved the hooker's job, the money was really good there. And the weigher's job wasn't hard to do, it was mostly you just weighed the steel and marked it on a schedule….

Interviewer: So when you were learning, originally, in this job or the job that led to the one you're describing, what was that learning like?

Jim: I sat behind, I sat right beside him and just watched what buttons — he had some buttons that went up and down, controls that moved the line backwards or frontwards. I mean, like it was just watching.

Some of the changes that emerged with technological changes appeared in our interviews in the descriptions of training others through production line mentoring. They now were the operators. Those they were training were not helpers. They were simply new to the job or, as in Tony's account, they were students from local colleges there for the summer. Here, from the point of view of the trainer, is Bill's description of his own training procedures around the time of the interview:

Well, I was training a student… I was training a student on a job about three weeks ago and he'd never been there before, and what I did was… it was a panel and what our particular job was putting billets into a furnace, charging them into a furnace. Then there were panels, I forget how many, there might be twenty, twenty-five buttons, but you'd have one part over here that brings the billets down. It's called "unscrambling." You straighten them out and then you go on to a roller line and you bring them up farther and then the other part is putting them into the furnace. Now, when the guy at the other end needed some more billets, he'd push a button and this big arm would come and push them in the furnace. So what I would do was, "Okay," I said, "watch me!" And so for the first half-hour or hour, he was just watching me do this job and as I'm doing it I'm explaining all these buttons on the panel and what we're doing and what we're supposed to be doing. Then I said, "Okay, come on over on this side," and I let him... like, it was three separate processes we were doing.... "Okay, you operate these ones... I'll take care of everything back here. You do this." So I did that for about... actually, it was only about half an hour because there wasn't much to it. Then I said, "Okay, come over on this side," and it was, "now I want you to look after all this." It was a little bit trickier and I left him there for, I guess, maybe about an hour or so just doing this, and I said, "Okay, now sit in the chair. Now you're looking after this part and that part; I'm going to look after this," so now he's doing two things. About an hour later, "Okay, now you just do the job" and I'd just be standing there. If he got behind or if he got in any kind of trouble, I would... I'd straighten it out for him. So by the end of the shift, he's pretty well... he's slow, but he knows what he's doing. If he makes a mistake, he's more kind of likely to remember. You know, if I say, "Don't do this because this is going to happen," well he's going to do it. Let him do it, it's fixed now. Now you get them out of trouble and off they go. To me that was the way to train somebody.

This is clearly a very different situation than the one in which Bill originally learned. In those earlier settings, the "helper" actively assisted, under the operator's direction, in getting the work done. He came to know it as a junior partner in a work process. Bill's account is of learning by watching how the operator controls a process through pressing "buttons" and then trying them out. Of course, as we see in the next part of the chapter, there was considerably more to be learned but this did not form part of the operator's responsibilities in training the person new to the job. On this job, at least, the trainee can be allowed to make mistakes and to build experience in that way. But it is a very different situation of learning than the earlier relationship between operator and helper.

According to Alex, the specialized crane crew that oversaw training and inspected the cranes disappeared in the 1970s — the period when, according to others we interviewed, foremen were ceasing to be promoted from within a given department but rather began to be hired externally. Training facilities for technicians disappeared in the mid-1980s, when, encouraged by the Ontario Ministry of Colleges and Training and with the financial help of the Ontario government, Stelco came to rely increasingly on courses designed to their specifications by community colleges. Earlier, the in-house formalized and informal training in steel plants created skills for the steel industry in general as well as for the provincial and national labour market for skilled labour. Progressively the costs of training for the general labour market has shifted from industry to the provincial government — and often onto the person who is learning. The kind of training that Steve reported for the earlier period has gone:

> Pretty well all the in-plant apprenticeship programs, all the equipment, has all disappeared. Now the training room where we had instruments and we had sample processes that you could tune controllers and train people on, is all gone. There is no in-plant training... now their goal seems to be... [to] try and hire somebody out of Mohawk College or somewhere.

In Steve's account we can see the move described earlier, the shifts in training from the plant to the community college, from at least a degree of control over the reproduction and transmission of skills among workers to control by state and capital in part through education regimes.

While we do know that Stelco adopted an interactive management training program for supervisors and established a quality and service committee for senior managers and also various joint management/labour committees (Livingstone 1993: 31; 1996: 19–20), we do not know precisely what kinds of changes in managerial technologies were being introduced into Stelco at this period;[31] similarly, we do not know how they operated concretely on a day-to-day basis and how they were received and/or managed by workers. We can guess at some of the changes in how the steel industry was organized internationally, not only in terms of its participation in a global marketplace, but also in such indications as its participation in the International Organization for Standardization (ISO). The ISO is an association of a hundred and fifty-nine member countries that is aimed at the establishment of globally consistent agreements on the technical specifications and criteria for materials, products and processes. Subscription to standards of this kind require the establishment of systematic and documented procedures for production processes. Alison, who is a health and safety representative, described her own involvement in documenting the procedures that she used in her job:

> Like I'm involved a lot now with trying to write procedures up and have it written down.... And like when I'm involved in doing these procedures I'm wondering why are we locking it out [i.e., turning it off for repair]? Are we locking it out for the mechanical to work on it or are we locking it out because the whole system is down? You know, like what's the whole process in locking it out? You know? Do we want to put the whole thing in it or do we just want to say "Okay, we're just taking it out of service to be worked on." That type of thing. And our procedures, like the format of them is basically we do a scope, exactly what you're trying to write down. And then you would do Safety Precautions, so anything involving like a process, whether it be gas hazard or, if you're pulling electrical disconnects, the proper procedure in how to do that, right. Then you also say like any reference material, right?

So there might be a reference material on how the process works, how to change from one pump to the other without disrupting the flow, you know, this type of thing, right. So you have to write that all down. And then, finally, you get down to "the procedure." I mean, it's just a step-by-step type thing. And the way they're written down is actually pretty good because you do Step 1, "shut valve off over here," and then in the comments section, we'll say why you're shutting it all off. Step 2, you do something else and then you'd say, again, why you're doing it.

Bill was cynical about the procedural manuals created to meet ISO requirements:

Bill: There is no standard training process…. I can get trained by four different people and four different people are going to tell me four different ways of doing something.

Interviewer: So there aren't procedure manuals that are associated with each [computer] stand or…?

Bill: There is now — but it wasn't Stelco generated. The ISO 9000 [a set of standards for quality management systems], whatever else, they demand that you have manuals, more or less training manuals for each job whatever else. There are manuals there now… but I've never seen somebody take one out and read it. I've read a couple of them but I've never seen somebody use them. That's as close as they come to a standardized procedure on each job….

Interviewer: Did you find that these manuals reflected what you knew… what you were doing?

Bill: Well, I know the guy that did them and the guy that did them — there was one guy they assigned but this was, like I said, it didn't come from inside Stelco. They thought, hey, you know, this would probably be a good idea if we standardize…. It was ISO demanded. They had to do it. That's the only reason. But I can take you down there and I can show you, you know, piles of dust on them or they're hidden under here or whatever else. It's the only reason they're there….

Interviewer: Do those manuals come out when there's an audit?

Bill: They'll dust them off.

Interviewer: They'll dust them off!

Bill: I'm serious, they'll dust them off. They'll go along and just… you know, they might be in a drawer or underneath a desk or sometimes it's right on the floor in the corner. The guy'll take them, dust them off, put them somewhere where they can be seen. I'm not kidding you.[32]

Even though the procedural manuals are not used to standardize training or routines, their availability becomes important when there are questions about whether proper procedures have been followed. In addition to ISO requirements, the documentation of procedures was required by the Health and Safety Committee (a joint union-company committee). Alison described how written procedures were used on account of liability issues in case of an accident:

> That's one of the things, whenever I go to an accident investigation. Because a lot of these accidents that I do attend are not in my department, the first thing I ask is "Where is the job procedure?" And that way the company has themselves covered. If there's no job procedure, it's like "Well, who instructed this person to do it?"

The extension of these types of managerial organization into the daily life of the plant exemplifies a marked shift from the type of organization that characterized the Compton Company described at the beginning of this section. The Compton Company provided us with a model of industrial organization in which there was no disjuncture between the knowledge and skills of the shop floor and that of the supervisory and even managerial staff. As the managerial organization of Stelco became increasingly hooked into the ruling relations, both nationally and internationally, whatever the technological requirements, there were also skills requirements of a type that could only by learned in formal education settings. Hence the supervisory staff are increasingly no longer recruited from the shop floor but are hired externally and may even have university degrees. The disjuncture between the experiential knowledge of people gained in the course of their everyday work, both out of their experience and as they themselves improved on what they had learned, and the knowledge of the supervisory staff became marked. Alex's account that follows points to another dimension of the disjuncture between the foreman's and the shop floor knowledge of work processes. He identified a relationship in which shop floor knowledge was consciously withheld from the outsider:

> *Alex:* Okay. In our service shop, that's where our foremen came from, the basic foremen. In the seventies it changed, where they hired outside, unrelated to the shop. Prior to that, it was always foremen, like foremen were made from within. After, in the seventies, they changed. They put an ad in the paper somewhere and they hired people to be supervisors. It was education and management skills that they were looking for instead of work skills. To be quite honest with you, I don't think it was the way to go. Only because — These were good people, some of them were good people but they didn't know anything. And I mean, we're like children down there, we're children down in that plant and —

Interviewer: You mean you're treated like children?

Alex: Well, we're treated like children but we're also children back. Like if you don't treat us nice, we're not going to tell you anything.... You know? And a supervisor can come out and if you don't know the job, if you don't know the basic skills of the job, I always call us a brotherhood, but the brothers, they can make you or break you or they can.... No, it's not a positive thing. See I would rather, you know, when you think about it, you have to have some knowledge of the basic job that's going on there... to understand what those guys are doing. If you look at a written word, a type sheet, well what has he done here? Not just take it for face value.

Experiential Learning

Our focus in the previous section of the chapter has been on the ways in which restructuring in the steel industry undermines the traditional ways in which informal skills in the use of tools and manual skills in general are reproduced. But, of course, experiential learning still goes on. What is disrupted or displaced is its integration into the industrial process on more than an individual basis. By the term "experiential learning," we mean learning that takes place in ways that are not mediated by the text-based systems characteristic of schooling and college. It is a historical process where a kind of "human capital" is stored in the individual's own history in the company and the community and available only as the individual continues to work there or passes it on to others. There is still little formal recognition of such knowledge with the exception of such rarely used devices as Prior Learning Assessment (PLAR).[33]

Everyday work settings are the contexts of experiential learning. An individual builds up a knowledge of how to do particular jobs, of the layout of the region of the plant that he or she has worked in, of the idiosyncrasies of particular machines, of how to solve particular problems and so on. By contrast, formalized skills are stored in texts of various kinds and transmitted in formalized settings of education and training. The transmission of experientially acquired knowledge and skill is from individual to individual in work situations which they share. The plant itself, its physical layout, its organization, its technologies, are essential settings in which experiential skills are developed; experiential skills are stored by individuals who have, as we have seen, actively built on their experience to transform it into skills and knowledge relevant to their own work and teachable to others. Yet, unless it is incorporated into institutionalized training processes such as apprenticeship, experiential learning has no *institutionalized* form of transmission. And apprenticeships as well become more modularized and less integrated with experiential learning.

The experiential knowledge and skills acquired by workers in the course of their everyday work activities is not well defined by, nor does it appear to be valued by, the company. Dan formulated this problem for us. In the following passage from our interview with him, Dan was arguing against the company policy, during the period of multi-tasking and multi-crafting in the 1980s, of taking those already trained in a craft and introducing them to production work so that they could apply their knowledge of a trade to the production process. He pointed out that this procedure was one that essentially wasted the experiential knowledge the production worker had built up over time. He asks: rather than introducing people in trades to production work, why not introduce production workers to the skills of a trade?[34]

> What does it matter what pipe he fits? Or he's a millwright, what does it matter what pump he works on? Or an electrician, the same thing and so on and so on. But a production worker, that's the guy that says "See that waviness in that strip going down that line? That tells me it's on gauge." "Well how do you know that? "Well, twenty years of watching it and relating it back to a gauge problem." Or "See that furnace? I've opened up the door and I looked in there. See the colour of that steel? That steel is about 2500 degrees, it's ready to roll." "Well how do you know that?" "Because I know that sheen that forms on there because for twenty years, I've watched that happen." And the guy beside me said, "See when you see that sheen? Roll it." And it's worked. That's where companies screw up. A perfect example of that down at Stelco was our combining of a production job with a trade job, in our basic end, we said "Let's take trades and let's put them on equipment, and let's put them on jobs so that if the equipment breaks down, the tradesman can fix it." Well, when you start going down that road what you're doing is you're minimizing or belittling the quality of the people you have on the production side. It would have been far better to say, "You know what? Let's take that production guy that we know is going to take twenty years to be proficient on his job, and let's give him a few years of, you know, every so often, training on the mechanical side to supplement our mechanical work for us." That's the way it should be going. But we don't look at it that way.

Extending Dan's reasoning suggests that we think of experiential learning — of solving problems, of recognizing colours of steel and so on — and its transmission as distinctive in this way: that it is built up biographically in an individual's everyday world of working.

In contrast to formalized learning, which is standardized and text-mediated, experiential learning secretes the historical specifics of a particular local situation, the way in which the particularities of a work setting come to be identified in an individual's consciousness as a historical pattern, repeated in a particular location, a particular configuration of a local setting, a machine process with a particular history. Since what counts as experiential learning is defined by the work or job it relates to, it's hardly surprising that it appeared in many forms in our conversations with respondents. And it is exactly this kind of experiential knowledge which is often lost as plants are technologically upgraded. Ironically, as machinery is modernized and breakdowns become less common on account of the machinery being well-engineered, even more knowledge is lost. When a malfunctioning modular component cannot be replaced — since it is cheaper to replace a component than to repair it — instrument technicians sometimes run into a peculiar problem, as Henry detailed concerning computerized distributive control systems (DCS). These systems allow for central operation of controllers, control valves and anything to do with control temperature, pressure flow level and PH levels:

> Yeah. So what has happened is that, if there is a problem, which is very seldom, even though I've got these courses, I may not have had to do it for three years, have any problems with this DCS, so if there is a problem, even *I* will probably call in engineering. So some of those jobs that are probably our jobs, and *should* be our jobs are passed on to engineering. So that's — some people do that because it's easier, and on the other hand it's also because they [engineers] have spent more time with it also.

Sanger reported management efforts to automate information handling whereby "workers become generalists":

> An example of this kind of change is the introduction of comput-erized controls in the heater operator's job in the No.1 Barmill. Whereas the operator previously checked the color of flames and fumes to gauge the readiness of steel blooms for the finishing op-eration, the computer does this automatically. The operator now receives information on the screen while the computer monitors the reheating furnace and makes appropriate adjustments. (Sanger 1988: 111–12)

Some experiential learning becomes built through repetition into an indi-vidual's bodily processes. Jim related how it becomes automatic:

> You had to make sure that area was cleaned up to put some stuff — You didn't want to put the new stuff on top of the old stuff, okay. Because usually the old stuff would be going out first, and then usually we used to hook it up with chains, you get the lifts over there, you can only pile them up so high. You used to have a tape measure. Used to be you could only go about six inches high, because of chains, you know, you don't want to do more than that. So for a while, I used to go with a measuring tape, but after a while, you can call [*Interviewer:* Eyeball.] yeah, eyeball, you knew it would be six plates you got half an inch there, you had a quarter inch. You knew exactly how many plates you could do.

What has first to be carefully observed, watched for, done slowly to make sure it's done right, becomes built into a bodily "habitus" (Bourdieu 1990), a practice of co-ordinating hand and eye that is a fundamental feature of acquiring bodily skills.

Tony worked on the caster, a dangerous job. He described how, though he was a health and safety rep, he went into certain situations without protective gear. He could count on responses to potential danger that he had built up over time to protect himself:

> A lot of times I see myself, and even as a rep I shouldn't, but I see myself standing in front of the steel without my safety equipment on. Because it's predictable to me, I know if it's going to splash, you know? I've done it so many times that "Okay, I don't need to put my coat on because we're dealing with this." But ninety percent of the time, it's a law that you need to wear your safety equipment but a lot of time I go in without it because I've seen the operation enough that I know I'm safe now. And all I've got to do is step back if anything happens.

What would be true for him, however, was not true for students on site during the summer months.

> But the students that come in, you don't want to see them get burned. And "just because I don't wear my gear doesn't mean that you can't. You put your gear on." And if I have to set an example for the person, I'll do the same thing [put my gear on]…. I don't want them coming back to me saying, "Well, Tony trained me but he didn't have his gear on either."… So, yeah, we bring them in and we try and teach them the right way.

We don't want to suggest by the term "experiential learning" that learning is passive, that individuals are somehow impacted by an environment which goes to work on them without their conscious participation. This is not at all what we learned from those we interviewed. They were actively interested in learning. "I love to learn," Bill told us and his account of how he went out of his way to observe and learn from others was typical:

> I think eighty percent of what I learn, I learn by watching, but if I see a particular guy that I think is good at a job, I'll go and talk to him about it. The other guys I just watch because, you know, for the most part people do things differently, like little different shortcuts they've [worked out] and I'll just watch them all, eventually figure the one I feel that makes the most sense.

Bill was attentive and selective; he learned by watching and mulling over what he saw in terms of how it made sense for his own practice. Casey, interviewed by Livingstone in 2004, described learning from an experienced worker how to gauge the quality of hot steel by burning wood in a process that relied on "feel" rather than instrumentation:

David: So in terms of reading the tolerances that you need, how much of that is eyeball, how much of that is computerized?

Casey: It is all eyeball because we burn wood against it.... That's the learning process, is figuring out what the steel is doing, or what grade, or what your tolerances are, and how it reacts with different types of wood, because you use two different types of softwood and one type of hardwood.

David: What are they by the way?

Casey: There's a soft pine that we use for very, very weak grades, like a lead and like low grades. I think it's birch that they use. We had cedar once, we had some cedar in there, and that was just wrong, because you couldn't read it at all, it blackened out right away. The smell was great! [Laughs.] But it was counterproductive.

David: The thing about the reading, you put the wood against the steel, the molten steel...

Casey: Where the two rolls that condense the steel, there'll be a line, it's called a "scale break," so when the bar comes in, it gets pushed down, the line that happens on the side is the scale break, that is what we read. We look there for size, you've got to make sure that it is hitting the path properly so it is like on and off of the whole type of a thing. The rolls can be skewed this way and that will give you a different reading, and there's a whole bunch of different ways to — to look for.

David: So you are using the wood to basically read the temperatures?

Casey: Temperatures, but more so, quality, and size.

David: Different impurities are going to give you...

Casey: Yeah, different things are going to react different with the wood, and that gives you a different reading.

David: So you've got wrenches to make adjustments, have you got water dials that you have to read?

Casey: No. It's all feel. I find a lot of time that I'm working, I do something because I know that it is going to give me the desired effect. The wood will tell me if I've done it right, or if I've done it wrong.

Another type of experiential learning involves the synthesis of multiple cues in an explicit formulation of a problem or state of affairs. However technologically standardized, a plant is a particular location. It has a history. Machines have histories. Histories are sedimented in actual performance or interconnections that are not recognized in or anticipated by what is formalized in management or in formal learning processes. They are, however, recurrent features, events and problems in the local setting:

> *Steve*: But the biggest thing is most things re-occur and most things that I fix, it's not because I was really smart, it's that I have a good memory and I would think back three years ago, on afternoon shift, I know it's up there, so I go and it might take me five minutes to refresh myself but sure enough it's the same problem as happened three years previous.

> *Interviewer*: So you know what you're looking for.

> *Steve*: You know what you're looking for. And three years previous it might have taken four hours to find the problem, now it's taking me ten minutes. And it's something that I don't think the company appreciates.

The standardization of formalized procedures, however refined, cannot escape the particularizing history of their everyday operation in the particular relations of a given setting, nor can it adequately substitute for the memory of the worker. It is this that experiential knowledge and experiential learning distinctively taps. We do not mean, of course, to suggest that experiential knowledge cannot be transmitted. On the contrary. But it belongs in the particular setting in which it is acquired and the particular configuration of relations it articulates. The following account from Steve about when he was working as an instrument technician provides an example:

> You're a lot more proficient when you've worked in an area for a long time, because you look at the charts, you look at the flow. Quite often the problem that you're experiencing isn't the instrument at all, it's something to do with the process. And you can look at the process and say "Well, you're doing this wrong and this is happening." A good example of that is one of the controls that we work on is where they wind up coils of steel, coils that are galvanized. We have a control that keeps the edge nice and straight. It's like a roll of toilet paper, the control follows where the strip is, so that you have a nice even edge on it. We've had a problem for years where when the [caster] really digs six-foot diameter coils you know, maybe 20-ton coils, that they'd end up a little bit like a dish. And our controls were working perfect. But what we found is, the inner steel was slipping on the steel mantle where it was being wound, and when it would slip, it would always seem to move to the same direction very slightly. So that by the time they finished this 20-ton coil, there would be a 4-inch dish to it. But our controls were working perfectly. So what we actually, how we demonstrated it, is we got them to take some peel-and-stick tape, put it on the mantle where it wouldn't slip — the coil would come out perfect, the next one. So then

they would take the trouble to wash the mantle off and make sure it was nice and clean. And everything would be fine for about six months. But after you've experienced the problem a few times, you'd go and show the supervisor of that mill, "Look, it's not our problem, look at these scratch marks in the coil, you see how they're curved? That's what's happening." And it's experience on the job.

Of course, as we can see from Steve's story, experiential learning is an active process. The tendency of the coil to develop a dish-shape is first observed and puzzled about; a procedure is devised to test possible solutions,[35] and a definite interpretation is arrived at.

Experiential learning operates within the framework of the productive process. This orientation defines what is relevant to be learned. It is an active process in which what is observed, looked for, practised and conceptually assembled is made relevant to the job at hand. As Alison's story illustrates, it complements the technology:

As Utilities Gas Tester, you're going to meet dangers of carbon monoxide, because I'm doing the gas test for everybody else, okay. As a Water Re-circulation Operator, because I carry this monitor around with me, I have learned just from walking around, where to expect gas. The carbon monoxide has no odour but what I find in the blast furnace area is that where you have a certain odour, the chances of you having a high carbon monoxide level are great. It's just this smell that you get. And so you can sort of tell, like sometimes it's so loud down there, you can't even hear your monitor but I'll smell this thing, right, and then I'll look down and I'll see the little red light that flashes when it has — like a beep-beep, I mean, you might have ear muffs on and so on. So if I smell this odour — And then I would tell that to anybody coming in, like, *that's* the odour. Like, "Smell that?" I might take them to a place where I know you get that smell: "Do you smell that? It sort of stings your nose a bit? Well, usually that means there is a lot of carbon monoxide associated with that." Not always but — You know it's just some of the things.

This process of learning goes from the experiential — what is perceived — to the conceptual level. What becomes knowledge cannot be observed but has to be assembled conceptually to be given relevance. An individual's own local history in their work is a resource which can be drawn upon to assemble a picture of what's going on or to find solutions to problems. Alison described a situation arising from an unanticipated interaction between two systems. She has built up over time a conceptual "model" of the relations among what is going on in different settings. Presumably, plant operations in these units are not directly co-ordinated with one another so workers in each setting do not experience the relations between what is going on where they work with what is going on in other units. Alison, however, moves around among different settings. Over time, she has come to assemble or relate events occurring in one setting with those in others so that, through pattern recognition, an event occurring in one setting can be linked to events in another, as we see in this account:

Alison: Yes. It's quite interesting where I work now because I can relate, like I know how each individual thing affects the other. Right?... So these people have always worked that job and they don't understand how their system would relate to our system, and they're looking at them like — Well you know that water — they never knew where that water — They just knew they pumped it somewhere but they didn't understand that they pumped — That it went over there, that we reused it for something else, you know, and so on and so forth...

Interviewer: Yeah. So you presumably kind of build up a larger picture of what the processes are in the plant?

Alison: Yes, it enters into your skills because, for instance, I had a problem a couple of weeks ago. I noticed that the water had turned a certain colour; I just noticed it while I was doing my samples. At the same time, I also had a problem — they had called me to the furnace because they were having a problem with the level control. We took care of that problem with the level control. And I never really gave it much thought. A couple of weeks later, we had the same problem with the level control and I noticed that the water was the same colour again. Hey! So then you're sort of there, thinking "Okay, now why is that?" And then you start delving in a little bit and you start thinking "Well, it's not the usual colour, what have they changed in their process?"... So then you talk to the Blower and you would say "Okay, what have you done?" He would tell me he did something or other and I would say "Oh, well maybe you should call me and tell me that you're doing this so I could shut a chemical off." Because this particular chemical, when he shut off his, he changed his process, then I should have changed my process, okay. Which we didn't, which in turn caused this level control to go screwy. So by noticing that the water colour had changed, I delved into a little bit of what he had done... And so now I can say "Okay, well from now on when you do this, please notify me. I will turn off my chemical and this will not cause us all this problem on this level control."... So it helps to be observant, you know, that type of thing.

Yet another form of experiential knowledge that was described is in a sense learned from the machine process itself. Again, we want to avoid suggesting that this is a passive process. In the following passage from our interview with Tony we can see a process of active reflection at work in how he learns:

This was a brand new machine — I don't know if they said it was [a] 300 million dollar casting machine. And actually from the very start (it was June

136

of '87) they had us in the plant. It was still under construction actually, the machine was. And what they were doing was they were sending us to Lake Erie Works to learn their casting machine out there… so I shuttled [back and forth]. They would take us up to Lake Erie…. We'd go up there and watch how their machine worked because ours wasn't ready yet. So in a way we were all learning together, back then. Now just from sitting there and watching the machine work and all, you look at it and think "Well, yeah, you can do this and you can do that." You learn things or pick up things on your own.

Tony worked as utility man on the caster that was installed at Stelco's Hilton Works. Though it is a continuous process, it has to be watched and controlled.

It's just massive, it's humungous, for one thing. To get to our worksite we have to go probably five stories up in the air. We're dealing with ladles of steel, liquid steel, 150 tons of liquid steel. And they get put on to this thing called a turret and then spun around into position…. The crane picks them [i.e., the ladles] up from one area and brings them up to us on the machine. And then from one aisle to the next [the turret] spins the ladle around into position; the ladle of liquid steel gets opened…. On top of this is a thing called a tundish. Basically it's just a giant bathtub. The tundish fills up from one end and on the other end, on the bottom, the steel comes out of these ceramic things called shrouds and it fills the mould. And then the steel runs through this machine that's shaped like a banana. The steel ends up going through the machine; it comes out horizontal. And in the end it's red hot but solid…. And there's a machine at the end of the line that cuts it up just like butter. For us back then, like for me in particular, it was — I'd never seen liquid steel before. From afar, yes. But to be standing right up close to it, you know, it's — I'd never seen it before. It's hot; it sparks; it's very dangerous; it's unpredictable. There's things you need to learn around liquid steel — like that water and steel don't mix. But just being around it, I guess, you learn. And that's where I've been for the past, well, what is it now, twelve, thirteen years?

Alex described his experience of training on the roll-grinders as an active process of observation of and reflection on the machine process itself.

Interviewer: And was it a difficult thing to sort of learn this job?

Alex: You would maybe watch for maybe one or two rolls. It was a hands-on learning experience, hands-on, strictly hands-on. So the more time you were allowed to actually do the work, the better you could absorb. Stuff that you had, because you were going from machine to machine, like I just took down notes, specifics like for the changeovers, I keep using that word, changeovers, but for setting up the machines, you know. I'd put that in a little book and you keep that book because when you started doing the relief, you didn't always want to be asking somebody, you wanted to feel you were a little bit confident doing your job, eh. So most of it was all hands-on, you learned hands-on.

Finally, there is another kind of learning altogether that is not defined by the job but arises from reflection on experiences in which individuals discover aspects of their relationship to the company. Tony learned from a potentially very serious accident:

Tony. There was a few times where I put myself into positions where I risked my life.... The last particular time was, I think, four or five years ago, I got splashed in the face with hot hydraulic fluid and I ended up getting second degree burns. And back then, like not so much myself but my family, like "Was it worth it? Like look at your face, look in the mirror. Your lips are burned, your nose, you know, you could have lost your eye." "Yeah, you're right, it's not worth it." So I'm at a point now where, if I see any danger at all, I just walk away. You know? The machine is the machine but my life is my life.

Interviewer. So when you look back on that accident, there was something that you did then that you felt...

Tony. I had to do it to keep the machine... I would never do it again, no.

Interviewer. You were trying to keep the machine going?

Tony. That's right. Now I would say, "If you want that machine to go," [say] to the supervisor, "Do it yourself." Like, back then I thought "Well, we got to keep the machine going." Well, it's more important to keep me going. Because I have to go home to my kids at the end of the day, I have to go home to my wife. You know.

Interviewer. So you were under some pressure from the supervisor at that time?

Tony. Sure. I was thinking yeah, that's part of my job, I need to change that hose. And even though it's under pressure, well it still needs to be done. Well, you know what? I don't think that's safe. And being a health and safety rep, I know that the government's always been on my side with the Occupational Health and Safety Act, to say if I refuse to do that job, it's not going to affect my position here. I'm doing it because I don't feel it is safe and I'm not here to get hurt or get killed. I don't want to do that job because it's unsafe. So I can refuse to do it under the Act, say "That's under pressure there. I'm not touching that." You know? You cool it down and make it proper for me and then I'll go in there because that's my job. But to go in there and risk getting burned? It happened to me before, it's not going to happen again. And then you look at the liquid steel. If a breakout occurs and I feel that I'm in danger of getting my legs burned and my arms burned, I'm going to run like hell. It's not worth it to me to go home maimed or burned or — To save what, to save a machine that they can rebuild in three days? No.

Interviewer: So there are other kinds of things that you learned that such a mixture of experience of working teaches you things.

Tony: Sure. It's more important for you to come out of there every day in one piece than to risk your life. In the position we're in, we're dealing with an extreme situation. Liquid steel going into this hole. I mean, it works, everything happens the way it's supposed to happen but at any time, something could occur and it's up to you. Like I called myself a babysitter when I do the Operator's job because essentially you're sitting there watching this machine work. If I feel at any time that my life is in danger, I know I can push the stop button that stops the flow of steel.

Interviewer: And you've got to get out of there.

Tony: And then get out of there. And then if there's any damage to the machine, well "Stelco, I'm sorry that that happened but I felt that my life was in danger, I needed to run."

Tony passed on the awareness of danger to students who trained with him:

That's the first thing I tell any student coming in... If ever you feel for your life, a gut feeling even, you turn around and walk back in the lunch room and then we'll talk about it in the lunch room, not on the job.

Like Tony, Alex has learned something about himself, his life and his relationship to Stelco. Not something easily communicable. It is a deep disillusion:

Stelco is a job, period. A job. You do enough to save your posterior, that's the end of it. Because you learn — I'm going to be honest here, like you learn within, if you don't learn within a year, you're going to be very frustrated. And I didn't learn within a year, you know. The way things are done down there, they're — Nobody wants to improve things. And I'm talking about supervision. And when you're there and you say "Well, why don't we do this" or "Why don't we do that?" "Well, we've done it like this for that many years, it stays that way." It's not a progressive thing, you know, it's not. And for anybody that cares, like you just get browbeaten and browbeaten and browbeaten. So you're better off just getting in that whole mould in there and stay in there. And like take pride in your ability to do your work well. And if they would ever question you on something, that you've got the right answers. That's where I come from at work. But as far as the pride at work, no. Like you just do the work well. I'm proud of my work in the sense that, at work, that it's done well. But I don't worry about it in the sense that this is contributing to Stelco, or this is contributing to Stelco... No. That's taken out of you a long, long time ago. That's taken out of you.

Conclusion: Skills and the Ruling Relations

The primary research resource on which this chapter is based is a series of interviews with people working at Stelco's Hilton Works whose work life experience spans the period before restructuring, starting in the late 1960s or early 1970s to 2003 when our interviewing concluded. This research was complemented by other sources in the ethnographic literature, an earlier study of the plastic industry by George Smith and Dorothy, and relevant government documents. Our interviews were focused on how people learned the kinds of skills they used in the plant and on the skills they had acquired in the context of the everyday relationships of family, neighbours and friends.

The introductory section of this chapter expanded on Harry Braverman's theme of the expropriation of working-class skills by the new forms of managerial methods he identified with Frederick Winslow Taylor's school of scientific management as paradigmatic of monopolistic management in general. His original conception was relocated here in an account of a more general reorganization of society that Dorothy (Smith 1990a and 1990b) has described as the emergence and increasing dominance of ruling relations based in various textual technologies, including print, film and so on. The interconnections of the ruling relations began to emerge in North America starting in the late nineteenth century. They include but go beyond the internal relations of the industrial enterprise — the focus of Taylor's work — into an expanding expropriation of localized forms of organization and agency. Though new forms of the organization of capitalist enterprise were central to the process of development, complementary forms of law, of organizing government as bureaucracies as well as the production and applications of knowledge in universities and professions created the social relational environment in which industrial and retail corporations could flourish and grow. The term "the ruling relations" identifies this increasingly interconnected, dense and expansive complex of objectified forms of organization and relations, elaborated well beyond Taylor's dreams by the increasing use of electronic forms of control and guidance.

The interviews enabled us to draw a picture of some of the ways in which a working-class community stored and transmitted manual/mechanical skills across generations and among peers. Working-class communities associated with the major industries of the previous era were sustained economically by the industries with which they were associated, but they also brought to those industries the "human capital"[36] that was regenerated invisibly in the community. The exchange of skills among community members in renovating homes, doing repairs, fixing cars and so on also contributed to its general wealth. The restructuring and/or relocation of industry undermine this social organization by radically reducing the number of high-paying industrial positions on which such communities were built. We do not know what the effects of this change may be, in part because these skills resources now provide the base for the smaller enterprises to which some at least of the original functions of the larger companies have been contracted out. Nonetheless, clearly the conditions that created this important reservoir of "human capital" are undermined with the undermining of the community's economic base.

The final part of the chapter, concerning the displacement of worker-controlled skills training, is its centrepiece. Its interest is in the transfer of skills training from among workers in the industrial setting to the formalized textually mediated forms of the ruling relations. An example of a plastics company in which the supervisory staff and even management had come from the shop floor is used to highlight the kinds of changes that have taken place in industry in general and in Stelco's Hamilton plant in particular. Drawing on the interview material, the kinds of training characteristic of the plant prior to the restructuring of the 1980s and 1990s are described, showing the extent to which in the previous period training was almost entirely from worker to worker, and foremen were drawn from the shop floor and shared the knowledge of operations with other workers. Restructuring, an uneven but continuous process from the late 1970s on, progressively substitutes formalized learning outside the plant for these informal types of learning. Formerly, almost all the training at Stelco was internal, supplemented for technicians by some community college or high school classes. Over the period explored, more and more of those hired into supervisory positions have higher formal education qualifications and no experience of the job they supervise. Increasingly also those few recently hired into the union bargaining unit have formal education qualifications beyond high school. The interests of government in reshaping the labour force to meet the demands of the new forms of management as well as of technology conjoin with those of industry. The community college has been reorganized to respond directly to the specific needs of industry. The complex of relations that displace the earlier forms of training controlled at the shop floor level now increasingly integrates industrial management with the education system, at least at the community college level.

In Experiential Learning, the final section before this conclusion, we brought into view aspects of learning experientially that are relied on yet remain largely invisible and transmitted to others only uncertainly. In contrast with formalized skills that are built up in formalized settings of training, experiential skills and knowledge are built up by individuals in the course of their work. We argue that, regardless of the technical niceties of technology, any machine or electronic process has a history, develops idiosyncrasies, is located in a particular setting and so on. Experiential learning is responsive to these particularities. It is an active, reflective process in which observations and events become lessons through the thoughtful way in which their relevance to the job is derived. This kind of learning goes on, will go on and is essential, yet generally lacks recognition and institutional forms in which it is transmitted from individual to individual. It could be said that it is perhaps only in the Health and Safety Committee, a joint committee of Stelco's Hamilton plant and Local 1005 of the United Steelworkers, that there is some determinate form in which what is learned under conditions of injury or illness is transformed into learning for the plant and in particular for safety at the shop floor level.[37] Of course, the Health and Safety Committee is also informed by advances in scientific and technical knowledge in this area, but it clearly also draws on what people know about their working lives and what can be discovered about the everyday working conditions that lead to accidents. Our research did not extend far into this area, but it would be a fruitful area to research in the future and a possible model for how experiential knowledge can be recognized, respected and incorporated into the working knowledge of industry.

We draw a picture that is multi-faceted. It locates a general process of expanding the "ruling relations" into the organization of skills training so that the primary basis of their reproduction is increasingly in the formalized settings of community colleges. We also suggest that the very process of restructuring itself and the undermining of the economic basis of working-class communities also disrupt the informal processes of transmitting skills that have been stored in those communities. Our discussion of how informal skills were learned in the course of work experience in the plant show learning as an active process in which intellect and manual skills are combined. Looking across time over the period encompassing the working lives of those we spoke to, we could trace a progressive diminishing of company support for the transmission of skills, particularly those learned experientially or from worker to worker. There is little to ensure that the store of skills built up by workers during their working lives in the plant will be reproduced in the next generation of workers.[38] The average age of workers in the plant in 2003 was fifty (see Chapter 1), and Stelco management never indicated an interest in perpetuating a workforce of the kind we spoke to. As the following chapter shows, Stelco was forced to start hiring on account of sheer attrition, but there are different issues now in terms of workforce recomposition. The dependence of Stelco — and now U.S. Steel — on college-trained supervisors and trainees and upon formalized courses tailormade for them by community colleges responded to the technological transformations. These transformations and the changes in how steelwork is learned have followed from the increased managerial deployment of computers to reduce worker control over the labour process.

Notes

1. We also draw on later interviews with Stelco workers undertaken by Livingstone and Dobson.

2. The Centre for the Study of Education and Work (CSEW) at the Ontario Institute for Studies in Education, University of Toronto (OISE/UT) has online project papers exploring this issue; see <nall.ca/res/index.htm> and <www.wallnetwork.ca>.

3. Michael Moore's documentary film *Roger and Me* (Moore [dir.] 1989), showing the devastating effects on Flint, Michigan, following upon the destruction of the GM auto production plant, refers to the multiple personal relationships of family and friends that were disrupted and destroyed. Along with the destruction of a way of life was, we suggest, a destruction of the informal systems of organizing and controlling the production and transmission of knowledges on which companies such as General Motors relied for so many years. See also Hamper (1986) for a biographical treatment of life in Flint and at the auto plant.

4. The project of expropriating worker knowledge and skills was, according to Taylor, a "burden" taken on by management in order to gather "together all of the traditional knowledge which in the past has been possessed by the workmen and then of classifying, tabulating, and reducing this knowledge to rules, laws, and formulae" (in Braverman 1974: 101).

5. Compare Braverman's comments on job classifications (1974: 428–30). The CWS is arguably the most complex job class system ever devised for manufacturing. Designed in the 1940s by management consultants and then implemented in the 1950s, the CWS has continued to be relied upon in order to deal with job changes — because management and the union could never agree on new language. Nonetheless, the number of job classes has been drastically reduced since that time. For more on the CWS, see Chapters 1 and 3.

6. Management efforts to capture the production and other knowledge of steelworkers and transfer it to them began in the nineteenth century (see Stone 1974). The Fordist organization, predicated upon mechanization involving the fragmentation and standardization of production, with the assembly line as a technology of control of the labour process that sets the pace of work (Braverman 1974: 372), and with associated "benefits" such as higher wages and productive efficiencies, had been deeply influenced by Taylor's "scientific management," which aimed at increased profitability through the separation of conception from task (see, e.g., Braverman 1974: 114; Foster 1988; Whitaker 1979: 81). A Taylorist core still remains in management theory and practice (see Waring 1991; Livingstone 1993: 15; Rinehart, Huxley and Robertson 1997: 46, 155). On Fordism, see also Chapter 1.

7. See Veblen (1954) on absentee ownership.

8. Such strategies for avoiding unionization did not always work as intended, as some of the transplanted production facilities were unionized in turn (High 2003: 119) or else the labour-displacing strategy ran aground on the shoals of over-productive capacity combined with shrinking markets (Yates, Lewchuk and Steward 2001: 533–44).

9. For Braverman's critique of studies arguing for "upgrading," see 1974: 424–25.

10. The term "deskilling" is a problematic concept. Foster for one perceptively points out that Braverman never used the term (1999: 15) , while Braverman repeats several times that the very notion of skill has itself become degraded (1974: 130, 444).
11. And then, of course, there were dissenting (e.g., T. Smith 2000) and middle positions (Hale 1980: 90–97).
12. Also compare Crompton and Jones's distinction between "technical" and "social" definitions of skill (1984: 1–2) and Darrah's argument concerning skill rhetoric as drawing analytic attention in two opposed directions — simultaneously towards "characteristics of workers" and towards "macroscopic processes" (1996: 10–13).
13. Braverman notes that Marx's definition of capital in *Das Kapital* is actually the entire text (Braverman 1974: 25n); similarly, Braverman's entire book is his definition of skill. As such, his final statement is found close to the end of his book, where he provides a definition of skill *from the worker's perspective*, which is to say as being like "craft mastery... the combination of knowledge of materials and processes with the practiced manual dexterities required to carry on a specific branch of production." This "mastery" of the labour process is lost with the onset of production through "scientific, technical, and engineering knowledge" such that "the very concept of skill becomes degraded along with the degradation of labor" (1974: 443–44; and cf. 7, 130).
14. Note Braverman's specification of the development of management:
    > Management has become *administration, which is a labor process conducted for the purpose of control within the corporation*, and conducted moreover as a labor process exactly analogous to the process of production, although it produces no product other than the operation and co-ordination of the corporation. From this point on, to examine management means also to examine this labor process, which contains the same antagonistic relations as are contained in the process of production. (1974: 267, emphasis in the original; see also 1974: 127)
15. The point here bears special emphasis. Engineering developed out of skills and knowledge that were originally acquired experientially and through apprenticeship; there occurred a differentiation in conjunction with emerging sciences which selected out and built upon aspects of those skills and displaced the authority of craft and trade types of organization. Engineering training was itself re-engineered to bring engineers and engineering in line with management and the relationship was not always stable. The issue of the "proletarianization" of engineering versus engineering as a "new middle class" (see Meiksins and Smith 1996) is not an overt issue in our study, as our interview focus was on trades and production workers; for now, compare Braverman's "general law of the capitalist division of labor" in which "a structure is given to all labour processes that at its extremes polarizes those whose time is infinitely valuable [e.g., some but not all engineers] and those whose time is worth almost nothing [e.g., some engineers and trade and production workers]" (1974: 83) and recall his comment on management as administration (footnote 14, above; see also Hales 1980: 50–58).
16. Alison is a bit unusual in that she learnt about tools from her father. (Her and

others' first names identifying the respondents' part in interviews are pseudonyms used to protect confidentiality.)

17. Willis described the deep alienation of the "lads" he engaged with in the field work leading to his book *Learning to Labor* (Willis 1988; see also Willis 1979; Dunk 1991). Conceptualized very differently, Arthur B. Shostak (1969) recorded similar patterns of alienation among those working class youth he labeled as "rebels" in contrast with "accommodators" in his 1969 study of "blue-collar life" in the United States. The "rebel" group is characterized as likely to become involved in "delinquent" activities. Those who accommodate stay in school, usually in a predominantly working-class high school, although they are likely to be steered into vocational courses. The "youth culture" of the "rebels" emphasizes

> fun and adventure; a disdain for scholarly effort; the more or less persistent involvement in "tolerated" status offenses like drinking, gambling, occasional truancy, "making out" in the sense of sexual conquest, driving cars before the appropriate age, smoking, swearing, and staying out late. (David Matza, quoted in Shostak 1969: 150)

Here and at other points in this account, a distinctive and traditional working-class culture of masculinity seems to surface. The lack of interest displayed by blue-collar youth in this group for continuing on to college even when they "possess high academic aptitude" (1969: 151) suggests that they may share the kinds of emphasis on manual rather than on "mental" skills suggested in the quotation from LeMaster above. The same would seem to surface in Shostak's account of educational and career decisions made by the group of blue-collar youth he describes as "the achievers" who successfully make their way into college. They appear to share values that downgrade non-manual skills, both in themselves and in relation to the kinds of occupations to which they can expect to get access. Every now and again, the "influence" of a senior generation becomes directly visible, though negatively valued, as when he writes of the "uneven and unreliable knowledge" of the labour market transmitted to blue-collar youth by "well-meaning parents, friends, and the mass media" (Shostak 1969: 153). For male attitudes towards the introduction of women into Hilton Works, see Luxton and Corman (1993: 125–32); Livingstone (1996: 55–62); Livingstone and Luxton (1989: 113–26).

18. Of course, an analogous investigation could be made of the ways in which such informal skills are stored and transmitted specifically among women.

19. This name is a pseudonym.

20. This and the other quotes in this section are from Smith and Smith, field notes (compressed) May 1986. The personnel manager of another company viewed this as a general feature of the plastics processing industry: it "has that 'promotability' from inside, from the plant floor, whether you be a material handler or what have you. And then again to trouble-shoot machines and start learning — a lot of that was just the same."

21. The term "foreman" is gender exclusive, but it is used here to label an older work organization and labour process that the gender-appropriate term "supervisor" does not capture.

22. The competency-based approach to curriculum design that Jackson (1995) describes is analogous to the modular approach referred to here.

23. Stephan's experience in the mid-1990s as a subcontractor working on a plastics company's quality control manual is an example of another permutation in the process described here. The manual writer was a former aviation engineer hired by management as part of its efforts to obtain ISO certification in order to be able to make sales to the Big Three auto manufacturers. Management did not have an understanding of how work was actually accomplished on the floor. The engineer undertook an analysis of the internal operations of the plan by itemizing step-by-step all work processes and thereby began a process of appropriating workers' knowledge. Ironically, one outcome of the exercise (in combination with other shop floor issues) was that the predominantly Filipino workforce *certified themselves* by joining a union.

24. Such prestations have not entirely disappeared from industry. At Stelco, according to union informants, contractors have been known to show up at foremen's doors at Christmastime with the gift of a case of whiskey.

25. Management efforts to break such "arbitrary" power of the foremen has a long pedigree; see, e.g., Nelson (1995: Ch. 3).

26. Nancy Jackson (1995) looks at the introduction of competency-based curriculum in a college on the West Coast that subordinates the discretion and autonomy of instructors to employers. At an earlier period, instructors in crafts and trades might appropriately have been seen as representing working-class control of the reproduction of skills *vested in the institutional settings of community colleges*. Developments of the kind recorded by Jackson are suggestive of another aspect of the overall savaging of working-class control of the reproduction of skills.

27. Through until the end of the 1980s, Dofasco focused its steelmaking on steel sheets and was a supplier of steel to the nearby auto making industry; Stelco for its part specialized in steel forms, sheet steel and shapes. Beginning in the early 1990s, during its period of corporate reorganization, Stelco began producing for the auto industry such that by the mid-1990s around 30 percent of its production was for that industry, up from 15 percent in the early 1980s (Sandberg and Bradbury 1988: 106–107; Frost and Verma 1997).

28. Henry added that the issue was not necessarily the value of the formal credential for the company, but rather that they would hire college graduates over high school graduates simply because the labour market allowed it, although he commented that they would still probably hire "big men."

29. Steve mentioned that the union put a stop to much of the hoarding, although Bill remembers one of his trainers wanting to "control the information." Dan mentioned the withholding of knowledge by another worker in the context of a short-cut involving a possible safety hazard. In the 1980s, however, there appears to have been some hesitancy for some workers to train other workers too well as this could mean losing their job to the person trained (see, e.g., Sanger 1988: 99–101).

30. As Warren Smith also pointed out, such calculations have particular effects within the Stelco chain of operations:

> So you can take a fairly modern plant that doesn't make any finished steel, like [Stelco's] Lake Erie [Works], pour slab, and run it through a hot strip mill, turn it into hot roll, load it on a truck, sold right off the other end, and say this is the most efficient plant in North America. Doesn't matter

that they are *only selling* semi-finished. The point is, they've only got one man-hour per ton, in that part. They take that same part and they ship it down to Hilton Works. Now we have to roll it into fine automotive stuff. We have to coat it, we have to meet all kinds of quality standards, and, we have to assume the one man-hour per ton that they've already got in it, but we get accused of being *four* man-hours per ton, and we are some sort of *inefficient* monster.

Management efforts to use such calculations against workers in bargaining with the union have not been successful.

31. We do know that Statistical Process Control (SPC), based on the work of W. Edwards Deming, preceded the period of ISO standardization; the issue is the global picture of the outcomes of the implementation of such fetishistic management fads.

32. The non-use of such standardization manuals is possibly widespread in heavy industry. Rinehart, Huxley and Robertson, for example, found that use of the CAMI Operating Standards (COSs) book declined over time (1997: 149).

33. See <nall.ca> for a general overview of PLAR. It is seldom used within the steel industry.

34. The context here would appear to be similar to the dispute between management and the union local over the creation of "maintenance-operator" positions (in which "skilled" trades workers were moved into production-type jobs); the union countered by negotiating "operator-maintenance" jobs (in which production workers were given training in basic maintenance tasks) (Livingstone 1996: 39). For the dispute, see Chapter 1.

35. The demonstration of the problem with the mantle is an example of what Sennett called "domain shift," that is, "how a tool initially used for one purpose can be applied to another task, or how the principle guiding one practice can be applied to quite another activity" (2008: 127).

36. Sennett (2008) uses the phrase "knowledge capital," which might be better.

37. However, government support for issues of health and safety has been moving backwards under conditions of fiscal restraint.

38. Indeed, until the hiring of so-called "millennial kids" in 1999–2000, there was virtually no next generation; see Chapter 3 for further discussion.

Chapter 3

The Future of Steel Jobs

D. W. Livingstone and Warren Smith

Our goal from the beginning of this [bankruptcy] process has been to build the foundations for a stronger and more viable Stelco.... We've become a much more focused, effective and efficient steel producer.... We've streamlined the organization by reducing the number of products we make and the number of processes needed to make them. We've managed to reduce the size of our labour force... through voluntary retirements without layoffs.... And we've worked hard at improving communications with you and at increasing the level of openness and trust between management, our unions and all personnel.... The new Stelco can be successful in all market conditions. — Courtney Pratt, President and CEO, Stelco, January 28 (2005: 1–2)

Stelco steelworkers are well aware of the dangers to us and Canadian sovereignty with the sellout of Stelco to the giant monopoly U.S. Steel. We are making full preparations to defend the well being and economic security of our active and retired members... We are under no illusions that USX [U.S. Steel] will guarantee jobs, pensions or anything of value in the community that comes in conflict with its primary mission to make profit for its U.S. owners.... The gross profiteering and injustice to our city and people during the Stelco bankruptcy and sellout cannot be allowed to pass without a just reckoning. — Rolf Gerstenberger, President, USWA Local 1005, September 14 (2007)

The North American steel industry... has great potential to contribute further to the kind of economy and society that all Canadians want for the future.... Our design and production of the materials we need is only limited by our imagination and dialogue about the environment, life style and economy we want for ourselves and our children. — Peter Warrian (2010a: 8, 12)

This chapter first offers an overview of conditions in the steel industry in the first decade of the twenty-first century in terms of global developments and the situation of integrated plants in the developed world. We summarize the particular condition of Canada's first large integrated steel company, from the bankruptcy process of Stelco to the takeover and reshaping of the company by U.S. Steel. The workplace restructuring now occurring in integrated plants is examined from the perspective of the Hamilton Works plant, with particular attention to the challenge of the loss of experienced steelworkers' knowledge and renewal of a future labour force. We then address the more general questions about the future of the steel industry and the sustainability of steel jobs in terms of alternative models of ownership (further foreign takeovers; repurchase by domestic private capital; creation of government [or crown] corporations; worker ownership) and different models of management-labour relations (hierarchical or consultative management; industrial democracy or worker self-management). Hamilton Works may be an extreme case in some respects among surviving integrated steel plants, but the basic challenges are common to all integrated steel plants in the developed world.

Global Consolidation and Local Conditions

During the first decade of the twenty-first century, the steel industry entered a stage of global consolidation. By the end of the decade, around 60 percent of steel was produced in developing countries and over 40 percent of steel produced was traded internationally (World Steel Association 2009). Current technology was available to anyone with the resources to buy it, and numerous joint ventures between varied configurations of steel firms in developed and developing countries were formed. These conditions enabled Lakshmi Mittal, from his origins in northwest India and a small steel mill in Indonesia, to orchestrate a series of mergers resulting in the formation of the largest steel company ever known, ArcelorMittal (see Bouquet and Ousey 2009). In 2008, this company produced over 100 million tons of steel, with employees in over sixty countries (World Steel Association 2009). Since the 1980s, growing pressures from more efficient mini-mills and cheaper steel from freer trade with developing countries has been forcing integrated mills in developed countries into joint ventures, mergers and bankruptcies and out of bulk commodity steel markets into higher value-added production of specialized steels, especially for the auto industry (Madar 2009: 123–30, and see Chapter 1). But increasing demand for basic steel fuelled by China and other developing economies led to nearly a 60 percent increase in crude steel production between 2001 and 2007, from 850 million tons to 1.35 billion tons, and a quadrupling of the average global price by July 2008. With increasingly global competition, steel prices were once more vulnerable to wide fluctuations, dropping by over 50 percent in the "great recession" of the following year. Global overcapacity at the end of the decade had reached 500 million tons or 40 percent of current productive capability. Steel employment continued to drop and productivity to rise in Western countries and also began to do so in developing countries (OECD Steel Committee 2009). General conditions for remaining integrated mills in developed countries could justly be described as "expensive, volatile and difficult" (Madar 2009: 173).

Steel technologies have become standardized globally, and innovations such as computerized processing, near net shape casting, improved energy efficiency and use of by-products, and enhanced steel recycling are now widely accessible, provoking continual change in steel production systems around the world (Renner, Sweeney and Kubit 2008; Madar 2009). Half of the types of steel produced today did not exist a decade ago. In this context of global consolidation and strong competition, there have been substantial gains in labour productivity through automation and computerization. Labour has become a minor cost factor for many steel companies in the developed world — around 5 percent of total costs among Western European companies paying the highest wages in the world (Renner, Sweeney and Kubit 2008). Mini-mills without front-end processing have even lower labour costs per ton. But integrated producers using virgin iron ore rather than scrap steel still have advantages in terms of the low impurities and metallurgical properties required in thin casting for autos, appliances and cans (Birat 1986; Warrian 2010b). These technical grades of steel with very high value added remain the refuge of integrated firms for the near future. While labour costs may be minor, steel producers in developed countries, especially remaining integrated producers with dwindling unionized workforces, have been compelled to pay closer attention to the concerns of their experienced workers and the capacities of new workers in order to ensure continuing efficient production (Fairbrother, Stroud and Coffey 2004a, 2004b). Steelworker numbers have continued to decline since the turn of the century, but retention of their loyalty and working knowledge has become a strategic priority for survival of the old integrated steel companies.

This was the general context faced by Canadian integrated producers over the past decade. Canada has become a minor player with about 1 percent of world production, its 15 million tons per year dwarfed by China's 500 million tons (World Steel Association 2009: 9). The three major integrated companies — Stelco, Dofasco and Algoma, all with established ties to lucrative North American markets for steel — became vulnerable to foreign takeovers and compelled to make basic choices in terms of ownership, product lines and worker retention and training in order to try to survive. Dofasco had become one of the most innovative and profitable steel companies in the world, which made it an attractive target for larger international steel companies seeking greater access to North American markets. In 2006, it was taken over by the largest steel company, ArcelorMittal, as part of one of the most complex corporate mergers ever accomplished (Bouquet and Ousey 2009). Smaller Algoma Steel had survived a generation earlier only with the aid of large-scale government subsidies and worker concessions (Heron 1988). In 2007, Essar Global, an Indian conglomerate with steel, oil, shipping and construction businesses, bought Algoma as a platform for growth in the North American market for steel plate, sheet, blanks and welded shapes and profiles. In January 2004, Stelco, after a series of large financial losses, carrying large legacy costs and facing a lack of investment capital, entered bankruptcy protection under the Companies' Creditors Arrangement Act (CCAA). The company left bankruptcy in March 2006, taken over by three hedge funds. These funds cashed in on their investment by selling out to U.S. Steel, the largest remaining North American steel producer, in August 2007.[1] By the end of the decade, eleven of the twelve largest Canadian steel companies had been purchased by larger international firms (Warrian 2010a: 37).[2] Only Lakeside Steel—earlier sold by Stelco, centred near Hamilton in Welland, Ontario, and producing only pipe and tubing — remained under Canadian ownership. The bulk of this chapter examines the recent restructuring of integrated North American steel companies from the perspective of Stelco and Hamilton Works.[3]

Bankruptcy and Double Takeover of Stelco

Stelco entered bankruptcy protection in 2004 after several years of heavy financial losses in the wake of increasing cheap imported steel and its unions' refusal to accept wage, pension and benefit concessions to slash hourly labour costs. Stelco was not insolvent (a legal requirement for CCAA protection) but successfully argued in a precedent-setting position, accepted by the court, that its mounting debts would drive it into bankruptcy in a matter of months if the court did not intervene. At the top of its list was a $1.3 billion pension shortfall. Weeks later, steel prices soared and the company posted record profits. Just prior to the CCAA, Courtney Pratt, a former CEO at other large Canadian corporations who had developed a reputation for progressive worker relations, was named to the top post at Stelco.[4] A year later, Pratt declared in the annual report that a restructuring plan begun under court protection had been largely successful so far but that the challenges of better labour relations and lack of capital remained serious:

> The operational achievements of the past year are attributable in large measure to the outstanding effort and commitment shown by the Company's employees. In the face of incredible challenges and change, the men and women of Stelco are working more produc-

tively and safely than ever before.... One of our priorities during the past year was to improve the Company's level of communication with its stakeholders.... We worked to promote a culture marked by openness and trust with our unions.... Our admitted lack of progress on this front... was a source of great disappointment in 2004.... The accomplishments of the past year can enable a much stronger Stelco to emerge from its Court-supervised restructuring.... To achieve this positive future, it is critical that Stelco succeed in obtaining the new capital needed to fund its capital expenditure programs, to reduce the funding deficiencies in its main pension plans, and to provide the liquidity that will enable the Company to weather the inevitable cyclical downturn in steel markets. (Stelco 2005: 5–6)

This restructuring involved focusing on the core integrated steel business in Lake Erie and Hamilton and more fully integrating the two plants. There was simplification of product lines and a focus on high-quality products for value-added markets. Inefficient facilities, such as the rod and plate mills and large slab mills, were closed, and subsidiary companies, including two mini-mills in Alberta and Quebec, were sold as part of the plan to generate new capital in order to remain competitive. After two years of negotiations among stakeholders, the Ontario government contributed $150 million to Stelco's pension shortfall. But the company still had hundreds of millions in stayed obligations to creditors. While now relatively healthy through market improvement and organizational streamlining, Stelco was at the mercy of the hedge funds that had been buying up its debt (Watson 2006).

Three venture capital firms — Brookfield Asset Management's Tricap Management Limited (a Toronto restructuring fund), Appaloosa Management (a U.S. hedge fund) and Sunrise Partners LP (a Toronto-based hedge fund) — became majority shareholders in the winning bid to take Stelco out of bankruptcy protection at the end of March 2006.[5] Bond holders got their money back and pensions were protected. But the ownership restructuring plan wiped out the shares of old shareholders. The new controlling shareholders were issued new shares that were valued at $5.50. On the first day of public trading, in April 2006, the new shares ran up to $19.49, suggesting that they had been seriously undervalued during the period when prior shareholders had been left with nothing. Rodney Mott, the new CEO and an experienced turnaround artist in bankrupt U.S. steel companies, almost immediately began to cut jobs in Hamilton, streamline labour relations and sell more company assets. He soon indicated that Stelco was open to resale. In the year after emerging from bankruptcy, Stelco lost over $200 million but the stock climbed on speculation that this last major Canadian strategic beachhead would soon fall to a larger international steel firm. By late 2007,

U.S. Steel, the largest and oldest remaining integrated U.S. steel producer, completed the purchase of Stelco for over $38 a share — $1.1 million in cash — plus $800 million in debt and around $1.5 billion in pension and health liabilities. The venture capital firms walked away with massive profits, and Mr. Mott left with over $60 million himself.

On completing the purchase of Stelco, John Surma, U.S. Steel CEO, declared:

> Our objective is to run [Stelco's operations], run them well, and run them for a long period of time…. The slab supply coming out of Hamilton now, which is 900,000 to one million tons of slabs, is very important to us because we can now finish them at our existing Midwest facilities. It fits in very, very nicely to our existing systems. Our company has tripled in size since the year 2000. We've added operations in several countries. We do this carefully, so the things we acquire fit nicely in with the rest of business. (quoted in Powell 2007: A1)

U.S. Steel's declared objective was to integrate the slab operations at the Hamilton plant with finishing mills in Detroit, Michigan, and Granite City, Illinois. Stelco was to become a provider of slabs as raw materials[6] for U.S. Steel operations south of the border. Announced elements of the deal included a contribution of U.S. $31 million to Stelco's underfunded pension plans and an endowed chair at McMaster University in Hamilton to facilitate the development of new steelmaking technology. Other undertakings, revealed later, included the following commitments:

1) invest Can. $200 million in capital expenditures at the former Stelco over five years, including $100 million at the firm's Hamilton plant;
2) provide $15 million for research and development over three years;
3) increase exports from Stelco by 10 percent; and
4) maintain 3,100 jobs in the company and retain at least 75 percent of management employees over the next three years (Powell 2009a).

In the wake of the economic recession starting in late 2008, U.S Steel shut down its Hamilton and Lake Erie blast furnaces indefinitely and began a series of large layoffs that by March 2009 led to the layoff of all hourly employees, about 1,700 workers at Hamilton Works and 1,100 at Lake Erie Works. When recovery occurred in 2009, U.S. Steel's American plants dramatically increased the amount of steel they produced for Canadian customers while the former Stelco plants sat idle. As steel markets continued to recover, U.S. Steel called back 800 workers in June 2009 to produce coke at Hamilton Works for U.S. Steel mills and to avoid costly severance payouts.

But the newer, more efficient Lake Erie Works remained idle and embroiled in bitter contract negotiations. The general situation provoked the Canadian federal government to sue U.S. Steel in July 2009 over breach of promise to increase Stelco production and maintain jobs. Both Lakeside Steel, the sole remaining Canadian steel company, and the steelworkers' union gained intervener status at these proceedings. U.S. Steel countered that favouring less-efficient Canadian facilities would increase losses and jeopardize the entire company. In August 2009, the Hamilton Works blast furnace was restarted. In November, U.S. Steel recalled some workers to Lake Erie Works to avoid severance costs. In April 2010, a no-raise contract which conceded defined contributions rather than defined benefit pensions for new workers was finally signed after very bitter negotiations, and full operation at Lake Erie Works was planned for that summer. In the meantime, U.S. Steel had sold off its share in the Wabash iron mine. U.S. Steel also acquired full ownership of the Z-Line at Hamilton Works and began using this relatively new line to finish steel from its Detroit plant for the Canadian auto industry. In April 2010, U.S. Steel sold the idle Hamilton Works bar and bloom mills to Max Aicher, a German steel company that had been interested in buying them for several years. This company aimed to use these mills to process high value steel directly for North American markets, in contrast to U.S. Steel's future plan for its Canadian plants largely to supplement U.S. operations. In June 2010, the federal court ruled that the government case against U.S. Steel could proceed under the terms of the Investment Canada Act, which requires foreign takeovers to have net benefit to Canada (Owram 2010: B1). This ruling raised the possibility, however remote, of the sale of Stelco–U.S. Steel Canada once more to Canadian interests. However, U.S. Steel is appealing the ruling (Freeman 2010).

Whatever the eventual court decision on this particular matter, the prospect of another Canadian industry becoming primarily a provider of raw materials to be finished in other countries for higher added value (or finished for use in Canada with added value going to foreign owners) becomes increasingly probable. Canadian steel companies had long been the outstanding exception to the dominant pattern of the Canadian economy as suppliers of raw materials for higher value-added production in other countries. At the time of writing, global steel firms (e.g., Thyssen) are about to import from abroad all raw materials up to the slab stage to new steel finishing facilities located close to local auto plants in the southeastern United States (Warrian 2010a: 46). The ownership of Stelco may be pivotal for the future of any independent Canadian steel production.

Workplace Restructuring in Integrated Steel Plants

Integrated steel plants that remain viable in developed countries early in the twenty-first century typically have the following features: secure supplies of iron ore and coke to make high-grade primary steel; efficient basic oxygen furnaces (BOFs) and continuous casters to produce basic shapes; well-established access to their regional markets; efficient finishing mills to provide timely specialized (technical grade) steel products to these relatively lucrative markets; and experienced workforces efficiently producing a changing array of specialized steels. Cheaper steels from developing countries and from mini-mills continue to take over more of the basic commodity steel market and encroach upon specialized steel markets. Integrated steel firms that have survived bankruptcy have continued to close older facilities and reduce the range of products and size of labour forces to focus on specific steels that they can still produce in a more timely way in large quantities and at high quality for such industries as auto, appliances, construction and canning. But the largest global firms with growing markets in developing countries are using their assets and international banking capital to take over weakening integrated steel plants in developed countries and gain control over even the most highly specialized steel markets, as we have seen in the past few years in Canada (see Bouquet and Ousey 2009; Warrian 2010a). The reorganizing of these integrated steel plants becomes ever more challenging.

The Canadian steel industry has gone through several historical stages:

1) 1870–1940: nation-building with high tariff protection;
2) 1940–45: government control of production and pricing;
3) 1945–75: fully integrated steel industry with mass consumer products;
4) 1975–2005: the period of expansion into the United States and free trade; and
5) 2006–present: global steel integration (see Warrian 2010a).

Within the latter period, Canadian ownership almost disappeared and the Canadian steel industry has become integrated into a global steel industry for the first time. However, this progression is not irreversible. The possibility of a sustainable, Canadian-owned and controlled steel industry in the future is at least suggested by the array of alternative bids for Stelco after it entered bankruptcy in 2004; the declared intention of Lakeside Steel to buy Stelco from U.S. Steel in the context of the Canadian federal court hearings on U.S. Steel's alleged breach of agreement; and other alternatives discussed below. Potential benefits of global integration could include access to investment capital and larger markets, but risks include lack of control over investment decisions and capacity shutdowns not in Canadian interests, as is claimed in the current federal case against U.S. Steel.

The most immediate consequence of global steel integration in Canada has been a sharp decline in the proportion of the domestic market supplied by Canadian steel producers as well as an increase in the proportion of steel shipments that are exported. In 2003, domestic producers supplied 60 percent of Canada's apparent domestic market. By 2006, this was down to 47 percent. The U.S. Steel company imports since taking over Stelco in 2007 have reduced this proportion further. In 2003, only 37 percent of Canadian steel output was exported. Foreign ownership oriented to large American markets is increasing this share significantly (Warrian 2010a: 76). Capacity utilization, human resource and R&D decisions have become increasingly mediated by head offices elsewhere. Some integrated steel plants involved in large mergers can benefit from sharing marketing and product development, R&D and purchasing costs, as well as lower raw material costs from suppliers, managerial staffing efficiencies and lower costs of distributing steel. A significant benefit to acquiring firms has been the lowering of labour costs by negotiating more flexible contracts with employees of the acquired firm (Klau and Mittelstadt 1986; OECD 1987; Kuhn 1997). A notable case is the United States in the wake of bankruptcies around the turn of the century. For example, the International Steel Group (ISG) acquired large bankrupt steel firms and negotiated labour agreements with the United Steel Workers union allowing greater outsourcing, fewer job classifications and the restructuring of compensation and pension plans. Warrian noted: "Allowing workers to perform a wider array of duties than before and for outsourcing during peak periods of demand ultimately boosted labour productivity and thus helped to reduce unit labour costs" (2010a: 42).

As noted above, after Stelco entered bankruptcy protection in 2004, older, less efficient facilities were closed. Facilities deemed non-core assets that retained market value, including two mini-mills and steel pipe and manufactured products outlets were sold to generate capital for technological upgrades of core facilities. Upgrades included the Lake Erie hot rolled mill, blast furnace and caster, and the refurbishing of the coke ovens, blast furnace and processing and finishing systems at Hilton Works. Needed processes deemed too costly to upgrade, such as the Hilton pickle lines, were outsourced. Some priority was given to ensuring the supply of iron ore and coal through retaining ownership of mines and the securing of supply contracts. The key restructuring strategy was to consolidate operations around production of profitable specialized steels, particularly for the auto market. The Stelco annual report for 2005 declared:

> Failure to meet the automotive industry's ever-more demanding requirements for product quality and service, and failure to provide the new grades of advanced high-strength steels will seriously jeop-

ardize Stelco's long-term participation in this market. Similarly, for Stelco to attain a competitive cost structure will require the ongoing selective implementation of new process technologies throughout its integrated steelmaking processes. (2006: 24)

When Stelco emerged from bankruptcy in March 2006, it had narrowed its production to more profitable specialized steels, completed selective technology upgrading, retained most of its established customers in these lines and reduced its labour force substantially through attrition. The new CEO, Rodney Mott, quickly moved to try to smooth labour relations. Under the bankruptcy process, no grievance issue had been able to proceed to arbitration, so the number piled up, especially ones related to layoff disputes. A new collective agreement at Hilton Works was settled in record time in June 2006. This contract contained substantive wage increases, profit sharing that actually paid out to Hilton workers and provisions for increased formal consultation. Mott directed human resources staff to go out onto the shop floor to instruct supervisors in the art of speedy resolution and had little time for supervisors who presented issues to upper management. By late 2006, very few grievances were being filed. The 2006 contract also reduced the number of job classes in the plant from twenty-eight to eight, provided for more plant-wide job mobility and established a management-union committee to deal with the contracting out of work. At the same time, worker retirements continued apace and Mott considered closing further product lines and sold off further assets — which generated some immediate revenue but arguably jeopardized secure supply of needed raw materials. This move in particular suggested that a primary objective was positioning the company for takeover by others with complementary resources.

U.S. Steel CEO Surma's statements at the takeover in August 2007 confirmed that Stelco front-end furnaces and caster would be assisted by U.S. Steel iron ore and coal supplies and would provide steel slabs for finishing in American steel plants. Most finishing mills at Hilton Works were closed in short order, a bar mill was later sold, and production at both Hilton Works and Lake Erie Works became relegated primarily to filling supplementary needs not met by U.S. Steel plants south of the border with similar production ability and lower wage costs.

In terms of labour relations, it should be recalled that the early twentieth-century plants that were the predecessors of current U.S. Steel plants were the primary source for the development of scientific management. The latter was a production system organized around a tight hierarchy of engineering/management at the top and underneath a mass of industrial workers regarded as having little skill. A primary objective of this system was to break down jobs into simpler, routinized components that, with sufficient monetary incentives, could be performed efficiently with little thought (Taylor 1911). The culmination of this approach was the codification by management consultants in the 1940s of the whole system of hourly rated jobs in the steel industry and its full-scale implementation in the 1950s as the Co-operative Wage Study (CWS) system (see Chapter 1). As Warrian (2010a) noted, this system gave the job structure in steel a uniquely hierarchical and fragmented character that still besets the industry. Stelco, along with U.S. Steel, had been among the most sustained adherents of this organizational structure, and it had been a major contributing historical factor undermining effective co-operation between workers and management in both companies. When U.S. Steel took over Stelco in late 2007, the old hierarchical management style was quickly reasserted. Current markets for steel were good, every ton was out the door as fast as it was made, and workers continued to get profit-sharing bonuses. But plant rules got tougher, dismissals jumped and Hilton Works (now "U.S. Steel Hamilton") began to feel like the old Stelco again. Workers were disciplined for the slightest infractions. Accidents precipitated full inquisitions that could last for up to five hours and often resulted in penalties against the workers. Lunch box searches at the gate became an expected inconvenience, and every amenity in the plant that made life there a little more pleasant was eliminated. Even small toaster ovens, which made meals more enjoyable, were trucked from the plant. With the market downturn in 2008 combined with layoffs, both grievances and voluntary retirements mounted.

Under Courtney Pratt's leadership during the bankruptcy process from 2004 to 2006, there were concerted efforts to develop fuller management-worker consultation. Under Mott's leadership in preparation for resale, concessions were made to workers to avoid costly production delays. But, as with the spasmodic efforts at more interactive management attempted since the 1980s, these gestures did little to alter the basically hierarchical organizational structure of Stelco. Under U.S. Steel ownership, management-labour relations became as adversarial as they had ever been at the old Hilton Works and more so than ever at the newer Lake Erie Works.

In terms of job structures, integrated steel plants have been compelled to increase the flexibility of the old CWS system to cope with technological changes and mill closures. The reduction to eight basic job classes contained within the 2006 contract between Stelco and Local 1005, along with greater plant-wide mobility procedures, enabled easier movement with shifting job requirements. Along with job amalgamation and multi-crafting, the development of more maintenance functions for machine operators and the assignment of more trades workers to specific mills were efforts to streamline the use of labour in relation to increasingly automated production systems.

The contracting out systems in old integrated plants also changed to greater reliance on temporary re-hire of retired workers at the same time as hiring younger workers to renew the core labour force became imperative. At Hilton Works, the absence of hiring until the end of the 1990s meant that Stelco has relied increasingly on rehiring retired 1005 members to deal with market upturns and refits while becoming more and more desperate to recruit and train a new core. The statement by Stelco in the 2006 contract with Local 1005: "our organization's most important asset is our employees" and several new items on training (Stelco–USWA Local 1005 2006: 115) reflect a heightened priority on recruitment and training for the effective restructuring and renewal of the labour force in this integrated steel plant, as in most other remaining integrated plants in North America.

The Challenge of Renewal and Loss of Knowledge

Labour force renewal is indeed a common problem in nearly all remaining integrated steel plants, the main difference between the various firms being how early they realized this and what actions they have taken to recruit new workers and to retain older workers' loyalty in order to nurture younger workers' knowledge.

Renewing the Numbers

Graphs 3.1 and 3.2 summarize the total size of the unionized Hamilton Works labour force throughout most of the decade as well as its age and seniority distributions. The continual reductions averaged over 400 workers per year. In late 2009, there were less than 1,000 workers left in the plant, running the trimmed down operation of coke ovens, blast furnace and caster, and doing maintenance as well as operating the Z-Line finishing mill. At that point, the unionized labour force was about 7 percent of its 1981 size. With the shutdown of the entire plant for much of 2009, many workers who wanted to continue were forced to retire in the wake of indefinite layoff because their pensions were greater than their unemployment benefits. Between the March 2009 shutdown and mid-2010, there were over 700 retirements; in late 2009, about 200 of the 942 workers in the plant were eligible to retire. Many of these workers were in their late forties and early fifties. By mid-2010, plant numbers were down to about 850 as many of those eligible for retirement at a fairly early age continued to take it. The issues of renewing this aging workforce and coping with the loss of the knowledge of these experienced workers were becoming painfully obvious to all.

With the layoff of those with low seniority followed by early retirements, most integrated steel companies were left with middle-aged labour forces marching toward retirement. The OECD Working Party of the Steel Committee observed:

> The effects of reduced recruitment and of measures to promote early retirement have distorted the age structure of the workforce....

Graph 3.1 Total Number of Workers, Age and Seniority Profile, Hamilton Works Local 1005 Labour Force, 2003–2009

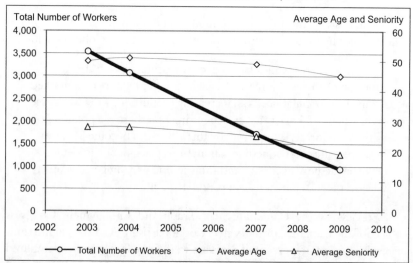

Sources: Stelco Active Employee Reports 2003, 2004, 2007, 2009

Graph 3.2 Age Profile, Hamilton Works Local 1005 Labour Force, 2003–2009

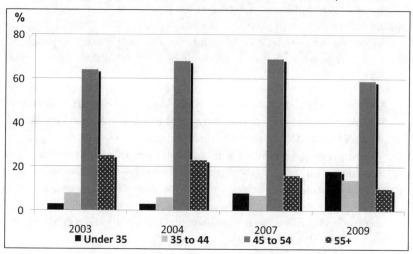

Sources: Stelco Active Employee Reports 2003, 2004, 2007, 2009

The sharp reduction in the recruitment of young steelworkers in recent years has been a major social and economic problem for some regions, and may in the longer term present problems for the steel industry itself in terms of an unbalanced age structure.... The uncertainty in job security will continue to contribute to an unbalanced age structure. It is evident that the generational bond to steel mill jobs is being broken. (1987: 4, 9)

A later analysis of the European Union steel workforce based on 1993–9 data stressed the same problem. Fairbrother, Stroud and Coffey concluded:

The EU steel companies face a growing problem with the age distribution of the workforce.... In each case there has been a marked aging of the populations as an increasing proportion of the workforce enters the 50–54 age bracket, suggesting that there is a polarization of the workforce. As time goes by this is likely to become acute, and raises very important questions about the replacement of older workers over the next five years and the training of younger workers to take on the jobs currently done. (2004b: 10)

A review by the Canadian Steel Trade and Employment Congress (CSTEC) of the Canadian primary steel workforce using 2001 data found similar results: almost 55 percent of workers were forty-five or older, compared to only 35 percent for manufacturing industries as a whole, whereas only 14 percent were under thirty-five compared to 33 percent in manufacturing generally. Their report declared: "Primary steel companies face potentially significant demographic issues, which could develop as older workers retire and the industry's experienced skill base disappears" (CSTEC 2005: 38).

Stelco was an extreme case of failure to address this renewal problem. The annual report for 2004 contained one of the first public admissions of the issue:

Approximately... 45% of the hourly workforce at Stelco are eligible to retire under the current provisions of the defined pension benefit plans. A further 35%... could retire in the next five years.... Stelco is currently recruiting individuals to satisfy its manpower requirements consistent with its succession plans and attrition rates. Retention of the skills and knowledge of the Corporation's employees, and the ability to attract and retain new employees where replacement is considered critical, is essential to the Corporation's continued operations. (Stelco 2005: 34)

As documented in Chapter 1, virtually nobody in the Hamilton plant in 1996 was under thirty-five. The drastic consequences of the lack of a labour replacement plan were becoming obvious (see Livingstone 1997, 1999b). But through the decade of the 1990s there were still virtually no new hires and little formal apprenticeship training for those younger workers in the plant who could have benefitted from it. Finally, during the 1999–2000 period, some new hiring was done — about 300 "millennium kids" as some called them. There was significant turnover among them in the uncertain conditions, and by the start of the bankruptcy process in 2004, still less than 10 percent of the decreasing workforce at Hamilton Works was under forty-five. The average age was fifty-one and the average seniority was twenty-eight years. Since 2004, some new hiring was needed just to keep basic operations going. By late 2007, half of the 2003 workforce had retired and the proportion under forty-five remaining was up to 15 percent. By late 2009, half of the 2007 workforce had retired and the proportion under 45 remaining was up to about a third and nearly 20 percent were under thirty-five. At that point, the dwindling Hamilton Works unionized labour force had an average age of forty-five and average seniority of nineteen years. This was still a relatively old, experienced labour force with hundreds approaching retirement.

Given the upheaval of so many retirements, the extensive plant restructuring and a generation gap between the older workers and most of the new millennial hires, transmission of working knowledge from older to younger workers at Hamilton Works was likely to be problematic. It should also be noted that because of the lack of hiring at Stelco generally between the early 1980s and 2000, the age and seniority profile at the Lake Erie plant, newly opened in 1980, and the older Hamilton Works plant had become very similar. In 2009, the average age at Lake Erie Works was forty-four and the average seniority was nearly seventeen years. While several hundred workers, making up about 40 percent of the current workforce at each plant, had been hired within the past ten years, a bulky half of the workers at each plant were in the forty-five to fifty-four age group, and a large gap between older workers and new hires was common to both plants. The most notable difference was that the total number of employees at the newer Lake Erie plant remained near the contractually mandated 1980 level, with greater continuity in production processes, making transmission of working knowledge potentially somewhat easier.

There were two basic choices to deal with this renewal problem: (1) keep chopping the permanent workforce while intensifying its workload and contracting out more and more work; or (2) develop a long-term hiring plan to create a permanent core workforce that will continue to do most of the work efficiently. Stelco persistently opted for the first choice at Hilton Works: mass layoffs and early retirement packages, followed by increased overtime and contracting out. The best available estimates suggest that in 1996 Hilton used about 3 million hours of overtime; the equivalent of over 1,500 full-time jobs. There may have been almost as many hours of contract labour. In the late 1990s, overtime averaged about 80,000 hours per month or 15 percent of gross hours; this amounted to between 500 and 750 full-time jobs. Subcontractors were paid about $100 million in 1997, another 450 jobs or so. The precise numbers can be disputed, but it is very clear that, from the

1981 strike and mass layoffs period onward, Stelco consistently relied on intensified overtime and hiring temporary non-union labour rather than renewing a permanent unionized workforce.

The second choice has been used by some successful integrated mills: keep most of the work in the plant for permanent workers and use phased retirement of experienced workers to train younger workers to continue as the main workforce. This option recognizes the knowledge of experienced steelworkers and the importance of passing it on to ensure effective steel production, as well as the prospect that workers who have adequate time for rest, family and community activities are both healthier and more productive. A number of European integrated steel plants that anticipated the problem of an aging workforce developed employment renewal plans. So did Slater Steels in Hamilton. A study of the Slater case concluded: "The true secret of success in age-related issues, as it is for many other workplace issues, is an effective (i.e., positive, constructive) relationship between the employer, its employees and their representatives" (Verma 1996). Dofasco's retention and new training strategy, discussed below, poses the most obvious alternative to Stelco's "slash and burn" approach.

So Stelco management only began new hiring in 1999–2000 when regular employment numbers had been reduced so far that new hires became imperative to continue effective operation. U.S. Steel has continued ad hoc new hiring and re-hiring retired workers when specific operations were threatened by small numbers. For example, when U.S. Steel restarted the Z-Line for the Canadian auto industry in early 2010, they found that the majority of the qualified operators in the plant before the 2009 shutdown (over forty of seventy operators) had retired. They were forced to re-hire retired operators (through a company called Staff Aid, originally founded by retired Stelco supervisors). Stelco management in the 1990s used a motto of "quality people" and U.S. Steel executives refer to retention of "intellectual capital." But neither management bothered to confer constructively with its workforce and union leaders to try to work out a long-term renewal plan to ensure that Hamilton Works and Lake Erie have a future.

Retaining and Nurturing Knowledge
The first comprehensive diagnosis of the human resource challenges of the Canadian steel industry in 2005 admitted that most steel companies had postponed dealing with these issues too long. Besides retirement and recruitment numbers issues, this CSTEC study recognized the major problem as ensuring effective transfer of workplace knowledge:

> The loss of retiring workers increases the risks that they will take their knowledge with them... particularly among the "older" sub-sectors... in which formal workplace knowledge transfer strategies

were very often absent. Firms face a greater need to ensure that approaches are in place to systematically capture and retain this workplace knowledge.... Retaining workplace skills and knowledge is central to a company's ability to adapt and apply new technology and maintain its competitiveness. A rapidly aging work force raises the question of the potential shortage and loss of workforce skills and increases the importance of knowledge transfer from older to younger workers.... This is further aggravated by the fact that a number of years may be required to fully understand many of the operations and maintenance jobs, to the point that even people with 10 years experience may encounter many production-related problems that they have not been exposed to before. (2005: xi, 77–78)

One of the most extensive international studies of transmission of knowledge in the steel industry similarly concluded that much of the transmission has occurred informally and the significance of this informal knowledge should be more fully recognized. Fairbrother, Stroud and Coffey stated:

> In the case of older workers... this is likely to be employees... whose approach to learning is not necessarily geared to formal methods of instruction. Indeed, the patterns of instruction in many steel plants may underwrite informal patterns of learning. (2004a: 19)

The authors expressed concern over the polarization of generations and the challenge of the remaining older workforce being able to pass on their knowledge to recent younger entrants with different formal education credentials and orientations. They noted that the skill profile of older steelworkers is severely underestimated because of their relative lack of formal credentials. In another report, Fairbrother, Stroud and Coffey suggested:

> A credentialist perspective of steelworkers' skills fails to properly contextualize a workforce skill profile. For instance, older workers' skills might not be credentialised in a formal way, even though they might be highly skilled individuals. Moreover, extensive workplace training does not always result in formal qualifications. (2004b: 9)

The fundamental problem of transmission of knowledge within steelworker communities across recent generations was dealt with in Chapter 2. More specifically, younger plant entrants need substantial opportunities for time with and mentoring from more experienced workers in order to learn to do their shifting jobs. This also applies to more experienced workers continuing to learn from each other. Even with extensive computerization, an integrated steel plant cannot be run effectively without experienced operators working closely with skilled trades. As a Local 1005 machine operator interviewed said: "As far as learning to operate this machine, it's something that over the years you just acquire a feel for." A repair electrician added: "We've learned from experience that if you want to find out what's wrong with a machine, you listen to the operator. The operators know the sounds."

Throughout the developed countries, the most evident problem in the transmission of workers' knowledge in the current steel industry has been a massive decline in apprenticeships (Fairbrother, Stroud and Coffey 2004a: 14; CSTEC 2005: xiii). Stelco in particular not only hired virtually no apprentices during the 1990s but provided few opportunities for previously hired production workers to enter apprenticeships — until such workers were too old to benefit significantly from them. More generally, in spite of appeals from union leaders in the late 1990s, Stelco increasingly relied on re-employing retired workers rather than new hiring. The large contingent labour force became primarily composed of retired 1005 members from every operating job and trade, back in the plant on either three- or six-month renewable contracts or in the employ of a contractor. While these temporary workers often had ample experience, their employment status gave them little opportunity or motivation to nurture younger workers. The effective abandonment of most organized in-plant training during the 1990s created large, difficult-to-fill gaps between the older experienced workers still in the plant and the younger workers needed to continue operating it. The most recent estimates indicate that, in addition to the age-polarized regular workforce of over 800 Local 1005 members in Hamilton Works, there are now from 500 to more than 800 temporary workers on a daily basis, at least half of whom are retired 1005 members (Howe 2010). These temporary experienced workers have even less chance to pass on their knowledge to new regular employees.

The organized training of steelworkers in skilled trades has become more modularized and classroom based with less mentoring from experienced trades workers (see Sanger 1988; CSTEC 2000). With growing retirements and computerization of production processes, it has become especially imperative to hire new workers with electrical trades qualifications. Since 2005, there have been concerted national and international efforts to recruit electrical trades to Hamilton Works. For example, over forty industrial electricians assigned to the steelmaking division were hired between 2005 and 2010. But less than half that many older electrical trades workers were left to mentor them. Given their more modularized formal training and limited possible mentoring, the transmission of useful working knowledge between generations will most likely be undermined. This situation is becoming even more serious for mechanical trades, with virtually no new hiring since the early 1980s and nearly all quickly approaching retirement.

The growing field of work and learning studies now provides ample evidence that the vast majority of job-related learning happens informally among workers and that incidental informal learning stimulates more intentional learning efforts (e.g., Livingstone and Sawchuk 2004b; Rubenson 2007; Livingstone 2010). The workforce near retirement at Hamilton Works contains a large amount of informal knowledge about how to run the plant. Will they be able to pass that knowledge on to younger workers effectively before it is too late?

Knowledge transmission is probably a far more pertinent issue than the frequently asserted concern about skill deficits or lack of human capital among both steelworkers and the general labour force. In terms of formal education qualifications, Canada now has the highest postsecondary education completion rate of any country in the world, as well as one of the highest rates of underemployment of these credentials (that is, the proportion who have formal credentials who can only get a job with lower education requirements for entry) (Livingstone 2009). So, in terms of credentials, over qualification or underemployment of workers is a much greater problem than under qualification or a general knowledge deficit. In international terms, Canadian steelworkers are also now relatively highly educated in formal terms. Since the 1960s, a high school diploma has been required to get a job in most Canadian steel plants. But by 2001, nearly 60 percent of primary steelworkers had at least some postsecondary education or a trades certificate (CSTEC 2005: 41). Canada has one of the most highly qualified steel labour forces in the world. The main problem in this regard is the divide between younger workers' formal qualifications and older workers' practical knowledge: younger steelworkers are increasingly more likely than older workers to have a college or university degree but less likely to have a trades certificate (CSTEC 2005: 45). The decline of trade certification among younger steelworkers is a reflection of the systemic underdevelopment of the Canadian apprenticeship system (Canadian Apprenticeship Forum. 2004) rather than of a relevant skill deficit among workers themselves. Both the steel labour force and the overall Canadian workforce are likely to have more general knowledge and greater computer skills than required for their jobs (Livingstone and Scholtz 2010). In addition, the most extensive studies to date comparing the match between job requirements and workers' formal education and informal job-related learning have been conducted in Canada. The most basic finding is that, whatever the formal match between requirements and formal education, workers continue to engage in extensive informal learning to keep up with changing job demands and to try to reshape their jobs (Livingstone 2009). The main question is whether the organization of their workplaces provides opportunities for effective job-related learning.

How steel companies utilize the large amount of learning that goes on within them depends to a large extent on how they are organized. An organization that involves rank-and-file workers in decision-making at various levels is likely to be one in which workers are more disposed to participate in and share recognized learning activities (CSTEC 2005: 115–20). In this regard, Stelco and U.S. Steel on the one hand and Dofasco on the other offer fairly striking current alternatives.[7] Warrian observed that Stelco "only learned what its engineers learned" (2010a: 120). Just as with U.S. Steel, Stelco had retained a very hierarchical organizational structure, not only with an authoritarian top-down management style and the strict skill hierarchy crystallized in the CWS system, but also a large engineering department separated from the shop floor. Prior to the global crisis, steel technical innovation was for the most part dependent on indigenous engineering talent within individual companies. Stelco engineering was the technical leader in Canada. For example, it developed the Stelco coil box in the late 1970s, an improvement that has been adopted around the world to enhance hot strip mill processing. But during the 1980s and 1990s, Stelco like most other integrated steel firms, virtually eliminated its R&D engineering department. Such departments were replaced by technology licensing and generic research consortia, whose research results became widely available for purchase by anybody. Innovation in steel plants became a matter of how adept steel companies were at processing and implementing solutions from these networks.

Dofasco's patriarchal organizational structure was less rigid than Stelco's, with occasional worker consultation and significant profit-sharing. When it became a fully integrated steel company in the mid-1950s, Dofasco deliberately adopted a more interactive networking, or "matrix," form of organizational development aimed at more inclusive participation by a larger portion of its workforce. When John Mayberry took over leadership in the 1990s, Dofasco systematically tried to make itself into a "learning organization." Communities of practice teams[8] were developed to deal with a diversity of organizational problems. Perhaps most significantly, Dofasco developed a labour force renewal plan that involved maintaining as many regular employees as possible and systematically using older workers as mentors, especially in a large new apprenticeship program beginning in the 1990s. Equally importantly, Dofasco followed the Japanese model and kept its laboratory close to the plant. Mayberry frequently declared that they had far fewer metallurgical engineers than Stelco but many more people working on "innovation." Dofasco presented itself as a leading North American "steel solutions provider." From the mid-1990s on, Dofasco reserved 1 percent of its total rolling time to experimenting and learning about new and improved grades of steel. It effectively turned its mill into a laboratory, then communicated the results to its staff and customers. These innovations were primarily based on refining and implementing new technologies drawn from steel knowledge networks through transfer or licensing and through involvement in consortia (like the Auto/Steel Partnership [A/SP]) rather than from an in-house engineering department. Dofasco became the most profitable and sustainable integrated steel producer in North America, more adept than its rivals at producing and marketing new steel products, partly because it learned quicker as an organization.

Over the past generation, the previously established hierarchical organization of recognized skills and responsibilities has been undermined by widespread computerized controls and continuous monitoring of production processes. As Warrian puts it: "Production workers and the metal itself couldn't wait for the engineers, lab technicians, etc. Responsibility for production control and ultimately quality control started to pass from the engineers to shop floor workers" (2010a: 67). The extent to which workers were enabled to apply their knowledge on the shop floor became increasingly strategic for effective steel production. Dofasco has been relatively successful in moving in this direction.

The basic structure of management-labour relations in privately owned steel and other manufacturing plants continues to constrain employee empowerment and involvement in decision-making as well as the extent to which employees' working knowledge is recognized and rewarded (see Livingstone and Sawchuk 2004b). For example, as noted in Chapter 1, the CWS was created by management consultants in the 1940s as a means of classifying and compensating workers; workers accepted the compensation clarification and gave up managerial prerogatives. This applied to non-unionized Dofasco as well as unionized Stelco. While the CWS system has now been massively reduced, the possibilities for shop floor workers to play equal decision-making roles and fully use their collective working knowledge remain highly constrained by managerial prerogatives in all private steel plants, at least when compared with the model of industrial democracy promoted by organized steelworkers both in their formative period and the 1990s (see discussion below). But, compared to the rigid hierarchical structure of Stelco and U.S. Steel, the more participatory organizational model that Dofasco initiated in the 1990s did demonstrate the greater potential of worker involvement in work teams and shop floor technology innovation for catching up with the Japanese organizational advances of the 1960s in use of workers' knowledge. Some successful international steel companies are now reorganizing operations to make knowledge management the central feature of their production systems. For example, Tenaris, a leading global manufacturer of steel pipe products for the energy industry, has developed a corporate university for many of its employees and declared: "Our employees around the world are committed to continuous improvement by sharing knowledge across a single global organization" (2010: 1). Whether such organizational changes will optimize the interplay of workers' formal and informal knowledge remains an open question. However, in the case of most of the Canadian steel industry,

Warrian (2010a: 71) observed: "With the recent change in ownership these innovations are now in limbo."

Alternative Futures

One of the most problematic aspects of foreign takeover of companies and industries is that decisions about future development are taken in the primary interest of the foreign companies. Capital investment, management-labour relations and technological innovation are all determined by how they are considered to affect the profitability and viability of the foreign firms. Foreign takeover can lead to short-term gains in terms of infusion of large pools of international capital, adoption of more effective models of labour relations, greater access to new technologies or opportunities in larger foreign markets. But ultimately domestic companies and industries that do not control decisions about their own development become branch plants whose future existence depends on the larger fortunes of private foreign companies. The sudden takeover of the Canadian steel industry in the past few years is a dramatic case in point, nearly ending domestic control of this industry.

Manufacturing still matters, both for producing essential materials and for the creation of synergies between manufacturing and job creation in newer economic sectors. This is particularly important in the present period in which accelerated concentration, transnationalization and centralization of capital have squeezed out so many manufacturing jobs. But throughout the history of industrial capitalism it has always been the countries, industries and companies that have gained autocentric or endogenous control over the allocation of resources that have flourished, gaining relative advantage and unequal exchange over more dependent ones (see Amin 1974). In spite of rhetoric about the inevitability of globalization and its benefits for all, there is no demonstrable reason to assume that economically dependent companies, industries and countries will now gain greater long-term benefits from foreign dependency as compared to such dependency in the past.

Dominant trends are not destiny. Social development is always affected by human agency. Future economic developments will be influenced by critical analyses, alternative visions, change strategies and mobilized social forces, as well as by ecological limits on growth. Warrian (2010a: 8) suggested in one of the opening quotes to this chapter that a major limit is our imagination. Canada has many potential comparative advantages for sustaining a future steel industry. We have one of the most highly educated labour forces in the world, high continuing education aspirations and extensive engagement in informal learning by workers with all levels of formal education, hence a labour force with excellent learning capacity. We have one of the most diverse multi-cultural demographic profiles in the world and an extensive history of export trade, hence are well prepared to engage in national and international knowledge and innovation networks in the steel industry. We have all the other basic features for a viable continuing integrated steel industry: ample supplies of iron ore and coke, efficient furnaces, casters and finishing mills, and access to large lucrative markets. We also have some of the most efficient mini-mills in the world. What Canada does not have at the moment is control over its own steel destiny. What are the future prospects? We will imagine alternatives in terms of: (1) ownership; (2) forms of management-labour relations; and (3) technological innovation and sustainable production.

Ownership

Whatever the longer term result of the Canadian federal court decision allowing the federal government suit against U.S. Steel to proceed may be, the preliminary decision in mid-2010 was indicative of at least dim recognition of the strategic importance of the loss of a viable steel industry in the country. Of the many hundreds of cases of foreign takeovers reviewed since 1985 by the federal government under the Industry Canada Act, only one prior case, involving radar satellite technology and national security, has been refused. The terms in the case of U.S. Steel are evident breaches of a specific purchase agreement. U.S. Steel makes the argument that there were market circumstances beyond its full control. But if Canada loses complete ownership control of its steel industry, the negative impact on other manufacturing industries is likely to become widely evident and the road back to viable, Canadian-based steel companies and sustainable industrial policy will become even more difficult. In any event, integrated steel mills in Canada will have to attract substantial future investment and reinvestment to remain viable. The "goalposts" may have shifted since the foreign takeovers of the last few years, but there are at least four plausible options for future ownership of the Canadian steel industry: (1) further foreign takeover; (2) repurchase by indigenous private capital; (3) government-owned (or crown) corporation; (4) worker ownership.

1. Further Foreign Takeover

U.S. Steel is the largest remaining North American-owned integrated steel company. Its survival strategy has involved closure of less efficient domestic plants and takeover of foreign companies in order to utilize more efficient portions of their plants and labour forces, primarily to remain competitive in North America. U.S. Steel has been engaged in such international diversification strategies since the 1970s in concert with large U.S. banks (Kamara 1983).

The company manufactures a wide range of value-added steel sheet and tubular products for the automotive, appliance, container, industrial machinery, construction and oil and gas industries. In mid-2010, it held integrated steel facilities in Indiana, Michigan, Illinois, Pennsylvania and Alabama, as well as Lake Erie Works, Hamilton Works and plants in the Slovak Republic and the Republic of Serbia. U.S. Steel is also involved in several steel finishing joint ventures in the United States, Brazil, Canada and Mexico. It produces coke at plants in each country, owns iron-bearing taconite mines in Minnesota and has a railroad and barge transportation subsidiary. There are three research and development facilities, in Pennsylvania, Michigan and Slovakia. The 2010 company profile declared: "US Steel continually looks for opportunities to strengthen our existing presence in the global arena and strives to meet and set world class standards in everything we do. At US Steel, creating value for our shareholders is a priority."

Two points are most pertinent here. Most shareholders remain in the United States and, wherever they are, profit maximization for shareholders remains the overarching goal regardless of any more local priorities for sustainable production. Second, there are no U.S. Steel research and development facilities in Canada. The prospect for nurturing innovation in Canadian steel plants diminishes.

If Warrian's assessment of the relatively limited innovative potential of the established hierarchical organizational structure of U.S. Steel and Stelco is accurate, then — regardless of the decision of the Canadian federal court — U.S. Steel itself remains vulnerable to takeover of its most efficient parts by even larger emerging steel conglomerates. Some speculate that concentrating and centralizing tendencies will lead to firms like ArcelorMittal, with over 100 million ton capacities, dominating the global steel industry in the near future (Payne 2003). Whether future ownership decisions are made at U.S. Steel's Pittsburgh head office or by an offshore conglomerate, the prospects increase for extended shutdown of foreign-owned Canadian steel plants, diminishing innovative opportunities for Canadian steelworkers and having widespread negative impact on the Canadian economy. Warrian observed:

> The recent temporary but extended shutdown of US Steel's facilities in Ontario may be considered a proxy for such an impact. Massive immediate job losses would be accompanied by crises for local businesses, a collapse of local public finances and the loss of a tax base for critical social and health services. (2010a: 24)

2. Repurchase by Canadian Private Capital
Lakeside Steel was founded in 2005 through the purchase of the former Stelco steel pipe and tubular plant in nearby Welland. Its primary owner has been a Canadian merchant bank called Jaguar Financial. From these beginnings, Lakeside looked for various types of acquisitions, intending to expand production. When U.S. Steel shut down its Canadian operations in 2009, Lakeside opportunely filed a motion asking the federal court of Canada to force U.S. Steel to sell it plants in Hamilton and Lake Erie because of vio-

lated commitments. The Lakeside and Jaguar CEO at that time, Vic Alboini, declared: "It is important for Stelco to be owned or controlled by a Canadian company, for the long-term benefit of Stelco's employees, customers and suppliers" (quoted in Powell 2009a). Lakeside itself is not big enough to make a plausible bid for Stelco but has involved large institutional investors both inside and outside Canada in preparing a bid. The Lakeside initiative drew some immediate support from both steelworker and autoworker unions who were sympathetic to repatriating Canadian ownership and, more urgently, keen to get back to work. Both the steelworkers union and Lakeside received intervener status in the federal court proceedings.

However, the federal government lawsuit does not ask the court to instruct U.S. Steel to actually sell Stelco, just to enforce monetary penalties.[9] If U.S. Steel were to decide to sell Stelco in the course of or as a consequence of these proceedings, it would be most likely to do so to the highest bidder. Such a bidder would most likely be a larger international conglomerate hoping to use the most efficient parts of Stelco — most obviously the newest integrated plant at Lake Erie — as a platform for greater access to lucrative North American steel markets. Even if Lakeside or another Canadian-centred bid were to be successful, there is little basis to assume that such a private capital initiative would be more concerned with making major investments in sustainable production facilities than U.S. Steel. The example of Tricap and other Canadian venture capitalists buying Stelco out of bankruptcy merely to flip it for windfall profits is only a few years old. The Industry Canada Act contains no provisions to protect against Canadian venture capitalists doing the same again, if former-Stelco assets were still attractive to offshore global steel firms. Even if the large institutional investors teamed with Lakeside Steel were mainly Canadian financial organizations reliant largely on Canadian investors themselves, the money managers of such firms are just as bound to profit maximization as U.S. Steel investors. Foregoing short-term profits for long-term sustainable development is not part of the equation.

3. Government-Owned (or Crown) Corporation[10]
From canals to railroads to hydro power to broadcasting to air transport and beyond, the sinews of Canada as a country have been built through innovative government enterprises. The uses of national policy tariffs and regional redistribution payments were defensive innovations that were instrumental in sustaining Canada as an independent nation-state. The centrality of Canada's public enterprise culture may have been forgotten by many, but it retains a large potential for contemporary national building and equitable international relations (see Hardin 1974 for the basic case). In spite of privatization efforts in recent decades by some federal and provincial governments to sell off public assets to reduce debt loads, crown corporations remain a basic part of economic life. Enabling legislation to create new ones is still in

place. Recent precedents are available for allocation of public funds to save strategic industries, most pertinently the Canadian and American bailouts of General Motors in 2009 involving share purchase as well as loans. We also had the example of government funding the survival of Algoma Steel in the early 1990s in conjunction with workers' purchase of some company shares.

Both the Ontario provincial government and the federal government contributed financially to ensuring the continued viability of Stelco at the end of the bankruptcy period in 2006. There is no overriding legal reason to prevent governments from now taking steps to encourage the sale of U.S. Steel Canada to public Canadian interests or to private ones that would commit to retaining steel profits in Canada for the strategic survival and revitalization of the Canadian steel industry. Such steps could include any combination of requiring sale for abrogation of the terms of the 2007 purchase agreement, providing tax incentives to Canadian investors and steel employees for the purchase of steel shares, converting the repurchased Stelco into a crown corporation with a mandate to retain strategic control of an essential industry and enforcing trade regulations to ensure Stelco and other Canadian-owned steel companies have a fair chance to compete in home markets. Whether any of these steps are taken is largely a question of political will, beginning with the mobilization of public awareness to the threat of the disappearance of a public enterprise culture and way of life that many Canadians still take for granted.

4. Worker Ownership

In 2009, the United Steel Workers union (USW), North America's largest industrial trade union, announced a new collaboration with Mondragon International (Mondragon Internacional, S.A.), the world's largest worker-owned co-operative, which is based in the Basque region of Spain (USW 2009; Davidson 2010). Leo Gerard, the Canadian-born president of USW, declared:

> We see this as a historic first step towards making union co-ops a viable business model that can create good jobs, empower workers, and support communities in the United States and Canada. Too often we have seen Wall Street hollow out companies by draining their cash and assets and hollowing out communities by shedding jobs and shuttering plants. We need a new business model that invests in workers and invests in communities. (quoted in Davidson 2010)

Basic features of Mondragon worker ownership are the following: all workers have a share and a vote according to the principle one worker, one vote; decisions on the direction of the firm are made in regular assemblies ("autogestation," meaning self-management); the highest-paid manager worker is not paid more than six times the rate of the lowest worker ("pay solidarity"); revenues are retained within the firm and the Mondragon co-operative system; the system is capitalized through its own co-operative bank (Caja Laboral Popular); and retirees can cash out their shares but cannot sell them to outsiders for speculative profit taking. In the Basque region, these co-operatives contain workshops, a co-operative university, R&D facilities, credit unions and vocational schools. These characteristics have been successfully reproduced since the co-operative system's origins in the economic ruins of the Spanish Civil War and World War II, and it now sells high-tech products, such as machine tools, motor buses, computer components and household appliances, throughout Europe very competitively, partly because profits are not taken by remote financial speculators (Whyte and Whyte 1991; MacLeod and Reed 2009). There are now around a hundred of these co-operatives linked together in a federative structure through apex organizations. Individual co-ops have a survival rate of over 95 percent, and workers in co-ops that fail are entitled to Mondragon unemployment benefits and are retrained and placed in another co-op within the Mondragon system (MacLeod 1997: 20–35, 51). In the USW–Mondragon model, worker owners will be union members who will reach collective bargaining agreements within their own ranks, but without the usual constraint that much of the profit has already been taken by other investors (Delaney and Peck 2010). In the wake of the thousands of manufacturing facilities that have closed since the onset of the recession in 2008, this moment of economic ruin in North America may be an opportune time for serious consideration of such an alternative.

The USW is starting on a modest scale to look for small business in appropriate sectors where current owners want to cash out, as well as for financial institutions such as co-operative banks and credit unions committed to productive investment. There is a long tradition of co-operative ownership in Canada, and co-operatively owned enterprises have flourished across the country (e.g., Quarter 1992: 15–40; Quarter, Mook and Armstrong 2009; MacPherson 2009: 166–75); indeed, the Antigonish movement of Maritime Canada, like Mondragon, is a regional system of linked co-operatives self-financed through credit unions (MacPherson 2010: 42). This tradition and the current network of co-operative social movements in Canada are arguably more supportive of the development of worker-owned co-operatives than is the case in the United States.

There is no fundamental reason why this model should be limited to small businesses; indeed, a number of Canadian crown corporations have their origins as co-operatives, notably the Canadian Wheat Board.[11] With comparable government legislative and financial support, Hamilton Works and Lake Erie Works could take a route towards co-operative ownership.[12] Once more the basic issue is political will and organizing skill. Numerous global justice and trade union activists, left organizers, green entrepreneurs and co-op movement members have expressed support for the USW worker-ownership plan. Davidson pointed out: "Lending a helping hand to the new initiative entails a good deal of investigation into the state of local businesses and conditions, plus building alliances, generating publicity, and contributing educational work among all those concerned" (2010). The positive experience of the Blue-Green Alliance involving the USW and the growing public and governmental appetites for investment of this kind could inspire state support and, as well, the pivotal "lender confidence" required for ongoing access to capital for development of such co-operative enterprises (see Sawchuk 2009). However, the notion of Stelco as a worker-owned enterprise has had virtually no discussion to date.

The option of worker buyouts of existing private enterprises should also be raised here. The experiences of Weirton Steel in the U.S. in the 1980s and Algoma Steel in Canada in the 1990s are well-known.[13] To date, such buyouts have been mostly rescues of failing firms, and an assessment by Strauss (2007: 794) summarized: "The experience with plant rescue buyouts has been fairly uniformly tragic… buyout arrangements are often put together so hastily that little thought is given to how the firm is to be run." But the proactive use of pension funds to gain equitable decision-making power in currently viable firms could, with careful planning, be another matter. In Canada, there are extensive co-operatives of various types (Co-operative Secretariat 2009) and, in the Quebec case at least, substantial producer co-operatives in the forest industry, a labour movement already using solidarity funds to support labour-friendly enterprises and a vibrant social economy supporting various non-profit activities (Neamtan 2005; Vaillancourt 2010). In this context, various forms of worker ownership can be "pathways of social empowerment as an experimental process in which we continually test and retest the limits of possibility and try, as best we can, to create new institutions which will expand those limits themselves" (Wright 2010: 373).

Management-Labour Relations

The most effective organizations have divisions of labour that enable those in different positions to use their talents as fully as possible. The technical division of labour is the allocation of designated sets of tasks in the production process to different jobs according to their presumed complexity and creativity. Beyond specific technical tasks, the most basic division of labour is in terms of the authority to decide which tasks are to be done. This social/managerial division of labour refers to the extent of authority one has to direct other workers' production activities, or the distribution of formal and informal degrees of supervisory authority through a workforce. Many have confused the technical division of tasks and the division of managerial authority among workers (see Murphy 1993). There has been a prevalent tendency to see the growth of managerial and supervisory positions as being a requirement of technological development. However, in cases of automated production, where the detailed technical division of labour became segmented and highly alienating for some line workers, technical tasks have been recombined in some organizations and, even when they are not recombined, workers with detailed technical tasks have been given increased authority to decide on which tasks are to be done. This reversal illustrates that technological development involves the interaction of technical divisions of tasks and managerial divisions of workers, rather than being simply machine-driven imperatives.[14] Choices about different models of managerial division of labour can have profound influences on effective utilization of workers' use of talents in technical tasks. At least four different models can be identified: (1) top-down hierarchical management; (2) consultative management; (3), industrial democracy; (4) worker self-management.

1. Top-Down Hierarchical Management
As mentioned previously, the traditional steel industry of the twentieth century was organized around a tight hierarchy of engineering/management at the top. Most CEOs were from the engineering staff in this earlier period. Beneath this hierarchy there was a mass of workers regarded as unskilled and semi-skilled. The scientific management model that grew with the steel industry aimed to break jobs into ever simpler tasks, and ultimately this model was developed into the most detailed technical division of labour ever devised, the CWS system. There was little prospect in this model of delegating any formal authority for decisions to the mass of workers. The collective bargaining agreements formed after World War II ceded authority prerogatives to management in exchange for secure working conditions, with no systemic provision for consultation with most of the workforce. U.S. Steel and Stelco were among the leading adherents to this model. While various forms of consultation with hourly employees have been added to some later agreements, such as the Stelco–Local 1005 contract in 2006, formal decision-making authority has remained resolutely with top management. There have been few genuine incentives for workers to share shop floor knowledge with management to aid in improving job design, and management-labour relations have tended to remain antagonistic.

2. Consultative Management
As noted above, the need for continuous monitoring of the expensive machinery of the steel production process via instrumentation has resulted in the increasing importance of the recognition of the exercise of shop floor workers' judgment. The success of the Japanese steel industry after World War II and of Dofasco from the 1960s on are both partly attributable to engaging more of the skills and talent of shop floor workers in the develop-

ment of more effective work processes. The use of consultative teams to make shop floor changes, regular interaction between engineering and shop floor workers and significant profit-sharing or bonuses as incentives to participate seriously in such information exchanges, have all led to productivity gains relative to more hierarchical models of management. But such consultation remains highly constrained in relation to workers' opportunities to contribute to major decisions about the development of the company. Top management's judgments and shareholders' profit priorities continue to prevail regardless of workers' general wisdom.

3. Industrial Democracy

In the formative period of the United Steel Workers union in the United States, the Steel Workers Organizing Committee (SWOC) engaged in a number of co-operative partnership experiments with steel employers.[15] Workers in these experiments shared their knowledge with employers to cut costs, identify production bottlenecks and set work standards, with the expectation that the profits and benefits of this process would be shared equitably between employers and employees. The basic case for such industrial democracy and the positive results of these experiments were laid out in a book promoted by some members of SWOC (Golden and Ruttenberg 1942). But some worker leaders remained highly sceptical of prospects for sharing in competitive capitalist market conditions. The sector-wide agreements forged in the wake of the World War II era of strikes were dominated by U.S. Steel and other firms steeped in top-down hierarchical engineering models. Further serious consideration of industrial democracy principles was pre-empted by preoccupation with wages and working conditions. Steel union leaders in both Canada and the United States have periodically promoted aspects of workplace democracy since that time, but without claims of aspiring to co-operative partnerships with employers and with no discernible interest from most steel employers.

4. Worker Self-Management

Worker self-management means that the managerial division of labour is either minimized or else eliminated entirely and all workers who are interested have a voice and a vote in major decisions within the workplace. The Mondragon worker-owned co-operatives provide a long-running example of high-tech firms in which each worker can vote in regular assemblies on general development issues. But workplace self-management can occur without exclusive worker ownership (for classic examples, see the discussion in Pateman 1970: Ch. 4; Dow 2003). There have been numerous examples of self-managed firms with much wider community ownership, such arrangements in Canada often being labelled community economic development (CED) in policy and community activist circles (e.g., McMurtry 2010). One of the most intriguing international examples has been the corporate plan of the Lucas Aerospace workers (Cooley 1987). In this aerospace plant, threatened with closure in the late 1970s, members of professional, trades and production workers' unions together developed detailed plans for an array of socially useful products oriented to community sustainability — including clean fuel buses and medical devices — to be produced by self-managed teams. The plan involved some government funding and was initially supported by the U.K. Ministry of Industry. The Lucas workers' plan continues to inspire similar initiatives (Wainwright and Green 2009), most of which require funding beyond the workplace itself to become viable.

Technological Innovation and Sustainable Production

None of the above models of ownership and management-labour relations is pre-ordained. Serious consideration of some of the less widely established alternatives may lead to new alternative sustainable forms. In any case, continuing technological innovation will be needed. Several important points need to be registered here.

The most important technological innovations of the twentieth-century steel industry were pioneered in Canada. The basic oxygen furnace, continuous casting and mini-mills all had early development in Canada (Warrian 2010a: 68; CSTEC 2005). However, in each instance, the idea was taken and developed fully elsewhere by others, financed by foreign capital. This is an old story. Throughout the last century, many fundamental innovations in many fields originating in Canada were taken and developed elsewhere because of the failure of Canadian investors to support them (Brown 1967). The major Canadian banks were primary culprits in this failure (see Naylor 1975).

Entrepreneurs and employees of the Canadian steel industry have clearly had the creative knowledge to generate leading steel innovations for generations. They still have the potential to generate new ones in the future. Canadian-centred research networks, such as CANMET (Canada Centre for Mineral and Energy Technology) and McMaster University, are strategically placed to create new technological advances drawing on both the critical mass of experienced metal scientists, technicians, skilled trades and production workers in the Hamilton region and on new international steel innovation networks. The central questions are whether such research centres will continue to be nurtured in Canada and whether Canadian investment capital will be applied to develop them domestically. With the sudden foreign takeover of the Canadian steel industry, prospects dim. However, if Stelco or other steel firms were to be returned to Canadian ownership in the near future, the creativity would continue to flow within the country. The alternative forms of funding and work organization to ensure developing Canadian steel ideas in Canada would need to be seriously reviewed by all supporters. The bid of Lakeside Steel before the federal court offers one immediate opportunity.

One thing needed to encourage more attention to sustainable production and effective job creation in steel as well as in many other industries is a reversal of the dominant optic stressing education and skill development as a primary solution to economic problems. Since the inception of industrial capitalism and mass schooling in the nineteenth century, schooling has been targeted in virtually every economic crisis as both cause and cure (Curti 1935; Schrag 2007). Advocates of human capital theory and a knowledge-based economy persistently argue for greater investment in all forms of formal education and skill development to respond to economic crises, including the current round of employment reductions in the steel industry. As noted above, such views ignore or evade growing evidence of a surplus of education attainments in relation to job requirements. While enhancing one's knowledge and upgrading specific skills is always valuable, the Canadian labour force and Canadian steelworkers are already among the most highly educated in the world and have continually engaged in lifelong learning to deal with knowledge gaps as they arise (see Livingstone 2009, 2010). Growing numbers of highly qualified workers are either unemployed or underemployed. The most relevant response to this situation is to identify and develop economic reforms that will permit more people to apply their already highly developed skills in decent jobs. Such reforms can include measures to redistribute work time, workplace democratization and creation of green jobs. For example, older workers could work shorter hours and move into phased retirement combined with mentoring programs for new steelworkers to aid the transmission of working knowledge, rather than sudden retirement for full-time jobs and then having some retired workers come back on an ad hoc basis. Second, there is a multitude of ways that workers could be given more latitude to apply their underutilized skills in current integrated steel plants, as long as those skills are given fair recognition and reward. Third, there are many new technologies under development that promise large reductions in CO_2 emissions, greater efficiencies in energy production, further improvements in recycling materials and lighter, stronger forms of steel. The 2009 manifesto of the European Confederation of Iron and Steel Industries (EUROFER) declared:

> Steel provides the foundation for innovation, durability and energy savings in applications as varied and vital as automotive, construction, medical devices, white goods and wind turbines. Steel is 100% recyclable — it loses none of its properties, no matter how many times it is remelted and reused — and therefore contributes significantly to the long-term conservation of fundamental resources for future generations. (2)

More and more steel-related jobs will go downstream to service centres and production of new machinery such as wind turbines. The point is that there will be many new green jobs related to steel, and, as primary steel jobs decline, steelworkers would be well qualified for many of them. The problem is not lack of relevant skills but lack of planning for new greener jobs.

Next Steps

Global corporations have become very footloose, often making much more than half of their sales outside their countries of origin. By the nature of their primary product, steel companies have been among the least mobile and most likely to keep their production facilities at home. But global steel trade has been significantly increasing for many years and global ownership has grown suddenly over the past decade. Even in this era of globalization, however, national sentiments can be powerful influences of resistance. Particularly in times of crisis, they can become of overwhelming concern. A current case in point is BP, one of the largest oil and gas conglomerates in the world, operating in a hundred countries. After its massive oil spill in the Gulf of Mexico in 2010:

> BP has become as British as Wimbleton.... As a result, it's possible the company will suffer harsher treatment at the hands of consumers and lawmakers. When things go bad, it turns out, internationals turn into homebodies. Since they can't rely on all nations in which they have outposts to come to their aid, they're effectively renationalized. (Gross 2010: 38)

Global private corporations could take on multi-divisional structures, much like General Motors did when it created semi-autonomous auto divisions in its expansionary era in the United States. But their overarching controlling bodies remain bound to profit-maximizing rules and insulated by country-of-origin corporation laws that are likely to turn them into homebodies when sentiments turn against them in the outposts. There is a prospect of this sort of development if Canadian national sentiments continue to rise in the wake of the shutdown in 2008 of U.S. Steel plants in Canada while its plants in the United States were reopened (Brennan 2010). If U.S. Steel executives continue to play hardball in Canadian federal court proceedings and if antagonistic management relations with employees at both Hamilton and Lake Erie Works persist, public support for Canadian takeback of Stelco is likely to rise.

Global steel companies like U.S. Steel have wielded massive economic and political power. In the absence of widespread mobilization of the democratic energies of Canadians, it is most likely that the foreign takeover will continue to hollow out the domestic steel industry. Increasing problems in labour force renewal and intergenerational transmission of workers' knowledge, diminishing opportunities for research and technological innovation, and accumulating production deficiencies versus plants in other countries are all likely to increasingly threaten the existence of the Canadian steel industry as anything more than hewers of another raw material.

But strategic weaknesses of large hierarchical organizations like U.S. Steel, not the least of which is a systemic organizational inability to engage workers' allegiances and creative working knowledge in the outposts, is also likely to continue to generate conditions for the rousing of national sentiments of resistance. Erecting economic walls around countries like Canada is no longer possible or desirable. But the accumulation of gigantic pools of privately controlled financial holdings drove the world to the gross inequalities that now exist both between and within countries and led to the economic upheaval that froze much economic activity, including the global steel industry, in 2008–9. When hedge fund managers continue to take over a billion dollars a year while unemployment mounts and poverty reaches obscene levels, there must be greater limits to global capital accumulation. Laxer concluded:

> Progressive advance means setting things the right way up in the economy so that people at large become masters of capital and not the other way around. Placing pools of capital in local, regional, and national holdings and democratizing both the control of capital and of the workplace needs to be the next great chapter in the history of democracy. (2009: 234)

When the Steel Company of Canada was established in 1910, it was created as part of a national policy that recognized that an industrially developed country needed its own domestically controlled steel industry. The alternative models of ownership and management-labour relations outlined in this chapter may offer some resources for hope of recovery if growing numbers of Canadians perceive the economic consequences of remote control of this industry and their destiny. In the wake of the shutdown of Stelco in 2008, a local steel union leader observed:

> There has been a significant turnaround in the attitude of the community and their perceptions of the steel industry and the steel plant. They see that the mill makes money for the community. They only see it with the shutdown of the mill. They now see it as the basis of the industrial heart of the country.... A complete shut down would devastate the community. (quoted in Warrian 2010a: 24)

Steelworkers continue mobilizing efforts to show how steel still matters in building the future infrastructure of this country. Whether Canadian steelworkers continue to matter will depend on how much support they get from other workers, other Canadians and their governments in the struggle for a more democratic workplace and economy.

Along with the relentlessly expanding conversion of evermore aspects of human life into vendible commodities, the displacement of labour by machinery in one sector after another has been a basic feature of industrial capitalism: from agriculture to manufacturing to an array of services. In our lifetimes, we have witnessed the most disruptive period of transition from manufacturing in the developed world. Many working-class communities have been badly damaged (e.g., Bluestone and Harrison 1982; Luxton and Corman 2001). On the positive side, we are producing more of what we need with much less labour. For the foreseeable future, steel will be an essential material for human societies. We now have the technological capacity to produce as much steel as we are likely to need with greater recycling and still diminishing numbers of steelworkers. The festering question is how much do we need. The ecosystem now screams out limits to industrial growth (e.g., McKibbon 2010). Reducing the impact of human activities on this ecosystem is now a survival imperative. The meltdown of employment in steel and other manufacturing industries in the developed world can also provide opportunities for more environmentally friendly work while still meeting established basic needs. Do we have the wit to envision and the courage to take up such sustainable practices?

Notes

1. For a detailed study of U.S. Steel, see Warren (2001).
2. The general account of consolidation of the Canadian steel industry in this chapter relies primarily on Warrian 2010a.
3. Facts not attributed in the remainder of this chapter are drawn from published articles by steel reporters (Steve Arnold, Naomi Power and Lee Prokaska) in the archives of the *Hamilton Spectator* and from the presidential records of Warren Smith.
4. For Pratt's own account of the Stelco bankruptcy process, see Pratt and Gaudet (2008).
5. According to Stelco's 2004 and 2005 annual reports, in November 2004 Deutsche Bank's "stalking horse" bid of $900 million was approved by Stelco's board of directors and in 2005 Deutsche Bank received a break fee of $11 million. The precise financial value of the Tricap restructuring fund approved by Justice Farley to take Stelco out of bankruptcy in 2006 has never been publicly released.
6. It should be noted here, as Warrian observes, that "in the past raw materials simply meant iron ore and coal, but now steel companies regard raw materials as including everything up to the slab stage and perhaps even the hotband stage" (2010a: xx).
7. See Warrian (2010a: 118ff) for a more detailed comparison of knowledge systems in Stelco and Dofasco.

8. For the concept of communities of practice, see the foundational text by Lave and Wenger (1991).

9. The Investment Canada Act does contain provisions allowing for a forced sale (Powell 2009d), and the federal government did make such a threat in May 2009 (Whittington 2009). USW sued U.S. Steel in 2009, seeking $44 million in restitution for lost wages and dues, and also asked for a court order compelling U.S. Steel to sell its Canadian holdings (Powell 2009c).

10. In Canada, a crown corporation is a wholly owned federal or provincial organization that is structured like private or independent enterprises but which has its own governance structure autonomous from the level of government that created it, and as such generally enjoys greater freedom from direct political or budgetary control than government departments. They are established to carry out regulatory, advisory, administrative, financial or other services or to provide goods and services, often in order to carry out government policy but at arm's length from the state itself.

11. In 2009, USW 1005 called on the government to create a steel marketing body mandated to buy steel and set prices in a fashion similar to the powers of the Canadian Wheat Board (Powell 2009b).

12. Despite a different political and economic context, the worker-recovered enterprises (ERT) movement in Argentina exemplifies one moral principle relevant to the Stelco–U.S. Steel situation, recalling the role of state money in keeping Stelco afloat. Some workers who had seized bankrupt workplaces and transformed them into co-operatives justified their occupations on the grounds that community ("state") subsidies had supported their workplaces and that, with bankruptcy, the firms should revert to the community in the form of co-operative ownership and management (Lewis 2004). On the ERT movement, see Lavaca Collective (2007); Vieta and Ruggeri (2009).

13. On Weirton Steel, see Beamer (2007); on Algoma Steel, see Quarter (1995).

14. See Livingstone (2009: 51–66) for fuller discussion of this distinction and Noble (1984) for its implications for job design.

15. See Hoerr (1988) for a detailed account of this process.

Postscript

As this book goes to press in late 2010, contract negotiations have broken down at Hamilton Works over U.S. Steel's demands of a two-tiered pension system without defined benefits for new workers and with the removal of indexing for current pensioners. The blast furnace has been shut down with no prospect of start up until spring 2011. Steel slabs and coils efficiently produced at Lake Erie Works are being shipped as "raw materials" to U.S. Steel finishing plants in the U.S. and re-imported to Canada. The Canadian government's Federal Court case against U.S. Steel drags on. The future of steel jobs in Canada looks increasingly bleak and the need for action on the positive alternatives discussed in this book becomes more urgent.

Bibliography

Adams, R.J. 1988. "The 'Old Industrial Relations' and Corporate Competitiveness: A Canadian Case." *Employee Relations* 20, 2.

Adams, R.J., and I. Zeytinoglu. 1987. "Labour-Management Dispute Resolution at the Hilton Works." In T. Hanami and R. Blanpain (eds.), *Industrial Conflict Resolution in Market Economies*. Boston: Kluwer.

Advisory Group on Working Time and the Distribution of Work. 1994. *Report of the Advisory Group on Working Time and the Distribution of Work*. Ottawa: Minister of Supply and Services (December).

Ahlburg, D., A. Carey, B. Lundgren, S. Barrett and L. Anderson. 1987. "Technological Change, Market Decline, and Industrial Relations in the U.S. Steel Industry." In D.B. Cornfield (ed.), *Workers, Managers and Technological Change: Emerging Patterns of Labour Relations*. New York: Plenum.

Albright, R. 1995. "A Mature Rivalry: Labor Relations in the American Steel Industry." In A. Verma (ed.), *International Conference on Workplace Change: Human Resources and Rationalization in the Global Steel Industry*. Toronto: Faculty of Management, University of Toronto.

Allan, D. 1985. "Analysis of the Steel Industry Labour Market and the Adjustments Facing Its Workforce." Paper presented at the Canadian Steel Trade Conference. Sault Ste. Marie, ON.

Allan, J. 1982. "Speech to the Conference Board of Canada Seminar." October 8. Reported in *Hamilton Spectator*, October 9.

Amin, S. 1974. *Accumulation on a World Scale: A Critique of the Theory of Underdevelopment*. New York: Monthly Review.

Auer, P. (ed.). 1991. *Work Force Adjustment Patterns*. Brussels: European Commission.

_____. 1992. "Further Education and Training for the Employees (FETE): European Diversity." Discussion Paper FS I 92–3. Berlin: Wissenschaftszentrum für Sozialforschung.

Aylen, J. 1986. "Hire and Fire Retires." *Steel Times International* (September).

Bacon, N., and P. Blyton. 2000. "Meeting the Challenge of Globalization — Steel Industry Restructuring and Trade Union Strategy. A Survey Report for the International Metalworkers' Federation." Nottingham: Nottingham University Business School.

Barnes, T., R. Hayter and E. Grass. 1990. "Corporate Restructuring and Employment Change: A Case Study of MacMillan Bloedel." In M. De Smidt and E. Wever (eds.), *The Corporate Firm in a Changing World Economy: Case Studies in the Geography of Enterprise*. London: Routledge.

Barnett, D.F. 1988. "The U.S. Steel Industry: Strategic Choices in a Basic Industry." In D. Hicks (ed.), *Is New Technology Enough? Making and Remaking the U.S. Basic Industries*. Competing in a Changing World Economy Project. Washington, DC: American Enterprise Institute for Public Policy Research.

Barnett, D.F., and R.W. Crandall. 1986. *Up From the Ashes: The Rise of the Steel Minimill in the United States*. Washington, DC: Brookings Institute.

Beamer, G. 2007. "Sustaining the Rust Belt: A Retrospective Analysis of the Employee

Purchase of Weirton Steel." *Labor History* 48, 3 (August).

Bell, D. 1973. *The Coming of Post-Industrial Society*. New York: Basic.

_____. 1989. "The Third Technological Revolution." *Dissent* (Spring).

Beniger, J.R. 1986. *The Control Revolution: Technological and Economic Origins of the Information Society*. Cambridge, MA: Harvard University Press.

Bensman, D., and R. Lynch. 1987. *Rusted Dreams: Hard Times in a Steel Community*. New York: McGraw-Hill.

Berg, I. (ed.). 1981. *Sociological Perspectives on Labor Markets*. New York: Academic Press.

Betheil, R. 1978. "The ENA in Perspective: The Transformation of Collective Bargaining in the Basic Steel Industry." *Review of Radical Political Economics* 10, 2 (Summer).

Birat, J.P. 1986. "Manufacture of Flat Products for the 21st Century." *Iron and Steelmaking* 14, 2.

Blackburn, R., and M. Mann. 1979. *The Working Class in the Labour Market*. London: Macmillan.

Blauner, B. 1964. *Alienation and Freedom: The Factory Worker and His Industry*. Chicago: University of Chicago Press.

Bluestone, B., and T. Harrison. 1982. *The Deindustrialization of America: Plant Closings, Community Abandonment and the Dismantling of Basic Industry*. New York: Basic.

Boklund, T. 1996. Participant in Roundtable Discussion: B. Berry, J. Lindsey, R. Higgins and B. Berry. "The Revolution in Technology. Roundtable Discussion of Executives from Leading Electric-Furnace Steelmakers." *New Steel* 12, 4 (April 1).

Bouquet, T. and B. Ousey. 2009. *Cold Steel: The Multi-Billion Dollar Battle for a Global Empire*. Toronto: Key Porter.

Bourdieu, P. 1990. *The Logic of Practice*. Stanford, CA: Stanford University Press.

Bowen, P. 1976. *Social Control in Industrial Organisations: Industrial Relations and Industrial Sociology, a Strategic and Occupational Study of British Steelmaking*. London and Boston: Routledge and Keegan Paul.

Braverman, H. 1974. *Labor and Monopoly Capital: The Degradation of Work in the Twentieth Century*. New York: Monthly Review.

_____. 1982. "The Degradation of Work in the Twentieth Century." *Monthly Review* 34, 1.

Brennan, R.J. 2010. "Ottawa Set to Take on U.S. Steel Giant: Laid-off and Locked-out Ontario Workers Watch Court Battle with Company that Bought Stelco." *Toronto Star*, January 4.

Brown, J. 1967. *Ideas in Exile: A History of Canadian Invention*. Toronto: McClelland and Stewart.

Burawoy, M. 1978. "Toward a Marxist Theory of the Labor Process: Braverman and Beyond." *Politics and Society* 8, 3.

_____. 1979. *Manufacturing Consent: Changes in the Labor Process Under Monopoly Capitalism*. Chicago: University of Chicago Press.

Buss, T.F., and F.S. Redburn. 1983a. *Shutdown at Youngstown: Public Policy for Mass Unemployment*. Albany: State University of New York Press.

_____. 1983b. *Mass Unemployment: Plant Closings and Community Mental Health*. Beverly Hills, CA: Sage.

Campbell, M., and F. Gregor. 2002. *Mapping Social Relations: A Primer in Doing Institutional Ethnography*. Aurora, ON: Garamond.

Canadian Apprenticeship Forum. 2004. *Accessing and Completing Apprenticeship Training in Canada*. <www.caf-fca.org/files/access/1-Report_jan04_e.pdf> accessed May 2007.

Castells, M. 1980. *The Economic Crisis and American Society*. Princeton: Princeton University Press.

_____. 2004. *The Networked Society: A Cross-cultural Perspective*. Northampton, MA: Edward Elgar.

Chandler, A. Jr. 1977. *The Visible Hand: The Managerial Revolution in American Business*. Cambridge, MA: Harvard University Press.

Chandler, H.E. 1985. "A Profile of Canada's Steel Technology." *Metal Progress* (April).

Cheung, C.S., I. Krinsky and B. Lynn. 1985. "The Canadian Steel Industry: Current State and Future Prospects." *Canadian Banker* 92, 2 (April).

Christmas, B. 1982. "It's Vital to Reopen Contract: Stelco." *Hamilton Spectator*, December 2.

_____. 1983a. "Workers Getting Steel Picture." *Hamilton Spectator*, July 27.

_____. 1983b. "Cec Taylor Ousted by a Single Vote." *Hamilton Spectator*, August 10.

_____. 1990. "Guess Who's Going to Dinner? Stelco Changing Relations with Workers by Taking Them Out for 'Pizza and Wings.'" *Hamilton Spectator*, September 21.

Clancy, P. 2004. *Micropolitics and Canadian Business: Paper, Steel, and the Airlines*. Peterborough, ON: Broadview.

Clark, G.L. 1987. "Corporate Restructuring in the Steel Industry." In G. Sternlieb and J. Hughes (eds.), *America's New Market Geography: Nation, Region, and Metropolis*. New Brunswick, NJ: Rutgers University Press.

Clement, W. 1981. *Hardrock Mining: Industrial Relations and Technological Changes at Inco*. Toronto: McClelland and Stewart.

Cohen, S. 1987. "A Labour Process to Nowhere?" *New Left Review* 165 (September–October).

Cohen, S., and J. Zysman. 1987. *Manufacturing Matters: The Myth of the Post-Industrial Economy*. New York: Basic.

Collins, R. 1979. *The Credential Society: An Historical Sociology of Education and Stratification*. New York: Academic Press.

Committee on New Directions in Manufacturing, National Research Council of the National Academies. 2004. *New Directions in Manufacturing: Report of a Workshop*. Washington, DC: National Academies Press. At <sites.nationalacademies.org/DEPS/DEPS_037539>.

Considine, T. 2005. "The Transformation of the North American Steel Industry: Drivers, Prospects and Vulnerabilities." University Park, PA: Department of Energy and Geo-environmental Engineering, Pennsylvania State University. April 21.

Contracting Out Committee. 1987. "Contracting Out Committee Report." *Steel Shots* (January–February).

Cooke, P. (ed.). 1995. *The Rise of the Rustbelt*. New York: St. Martin's.

Cooley, M. 1987. *Architect or Bee? Human Cost of Technology*. London: Hogarth.

Co-operatives Secretariat. 2009. "Co-operatives in Canada (2006 Data)." AAFC No. 11066B. Ottawa: Co-operatives Secretariat. At < www.agr.gc.ca/index_e.php>.

Corman, J. 1990. "Dissension Within the Ranks: The Struggle over Employment Practices During a Recession." *Studies in Political Economy* 32 (Summer).

Corman, J., D.W. Livingstone, M. Luxton and W. Seccombe. 1985. "What You Think about Working at Stelco and How It Affects Your Lives and Families." *Steel Shots* (September).

Corman, J., M. Luxton, D.W. Livingstone and W. Seccombe. 1993. *Recasting Steel Labour: The Stelco Story*. Halifax, NS: Fernwood.

Correnti, J. 1994. "Smart Workers, Smart Machines." Panel discussion. *New Steel* 10, 8 (August).

Cowie, J., and J. Heathcott. 2003. *Beyond the Ruins: The Meanings of Deindustrialization*. Ithaca, NY: Cornell University Press.

Crompton, R., and G. Jones. 1984. *White Collar Proletariat: Deskilling and Gender in Clerical Work*. London: MacMillan.

Crone, G. 1988. "Mood at Stelco 'Volatile' Says Union." *Hamilton Spectator*, September 6.

CSIA (Canadian Steel Industry Association). 1983. *The Canadian Steel Industry Factbook*. Toronto: CSIA.

_____. 1988. *The Canadian Steel Industry Factbook*. Toronto: CSIA.

CSTEC (Canadian Steel Trade and Employment Congress). 1993. "Skills Training Program." Toronto: CSTEC.

_____. 1996. "About CSTEC." Toronto: CSTEC.

_____. 2000. "Steel Industry Trades Replacement Program (SITRP) Hamilton Pilot." Hamilton, ON: CSTEC/Mohawk College.

_____. 2005. "Human Resources Study of the Broader Canadian Steel Industry: Final Report." Toronto: CSTEC. At <cstec.ca/Docs/FinalReport.pdf>.

Cunningham, J., and P. Martz (eds). 1986. *Steel People: Survival and Resilience in Pittsburgh's Mon Valley*. Pittsburgh: University of Pittsburgh School of Social Work.

Curti, M. 1935. *The Social Ideas of American Educators*. Paterson: Littlefield, Adams.

Cusumano, M.A. 1985. *The Japanese Automobile Industry: Technology and Management at Nissan and Toyota*. Cambridge, MA: Harvard University Press.

Darnell, H., T.P. Miles and H.C. Morrison. 1984. *Steel: Future of the U.K. Industry*. London: Technical Change Centre.

Darrah, C.N. 1996. *Learning and Work: An Exploration in Industrial Ethnography*. Studies in Education and Culture, 8/Garland Reference Library of Social Science, 1069. New York: Garland.

Davidson, C. 2010. "U.S. Steelworkers Plan to Experiment with Factory Ownership." *CCPA Monitor* February.

Davie, M. 1989. "Mitsubishi Role at Stelco Seen as Valuable Boost." *Hamilton Spectator*, November 4.

_____. 1990a. "Return of Stelco." *Hamilton Spectator*, February 24.

_____. 1990b. "Stelco Studies Outright Sale, Mill Closings." *Hamilton Spectator*, September 21.

_____. 1991. "The Survival of Steel." *Hamilton Spectator*, April 6.

_____. 1992a. "Brave New World for Stelco Workers." *Hamilton Spectator*, October 10.

_____. 1992b. "Hold On, 1005 Tells Stelco: Layoff Plans Too Fast, Martin Says." *Hamilton Spectator*, October 16.

_____. 1992c. "Co-operation the Key as Steelworkers Decide." *Hamilton Spectator*, November 14.

_____. 1994. "First the Good News..." *Hamilton Spectator*, October 28.

_____. 1996. "Hamilton 9002: Stelco: A World-class Ranking." *Hamilton Spectator*, February 20.

Daw, J. 1989. "Steelmakers Set Up Firm to Try for Breakthrough." *Toronto Star*, October 21.

_____. 1991. "Embattled Steelmakers Lobby for Import Restraint." *Toronto Star*, May 5.

Delaney, K., and M. Peck. 2010. "Keynote Speakers Ken Delaney (United Steelworkers) and Michael Peck (Mondragon International)." National Summit on a People-Centred Economy. May 30. Ottawa.

Deming, Edwards W. 1982. *Out of the Crisis*. Cambridge, MA: MIT Press.

Dennison, J.D., and P. Gallagher. 1986. *Canada's Community Colleges: A Critical Analysis*. Vancouver: University of British Columbia Press.

Docquier, G. 1989. "Labour Relations in the Canadian Steel Industry: Are We Really Getting Anywhere?" Address given to the Canadian Steel Production Association.

October.

Dofasco. 1990. "1989 Annual Report." Hamilton, ON: Dofasco.

Donaldson, M. 1982. "The State, the Steel Industry and BHP." *Australian and New Zealand Journal of Sociology* 18, 3 (November).

Dow, G. 2003. *Governing the Firm: Workers' Control in Theory and Practice*. Cambridge, MA: Cambridge University Press.

Dunk, T. 1991. *It's a Working Man's Town: Male Working-class Culture*. Montreal: McGill–Queen's University Press.

Edwards, R. 1979. *Contested Terrain: The Transformatiion of the Workplace in the Twentieth Century*. New York: Basic Books.

Eichler, M. 2005. "The Other Half (or More) of the Story: Unpaid Household and Care Work and Lifelong Learning." In N. Bascia, A. Cumming, A. Datnow, K. Leithwood and D.W. Livingstone, *International Handbook of Educational Policy*, 54. At <wallnetwork. ca/resources/workingpapers.htm>.

Elbaum, B. 1984. "The Making and Shaping of Job and Pay Structures in the Iron and Steel Industry." In P. Osterman (ed.), *Internal Labor Markets*. Cambridge, MA: MIT Press.

Estock, D. 1987a. "O.T.: Steelworkers Fear Overtime Is Costing People Their Jobs." *Hamilton Spectator*, March 26.

_____. 1987b. "Steel Takes Stock." *Hamilton Spectator*, May 30.

EUROFER (European Confederation of Iron and Steel Industries). 2009. "Manifesto of the European Steel Industry for Members of the European Parliament 2009–2014." Brussels: EUROFER.

Fairbrother, P., D. Stroud and A. Coffey. 2004a. "New Steel Industry Challenges." Working Paper Series, 52. Cardiff: Cardiff School of Social Sciences.

_____. 2004b. "The Changing European Steel Workforce." Working Paper Series, 55. Cardiff: Cardiff School of Social Sciences.

Fennessy, B. 2009. "Communities and Leaders at Work in the New Economy: A Comparative Analysis of Agents of Transformation Pittsburgh, Pennsylvania and Hamilton, Ontario." PhD diss. Toronto: Department of Sociology Education and Equity Studies in Education, University of Toronto.

Fennessy, B., and W. Smith. 2006. "The Human Factor in Technological Change at Stelco: A Union Leader's Perspective." Paper prepared for Rethinking Work and Learning: Research Findings and Policy Challenges Conference. Toronto: Ontario Institute for Studies in Education/University of Toronto, June 4. At <wall.oise.utoronto.ca/resources/Fennessy-Smith%20WALL2006.pdf>.

Flood, M. 1970. *Wildcat Strike in Lake City*. Ottawa: Queen's Printer.

Florida, R.L. 2002. *The Rise of the Creative Class: And How It's Transforming Work, Leisure, Community and Everyday Life*. New York: Basic.

Forde, D. 1985. "Change Is Sweeping This Company." *Steel Shots* (October).

Foster, J.B. 1988. "The Fetish of Fordism." *Monthly Review* 39, 10 (March).

_____. 1999. "Classic of Our Time: *Labor and Monopoly Capitalism* After a Quarter Century." *Monthly Review* 50, 8 (January).

Fowlie, L. 1992. "Stelco to Cut 1200 Jobs at Hilton Works." *Financial Post*, September 24.

Freeman, B. 1982. *1005: Political Life in a Union Local*. Toronto: James Lorimer.

Freeman, B., and M. Hewitt (eds) 1979. *Their Town: The Mafia, the Media, and the Party Machine*. Toronto: Lorimer.

Freeman, S. 2010. "U.S. Steel, Ottawa Legal Battle Could Drag On for Years." *Hamilton Spectator*. June 30.

Frost, A.C. 2000. "Explaining Variation in Workplace Restructuring: The Role of Local Union Capabilities." *Industrial and Labor Relations Review* 53, 4.

Frost, A.C., and A. Verma. 1997. "Restructuring in Canadian Steel: The Case of Stelco, Inc." In A. Verma and R.P. Chaykowski (eds.), *Contract and Commitment: Workplace Change and the Evolution of Employment Relations in Canadian Firms*. Kingston, ON: IRC Press.

Galbraith, J.K. 1985. *The New Industrial State*. Fourth edition. New York: Mentor.

Gaskell, J.S. 1992. *Gender Matters From School to Work*. Toronto: OISE Press.

Gerstenberger, R. 1982. "What Is the Company Trying to Accomplish?" *Steel Shots* (July).

_____. 2007. "Union Braces to Defend Steelworkers." *Hamilton Spectator*, September 14.

Godfrey, J. 1990. "Stelco and Its Workers Suffer Burden of History." *Financial Post*, June 8.

Golden, C., and H. Ruttenberg. 1942. *The Dynamics of Industrial Democracy*. New York: Harper.

Gordon, P. 1982. "A Report from the Chairman of the Board." In Stelco, "Stelco Annual Report 1981." Hamilton, ON: Stelco.

Griffith, A.I., and D.E. Smith. 2005. *Mothering for Schooling*. New York and London: RoutledgeFalmer.

Groom, M. 1990. "The Ultimate Threat." *Steel Shots* (June).

Gross, D. 2010. "Death on Our Shores." *Newsweek*, June 28 and July 5.

Hales, M. 1980. *Living Thinkwork: Where Do Labour Processes Come From?* London: Conference of Socialist Economists.

Halle, D. 1984. *America's Working Man: Work, Home and Politics Among Blue Collar Property Owners*. Chicago: University of Chicago Press.

Hallman, M. 1987. "Documents Show Stelco Knew Overtime Was Illegal: Mackenzie." *Hamilton Spectator*, December 17.

_____. 1989. "Stelco Says It Would Not Resist Takeover Attempt." *Financial Post*, November 24.

_____. 1990. "Stelco Slashes Dividend, Cuts Manager's Salaries." *Financial Post*, September 19.

Hamper, B. 1986. *Rivethead: Tales From the Assembly Line*. Foreward: M. Moore. New York: Warner.

Hardin, H. 1974. *A Nation Unaware: The Canadian Economic Culture*. Vancouver: J.J. Douglas.

Harper, D. 1987. *Working Knowledge: Skill and Community in a Small Shop*. Berkeley and Los Angeles: University of California Press.

Harris, C.C., R.M. Lee and L.D. Morris. 1985. "Redundancy in Steel: Labour-market Behaviour, Local Social Networks and Domestic Organisation." In B. Roberts, R. Finnegan and D. Gallie (eds.), *New Approaches to Economic Life: Economic Restructuring, Unemployment and the Social Division of Labour*. Manchester: Manchester University Press.

Haughton, G. 1989. "Community and Industrial Restructuring: Responses to the Recession and Its Aftermath in the Illawarra Region of Australia." *Environment and Planning*, 21.

Heron, C. 1982. "Hamilton Steelworkers and the Rise of Mass Production." *Historical Papers/Communications historiques* 17, 1. Ottawa: Canadian Historical Association.

_____. 1988. *Working in Steel: The Early Years in Canada 1863–1935*. Toronto: McClelland and Steward.

Heron, C., S. Hoffmitz, W. Roberts and R. Storey (eds.). 1981. *All That Our Hands Have Done: A Political History of the Hamilton Workers*. Hamilton, ON: Mosaic.

Heron, C., and R. Storey. 1989. "Work and Struggle in the Canadian Steel Industry." In C. Heron and R. Storey (eds.), *On the Job: Confronting the Labour Process in Canada*.

Montreal: McGill–Queen's University Press.

Herron, S.N. 1996. "Labor's Day: 25,000 March in a Peaceful Protest." *Hamilton Spectator*, February 24.

Hicks, D.A. 1985. *Advanced Industrial Development: Restructuring, Relocation and Renewal*. Boston: Oelgeschlager, Gunn and Hain.

High, S. 2003. *Industrial Sunset: The Making of North America's Rust Belt, 1969–1984*. Toronto: University of Toronto Press.

Hirschhorn, L. 1984. *Beyond Mechanization: Work and Technology in a Postindustrial Era*. Cambridge, MA, MIT Press.

Hoerr, J. 1988. *And the Wolf Finally Came: The Decline of the American Steel Industry*. Fourth edition. Pittsburgh Series in Social and Labour History. Pittsburgh: University of Pittsburgh Press.

Hogan, W.T. 1985. *Steel in the United States: Restructuring to Compete*. Lexington, MA: D.C. Heath.

Holt, J. 1996. "Six-year Contract Offered to 1005." *Hamilton Spectator*, March 26.

Houseman, S.N. 1991. *Industrial Restructuring with Job Security: The Case of European Steel*. Harvard: Harvard University Press.

Howe, G. 2010. Personal communication. July 28.

Howell, T.R., W.A. Noellert, J.G. Kreier and A.W. Wolff. 1988. *Steel and the State: Government Intervention and Steel's Structural Crisis*. Boulder, CO: Westview.

Hrynyshyn, D. 2002. "Technology and Globalization." *Studies in Political Economy* 67 (Spring).

Hudson, R., and D. Sadler. 1989. *The International Steel Industry Today*. London: Routledge.

Hull, J.P. 1998. "Strictly by the Book: Textbooks and the Control of Production in the North American Pulp and Paper Industry." *History of Education* 27, 1.

_____. 2003. "Working with Figures: Industrial Measurement as Hegemonic Discourse." *Left History* 8, 2.

Human Resources Development Canada. 1994. "Program Evaluation Study of the Canadian Steel Trade and Employment Congress: Phase II — September 19." Ottawa: HRDC.

Humphreys, A. 1995. "Local 1005 President Charged with Assault." *Hamilton Spectator*, October 12.

Humphreys, A., and K. Peters. 1990. "It's Crunch Time on Picket Lines: Union Boss." *Hamilton Spectator*, September 29.

IISI (International Iron and Steel Institute). 2004a. *World Steel in Figures*. Brussels: IISI.

_____. 2004b. *Steel Statistical Yearbook 2004*. November 18. Brussels: IISI.

ILO (International Labour Organization). 2003. "Key Indicators of the Labour Market. Employment by Sector." At <ilo.org/public/english/employment/stat/kilm04.htm>.

ILO (International Labour Organization) Metal Trades Committee. 1983. *"Training and Retraining of Men and Women Workers in the Metal Trades, With Special Reference to Technological Changes."* Geneva: ILO.

ISTC (Industry, Science and Technology Canada). 1992a. "Competitiveness of Canada's Steel Industry. Technology Change in the 1990s." Draft. Ottawa: Special Projects Branch, Industry, Science and Technology Canada. January.

_____. 1992b. "How Might Canadian Establishments Meet the Competitiveness Challenge?" Ottawa: Special Projects Branch, Industry, Science and Technology Canada.

Jackson, N. 1995. "'These Things Just Happen:' Talk, Text, and Curriculum Reform."

In M. Campbell and A. Manicom (eds.), *Knowledge, Experience, and Ruling Relations: Studies in the Social Organization of Knowledge*. Toronto: University of Toronto Press.

Jones, K.A. 1986. *Politics vs Economics in World Steel Trade*. London: Allen and Union.

Kamara, J. 1983. "Plant Closings and Apartheid: The Steel Connection." *Antipode* 15, 2.

Keeling, B. 1988. *World Steel: A New Assessment of Trends and Prospects*. New York and London: Economist Intelligence Unit.

Kelly, J.E. 1988. *Trade Unions and Socialist Politics*. New York: Verso.

Kervin, J., M. Gunderson and F. Reid. 1984. *Two Case Studies of Strikes: Final Report*. Toronto: Centre for Industrial Relations, University of Toronto.

Kilbourn, W. 1960. *The Elements Combined: A History of the Steel Company of Canada*. Toronto: Clark Irwin.

Klau, F., and A. Mittelstadt. 1986. *Labour Market Flexibility*. Paris: OECD. At <oecd.org/dataoecd/55/25/35558438.pdf>.

Kleiman, D. 1995. "Restructuring the United States Steel Industry Through Collective Bargaining: USWA Agreements Designed to Ensure the Future of the Integrated Steel Industry and Long Term Employment and Benefit Protection for Steelworkers." International Conference on Workplace Change: Human Resources and Rationalization in the Global Steel Industry. Toronto: Faculty of Management, University of Toronto. June 5–6.

Klein, K.H., and G. Paul. 1996. "Upgrading of Management Philosophy, Equipment and Operation at Badische Stahlwerke AG." London: The Institute of Metals.

Kruger, A.M. 1959. "Labour Organization and Collective Bargaining in the Canadian Basic Steel Industry." PhD diss. Cambridge: Massachusetts Institute of Technology.

Kuhn, P. 1997. "Canada and the 'OECD Hypothesis:' Does Labour Market Inflexibility Explain Canada's High Level of Unemployment?" Canadian International Labour Network (CILN). Hamilton, ON: Department of Economics, McMaster University. April. At <ciln.mcmaster.ca/papers/cilnwp10.pdf>.

Kusterer, K.C. 1978. *Know-how on the Job: The Important Working Knowledge of "Unskilled" Workers*. Boulder, CO: Westview.

Kutscher, H. 1986. "Forces for Restructuring the Industry and Its Facilities." Institute of Metals (ed.), *Restructuring Steelplants for the Nineties*. London: The Institute of Metals.

Kymlicka, B.B. 1987. *Canadian Steel Industry in Washington*. London, ON: National Centre for Management Research and Development, University of Western Ontario.

Lanthier, J. 1990a. "Stelco Workers Headed for Strike." *Financial Post*, June 7.

_____. 1990b. "Stelco Strike Could Be Road to Ruin: Analysts." *Financial Post*, July 31.

Larson, M.S. 1977. *The Rise of Professionalism: A Sociological Analysis*. Berkeley and Los Angeles: University of California Press.

Lavaca Collective. 2007. *Sin Patrón: Stories from Argentina's Worker-run Factories*. Trans. K. Kohlstedt. Chicago: Haymarket.

Lave, J., and M. Wenger. 1991. *Situated Learning: Legitimate Peripheral Participation*. Cambridge: Cambridge University Press.

Laxer, J. 2009. *Beyond the Bubble: Imagining a New Canadian Economy*. Toronto: Between the Lines.

Lazonick, W. 1983. "Technological Change and the Control of Work: The Development of Capital–Labour Relations in U.S. Mass Production Industries." In H.F. Gospel and C.R. Littler (eds.), *Managerial Strategies and Industrial Relations: An Historical and Comparative Study*. London: Heinemann.

Lefaive, D., and R. Hughes. 1990a. "1005 Turns Its Back on Brother Locals." *Hamilton Spectator*, November 1.

_____. 1990b. "We Have to Stop Fighting." *Hamilton Spectator*, November 5.

_____. 1990c. "It Paid Off, 1005 Boss Says." *Hamilton Spectator*, November 5.

Leicht, K. 1989. "Unions, Plants, Jobs and Workers: An Analysis of Union Satisfaction and Participation." *Sociological Quarterly* 30, 2.

LeMasters, E.E. 1975. *Blue-collar Aristocrats: Life-styles at a Working-class Tavern.* Madison, WI: University of Wisconsin Press.

Lerner, M.J., and D.G. Somers. 1989. "Worker Responses to Plant Closures." Final report submitted to Plant Closure Review and Employment Adjustment Branch of the Ontario Ministry of Labour. Toronto: Ontario Ministry of Labour.

Lewis, A. (dir.). 2004. "The Take." Toronto: National Film Board of Canada.

Litvak, I., and C. Moule. 1986. "The Canadian Aluminum and Steel Industries." In D. McFetridge (ed.), *Technological Change in Canada.* Toronto: University of Toronto Press.

Livingstone, D.W. 1993. "Working at Stelco: 'Re-Tayloring' Production Relations in the Eighties." In J. Corman, M. Luxton, D.W. Livingstone and W. Seccombe (eds.), *Recasting Steel Labour: The Stelco Story.* Halifax, NS: Fernwood.

_____. 1996. "Steel Work: Recasting the Core Workforce at Hilton Works, 1981–96." Final Report of the Workplace Change Section of the Steelworker Families Project, 1983–96. Toronto: Ontario Institute for Studies in Education/University of Toronto.

_____. 1997. "Renewing the Hilton Workforce." *Steel Shots* (August–September).

_____. 1999a. *The Education–Jobs Gap: Underemployment or Economic Democracy.* Toronto: Garamond.

_____. 1999b. "1005 Disaster Scenario: Hire or Die." *Steel Shots* (February).

_____. 2002. *Working and Learning in the Information Age: A Profile of Canadians.* CPRN Discussion Paper W/16. Ottawa: Canadian Policy Research Networks.

_____. (ed.). 2009. *Education and Jobs: Exploring the Gaps.* Toronto: University of Toronto Press.

_____. (ed.). 2010. *Lifelong Learning in Paid and Unpaid Work: Survey and Case Study Findings.* London: Routledge.

Livingstone, D.W., D. Hart and L. Davie. 1987. *Public Attitudes Toward Education in Ontario 1986.* Toronto: OISE Press.

Livingstone, D.W., and M. Luxton. 1989. "Gender Consciousness at Work: Modification of the Male Breadwinner Norm Among Steelworkers and Their Spouses." *Canadian Review of Sociology and Anthropology* 26, 2.

Livingstone. D.W., and J.M. Mangan (eds.). 1996. *Recast Dreams: Class and Gender Consciousness in Steeltown.* Toronto: Garamond.

Livingstone, D.W., and P.H. Sawchuk. 2004a. "Beyond Cultural Capital Theories: Hidden Dimensions of Working-Class Learning." In D.W. Livingstone and P.H. Sawchuk (eds.), *Hidden Knowledge: Organized Labour in the Information Age.* Aurora, ON: Garamond.

_____ (eds.). 2004b. *Hidden Knowledge: Organized Labour in the Information Age.* Aurora, ON: Garamond.

Livingstone, D.W., and A. Scholtz. 2010. "Work and Learning in the Computer Era: Basic Survey Findings." In D.W. Livingstone (ed.), *Lifelong Learning in Paid and Unpaid Work: Survey and Case Study Findings.* London: Routledge.

Locker, M. 1991. *The Canadian Steel Industry: Crisis and Prospects.* New York: Locker.

Lojkine, J. 1986. "From the Industrial Revolution to the Computer Revolution." *Capital and Class* 29 (Summer).

Luxton, M., and J. Corman. 1991. "Getting to Work: The Challenge of the Women Back into Stelco Campaign." *Labour/Le Travail* 28 (Fall).

_____. 1993. "Getting to Work: The Challenge of the Women Back into Stelco

Campaign." In J. Corman, M. Luxton, D.W. Livingstone and W. Seccombe (eds.), *Recasting Steel Labour: The Stelco Story*. Halifax, NS: Fernwood.

_____. 2001. *Getting By in Hard Times: Gendered Labour at Home and On the Job*. Toronto: University of Toronto Press.

Lynn, L.H. 1982. *How Japan Innovates: A Comparison with the U.S. in the Case of Oxygen Steelmaking*. Boulder, CO: Westview.

MacLeod, G. 1997. *From Mondragon to America: Experiments in Community Economic Development*. Sydney, NS: University College of Cape Breton Press.

MacLeod, G., and D. Reed. 2009. "Mondragon's Response to the Challenges of Globalization: A Multi-localization Strategy." In D. Reed and J.J. McMurtry (eds.), *Co-operatives in a Global Economy: The Challenges of Co-operation Across Borders*. Newcastle upon Tyne: Cambridge Scholars Publishing.

MacPherson, D. 2002. "Meeting Training and Skill Development Needs in the Steel Industry." Ottawa: Canadian Policy Research Network.

MacPherson, I. 2009. *A Century of Co-operation*. Ottawa: Canadian Co-operative Association.

_____. 2010. "Co-operatives and the Social Economy in English Canada: Circles of Influence and Experience." In J.J. McMurtry (ed.), *Living Economics: Canadian Perspectives on the Social Economy, Co-operatives, and Community Economic Development*. Toronto: Emond Montgomery.

MacRury, A. 1996. "Stelco and Dofasco Still Largest Single Employers." *Hamilton Spectator*, February 26.

Madar, D. 2009. *Big Steel: Technology, Trade and Survival in a Global Market*. Vancouver: University of British Columbia Press.

Mangum, G.L., S.-Y. Kim and S.B. Tallman. 1996. *Transnational Marriages in the Steel Industry: Experience and Lessons for Global Business*. Westport, CT: Quorum.

Mann, B. 1989. "Jobs Under Attack." *Steel Shots* (December).

Marcus, P.F., and K.M. Kirsis 1988. "The Rebound of the Threatened North American Iron Ore Industry." *Steel Strategist* (June).

_____. 1995. "World Steel Export Process Down Sharply Again (Yet, We Are Increasingly Optimistic about Price Trends Next Year)." Presented to United Steelworkers of America Board Meeting. September 28. Englewood Cliffs, NJ: World Steel Dynamics.

Martin, J. 1986. "Does Stelco Really Care?" *Steel Shots* (January).

_____. 1988. "Dental Plan Restored." *Steel Shots* (October).

_____. 1989. "President's Comments." *Steel Shots* (December).

Marx, K. 1954. *Capital: A Critique of Political Economy*. Vol. 1: The Process of Production of Capital. Moscow: Progress.

Masi, J. 1991. "Structural Adjustment and Technological Change in the Canadian Steel Industry, 1970–1986." In D. Drache and M. Gertler (eds.), *The New Era of Global Competition: State Policy and Market Power*. Montreal: McGill–Queen's University Press.

McCoy, L. 1999. "Accounting Discourse and Textual Practices of Ruling: A Study of Institutional Transformation and Restructuring in Higher Education." PhD diss. Toronto: University of Toronto.

McGannon, H.E. (ed.). 1971. *The Making, Shaping and Treating of Steel*. Pittsburgh: U.S. Steel.

McKibbon, B. 2010. *Earth: Making a Life on a Tough New Planet*. Toronto: Knopf Canada.

McManus, G.J. 1988a. "Computers Are Putting Steel Together." *Iron Age* (June).

_____. 1988b. "Getting Down to One Manhour per Ton." *Iron Age* (October).

McMulkin, F.J. 1964. "Ten Years of Oxygen Steelmaking at Dofasco." *CIM Bulletin* 57 (October).

McMurtry, J.J. (ed.). 2010. *Living Economics: Canadian Perspectives on the Social Economy, Co-Operatives, and Community Economic Development*. Toronto: Edmond Montgomery.

Meiksins, P., and C. Smith. 1996. "Introduction: Engineers and Comparative Research." In P. Meiskins and C. Smith (eds.), *Engineering Labour: Technical Workers in Comparative Perspective*. New York: Verso.

Meissner, M. 1971. "The Long Arm of the Job: A Study of Work and Leisure." *Industrial Relations* 10.

Mény, Y., and V. Wright. 1985. *Le crise de la sidérurgie européene, 1974–1984*. Paris: Presses Universitaires de France.

Metzgar, J. 1984. "The Humbling of the Steelworkers." *Socialist Register* 75–6.

Milbourne, R.J. 1990. "Stelco Steel — The Agenda for the '90s." Speech given to the Niagara Chapter of the American Iron and Steel Engineers, November 6.

Mills, C.W. 1951. *White Collar: The American Middle Classes*. New York: Oxford University Press.

Ministry of State, Science and Technology. 1988. *Industry Profile: Primary Iron and Steel*. Ottawa: Department of Regional Industrial Expansion.

Mitchell, P. 1984a. "John Allan Takes Over a Streamlined Stelco." *Hamilton Spectator*, May 1.

_____. 1984b. "It's a 'New Stelco:' World Class Status for Hilton Plant." *Hamilton Spectator*, December 15.

_____. 1992. "Stelco Is Out to Make Winners with Fortnight Seminars." *Hamilton Spectator*, April 28.

_____. 1995. "Union Irate at Stelco Exec Pay Packages." *Hamilton Spectator*, March 31.

Mitchell, P., and M. Wickers. 1982. "Stelco 2001: Lake Erie May Outstrip Aging Hilton, Gordon Says." *Hamilton Spectator*, January 5.

Moinov, S. 1995. "Privatization in the Iron and Steel Industry." Working paper SAP 2.47/WP.93. Geneva: International Labour Organization.

Moore, M. (dir.). 1989. "Roger and Me." Warner Bros.

Morgan, K. 1983. "Restructuring Steel: The Crisis of Labour and Locality in Britain." *International Journal of Urban and Regional Research* 7, 2.

Morrison, J. 1991. "Stelco Denies Hilton Works Closing Down." *Hamilton Spectator*, June 11.

_____. 1992. "Opening Books to Union Sets Precedence at Stelco." *Hamilton Spectator*, May 6.

Morton, D. 1984. *Working People: An Illustrated History of the Canadian Labour Movement*. Rev. Ottawa: Deneau.

Murphy, J.B. 1993. *The Moral Economy of Labour: Aristotelian Themes in Economic Theory*. New Haven: Yale University Press.

Nash, J. 1989. *From Tank Town to High Tech: The Clash of Community and Industrial Cycles*. SUNY Series in the Anthropology of Work. New York: State University of New York Press.

National Center for Policy Analysis. 2003. "Decline in Manufacturing Jobs Is Global." *Daily Policy Digest* (October 22). At <ncpa.org/iss/eco>.

Naylor, T. 1975. *The History of Canadian Business, 1867–1914*. Vol. 2: Industrial Development. Toronto: James Lorimer.

Neamtan, N. 2005. "The Social Economy: Finding a Way Between the Market and the State." *Policy Options* (July–August).

Nelson, D. 1995. *Managers and Workers: Origins of the Twentieth-century Factory System in the United States 1880–1920*. Second edition. Madison, WI: University of Wisconsin Press.

Noble, D.F. 1977. *America by Design: Science, Technology, and the Rise of Corporate Capitalism*. New York: Knopf.

_____. 1984. *Forces of Production: A Social History of Industrial Automation*. New York: Oxford

University Press.

Noirel, F. 1980. *Vivre et lutter á Longwy*. Paris: Maspero.

O'Brien, D. 1989. "Let's Look at the Idea of Multicrafting." *Steel Shots* (April).

O'Grady, J., and P. Warrian. 2010. "Human Resources Trends in the Canadian Steel Sector." Toronto: Prism Economics Analysis.

OECD (Organisation for Economic Co-operation and Development). 1987. *Labour Market Flexibility: Report by a High Level Group of Experts to the Secretary General*. Paris: OECD.

_____. 2003. *Labour Force Statistics*. Paris: OECD.

OECD (Organisation for Economic Co-operation and Development) Steel Committee. 2009. "Presentation for the Council Working Party on Shipbuilding." July 9. Paris: OECD.

OECD (Organisation for Economic Co-operation and Development), Working Party of the Steel Committee. 1987. "Study of the Age Structure and Technical Qualifications of the Steel Industry Workforce." SC/WP (87) 38. Paris: OECD.

Ollman, B. 1976. *Alienation: Marx's Conception of Man in Capitalist Society*. Second edition. Cambridge: Cambridge University Press.

Ontario, Government of. 1963. "Report of the Select Committee on Manpower Training, Hon. J.R. Simonett, Chairman." February. Toronto: Government of Ontario.

Ontario, Ministry of Colleges and Universities (Manpower Training Branch). 1974. "Training for Ontario's Future: Report of the Task Force on Industrial Training." Toronto: Government of Ontario.

Ontario Premier's Council. 1988. "The Case of Steel Manufacturing." *Competing in the New Global Economy*. Vol. 1: Industry Studies. Toronto: Queen's Printer.

Orr, J.E. 1996. *Talking About Machines: An Ethnography of a Modern Job*. Collection on Technology and Work. Ithaca, NY and London: ILR/Cornell University Press.

OTA (Office of Technology Assessment). 1980. *Technology and Steel Industry Competitiveness*. Washington, DC: U.S. Government Printing Office.

Owram, K. 2010. "U.S. Steel Could Be Forced to Sell Stelco." *Toronto Star*, June 15.

Palloix, C. 1978. "The Labour Process: From Fordism to Neo-Fordism." *The Labour Process and Class Strategies*. London: Committee of Socialist Economists.

Palmer, B. 1979. *A Culture in Conflict: Skilled Workers and Industrial Capitalism in Hamilton, Ontario, 1860–1914*. Montreal: McGill–Queen's University Press.

Papp, L. 1991. "Firm, Staff Not Guilty of Excess Overtime." *Toronto Star*, April 6.

_____. 1992. "Steelworker Urges Action on Economy." *Toronto Star*, September 24.

_____. 1993. "Three-Year Deal Reached for 6,000 Workers at Stelco." *Toronto Star*, May 3.

Parr, J. 1990. *The Gender of Breadwinners: Women, Men, and Change in Two Industrial Towns 1880–1950*. Toronto: University of Toronto Press.

Pateman, C. 1970. *Participation and Democratic Theory*. Cambridge: Cambridge University Press.

Patrick, V. 1985. "Dear Bob…" *Steel Shots* (October).

_____. 1989. "Changing Times." *Steel Shots* (December).

Payne, M. 2003. "How Big Is Big in the Global Steel Industry?" *Steel Times International* 27, 2 (February–March).

Peck, J. 1996. *Work-place: The Social Regulation of Labor Markets*. New York: Guilford.

_____. 2001. *Workfare States*. New York: Guilford.

Pegden, R. 1980. "The Greening of Nanticoke." *Industrial Management* 4, 3 (April).

Petersen, J., and R. Storey. 1986. "Final Report Prepared for Local 1005 on Technological Change." Hamilton, ON: Department of Sociology, McMaster University.

Pettapiece, M.N. 1983. "Angry Steelworkers Shout Down 1005 Chief." *Hamilton Spectator*,

April 27.

Phillips, C. 1996. "Just How Many Protested?" *Hamilton Spectator*, February 27.

Pilat, D., A. Cimper, K. Olsen and C. Webb. 2006. "The Changing Nature of Manufacturing in OECD Economies." STI Working Paper 2006/9. DSTI/DOC(2006)9. Paris: Organization for Economic Co-operation and Development.

Poling, J. 1996. "Protest Shuts Down Factories." *Hamilton Spectator*, February 24.

Polyani, M. 1966. *The Tacit Dimension*. Garden City, NY: Doubleday.

Powell, N. 2007. "Hamilton Steel May Get $100m Upgrade." *Hamilton Spectator*, August 27.

_____. 2009a. "Lakeside Steel Making Bid for Stelco: Says Plants Better Off in Canadian Hands." *Hamilton Spectator*, August 5.

_____. 2009b. "Open Steel Plants, Or Else… Let Feds Take Over, Says Union President." *Hamilton Spectator*, April 17.

_____. 2009c. "Union Seeks $44 Million for U.S. Steel Shutdown." *Hamilton Spectator*, September 10.

_____. 2009d. "Retirements Shrink U.S. Steel: Canadian Workforce About 500 Short of Average Promised in '07 Purchase Deal." *Hamilton Spectator*, December 3.

Pratt, C. 2005. "Statement to All Employees from the President and Chief Executive Officer." January 28. Hamilton, ON: Stelco.

Pratt, C., and L. Gaudet. 2008. *Into the Blast Furnace: The Forging of a CEO's Conscience*. Toronto: Vintage Canada.

Prokaska, L. 1994a. "Vets Square Off in Contest for Stelco's Top Union Job." *Hamilton Spectator*, April 4.

_____. 1994b. "Despite Success, 243 Workers Facing Layoff From Stelco." *Hamilton Spectator*, October 28.

_____. 1996a. "Local 1005 Backs Labour Protest." *Hamilton Spectator*, January 24.

_____. 1996b. "Stelco Workers Irate Over $1.68." *Hamilton Spectator*, March 29.

_____. 1996c. "How Stelco Deal with 1005 Died." *Hamilton Spectator*, April 4.

_____. 1996d. "We're Pawns in Talks: Workers." *Hamilton Spectator*, April 11.

_____. 1996e. "Local 1005 Says Yes." *Hamilton Spectator*, April 25.

Pron, N., and L. Papp. 1990. "Stelco Workers Show Little Joy as Deal Unveiled." *Toronto Star*, November 1.

Quarter, J. 1992. *Canada's Social Economy: Co-operatives, Non-profits, and Other Community Enterprises*. Toronto: James Lorimer.

_____. 1995. *Crossing the Line: Unionized Employee Ownership and Investment Funds*. Toronto: James Lorimer.

Quarter, J., L. Mook and A. Armstrong. 2009. *Understanding the Social Economy: A Canadian Perspective*. Toronto: University of Toronto Press.

Quinlan, M. 1986. "Managerial Strategy and Industrial Relations in the Australian Steel Industry, 1945–1975: A Case Study." In M. Bray and V. Taylor (eds.), *Essays in the Political Economy of Australian Industrial Relations*. Sydney, NS: McGraw-Hill.

Radforth, I. 1987. *Bushworkers and Bosses: Logging in Northern Ontario 1900–1980*. Toronto: University of Toronto Press.

Renner, M., S. Sweeney and J. Kubit. 2008. "Green Jobs: Towards Decent Work in a Sustainable, Low-Carbon World." UNEP/ILO/IOE/ITUC and Washington, DC: Worldwatch Institute. September. At <unep.org/labour_environment/PDFs/Greenjobs/UNEP-Green-Jobs-Report.pdf>.

Rhodes, M., and V. Wright. 1988. "The European Steel Unions and the Steel Crisis, 1974–84: A Study in the Demise of Traditional Unionism." *British Journal of Political Science* 18, 2 (March).

Rinehart, J., C. Huxley and D. Robertson. 1997. *Just Another Car Factory? Lean Production and Its Discontents*. Ithaca, NY: Cornell University Press.

Robins, K., and F. Webster. 1988. "Athens Without Slaves... or Slaves Without Athens? The Neurosis of Technology." *Science and Culture* 3.

Rose, J. 2001. *The Intellectual Life of the British Working Classes*. New Haven: Yale University Press.

Roy, W.G. 1997. *Socializing Capital: The Rise of the Large Industrial Corporation in America*. Princeton, NJ: Princeton University Press.

Rubenson, K. 2007. "Determinants of Formal and Informal Canadian Adult Learning: Insights from the Adult Education and Training Surveys." Ottawa: Human Resources and Social Development Canada. At <hrsdc.gc.ca/eng/publications_resources/research/categories/llsd/2007/sp_792_10_07/page02.shtml>.

Samways, N.L. 1988. "Revitalization of the Stelco Hilton Works." *Iron and Steel Engineer* 65, 1 (January).

Sandberg, L.A., and J. Bradbury. 1988. "Industrial Restructuring in the Canadian Steel Industry." *Antipode* 20, 2.

Sanger, M. 1988. "Transforming the Elements: The Reorganization of Work and Learning at Stelco's Hilton Works." M.A. thesis. Toronto: Department of Education, University of Toronto.

Sawchuk, P.H. 2009. "Learning, Labour and Environmentalism: Canadian and International Prospects." *Canadian Journal for the Study Adult Education* 21, 2.

Scherrer, C. 1991. "Seeking a Way Out of Fordism: The U.S. Steel and Auto Industries." *Capital and Class* 44 (Summer).

Scheuerman, W. 1986. *The Steel Crisis: The Economics and Politics of a Declining Industry*. New York: Praeger.

Schor, J. 1991. *The Overworked American: The Unexpected Decline of Leisure*. New York: Basic.

Schrag, P. 2007. "Schoolhouse Crock: Fifty Years of Blaming America's Education System for Our Stupidity." *Harper's* 315, 1888.

Scott, A. 1988. *New Industrial Spaces*. London: Pion.

Scott, J.C. 1990. *Domination and the Arts of Resistance: Hidden Transcripts*. New Haven: Yale University Press.

Seccombe, W., and D.W. Livingstone. 1999. *Down to Earth People: Beyond Class Reductionism and Post-modernism*. Toronto: Garamond.

Sennett, R. 2008. *The Craftsman*. New Haven and London: Yale University Press.

Shalom, F. 1991. "Steel Industry Must Cut Back, Conference Told." *Montreal Gazette*, October 8.

Shostak, A.B. 1969. *Blue Collar Life*. New York: Random.

Sloan, A. 1964. *My Years with General Motors*. New York: Doubleday.

Smith, D.E. 1988. "Determining Training Needs in the Plastics Processing Industry." The Nexus Project. Occasional Paper, 5. Toronto: Department of Sociology in Education, Ontario Institute for Studies in Education.

_____. 1990a. *The Conceptual Practices of Power: A Feminist Sociology of Knowledge*. Toronto; University of Toronto Press.

_____. 1990b. *Texts, Facts and Femininity: Exploring the Relations of Ruling*. London: Routledge.

_____. 1999. "The Ruling Relations." In D.E. Smith, *Writing the Social: Critique, Theory, and Investigations*. Toronto: University of Toronto Press.

_____. 2005. *Institutional Ethnography: A Sociology for People*. New York: Altamira.

Smith, D.E., and G.A. Smith. 1990. "The Job–Skills Training Nexus: Changing Context and Managerial Practice." In J. Muller (ed.), *Education for Work, Education as Work:*

Canada's Changing Community Colleges. Toronto: Garamond.

Smith, T. 2000. *Technology and Capital in the Age of Lean Production: A Marxian Critique of the "New Economy."* New York: State University of New York Press.

Spenner, K. 1983. "Deciphering Prometheus: Temporal Change in the Skill Level of Work." *American Sociological Review* 48, 6.

Statistics Canada. 2006. "Women in Canada: A Gender-Based Statistical Report." Fifth edition. Catalogue No. 89-503-XIE. Ottawa: Statistics Canada. At <statcan.gc.ca/pub/89-503-x/89-503-x2005001-eng.pdf>.

Stelco. 1960–2006. Annual Reports. Hamilton, ON: Stelco.

_____. 1980–2006. Personnel Reports. Hamilton, ON: Stelco.

_____. 1989. "Stelco Steel Turnover Report." October 6. Hamilton, ON: Stelco.

_____. 1995. "Stelco Annual Report 1994." Hamilton, ON: Stelco.

_____. 1996. "Stelco Hilton Works Personnel Reports." November. Hamilton, ON: Stelco.

_____. 2005. "Stelco Annual Report 2004." Hamilton, ON: Stelco.

_____. 2006. "Stelco Annual Report 2005." Hamilton, ON: Stelco.

Stelco–USWA Local 1005. 1993. "Basic Agreement Between The Steel Company of Canada and United Steelworkers of America." Hamilton, ON: Stelco-USWA Local 1005.

_____. 1996. "Basic Agreement Between The Steel Company of Canada and United Steelworkers of America." Hamilton, ON: Stelco–USWA Local 1005.

_____. 2006. "Basic Agreement Between The Steel Company of Canada and United Steelworkers of America." Hamilton, ON: Stelco–USWA Local 1005.

Stieber, J. 1980. "Steel." In G. Somers (ed.), *Collective Bargaining: Contemporary American Experience.* Madison, WI: Industrial Relations Research Association.

Stinson, M. 1991. "Stelco Galvanizes New Order." *Globe and Mail Report on Business,* June 3.

Stock, R. 2001. "Socio-Economic Security, Justice and the Psychology of Social Relationships." Geneva: Infocus Programme on Socio-Economic Security, International Labour Organization. April. At <ilo.org/gimi/RessShowRessource.do?ressourceId=8862>.

Stone, K. 1974. "The Origins of Job Structures in the Steel Industry." *Review of Radical Political Economics* 6, 2 (Summer).

Storey, R.H. 1981a. "Workers, Unions and Steel: The Shaping of the Hamilton Working Class." PhD diss. Toronto: Department of Sociology, University of Toronto.

_____. 1981b. "The Dofasco Way." In C. Heron, S. Hoffmitz, W. Roberts and R. Storey (eds.), *All That Our Hands Have Done: A Political History of the Hamilton Workers.* Oakville, ON: Mosaic.

_____. 1994. "The Struggle For Job Ownership in the Canadian Steel Industry: An Historical Analysis." *Labour/Le Travail* 33 (Spring): 75–106.

_____. 1996. "Behind the Union Drive at Dofasco: Efforts to Bring in a Union Began at Dofasco even Before Stelco, but the Company Has Kept Them at Bay." *Hamilton Spectator,* December 17.

Storey, R., and J. Petersen. 1987. *The Impact of Technology at Hilton Works.* Ottawa: Labour Canada.

Storper, M., and R. Walker. 1989. *The Capitalist Imperative: Territory, Technology and Industrial Growth.* Oxford: Blackwell.

Strauss, G. 2007. "Worker Participation—Some Under-considered Issues." *Industrial Relations: A Journal of Economy and Society* 45, 4

Taylor, C. 1982. "Equal Partners." *Steel Shots* (January).

Taylor, F.W. 1911. *Principles of Scientific Management.* New York: Harper.

Telmer, F.H. 1994. "Managing Change Key to Economy Recovery." *Canadian Speeches: Issues of the Day* 8, 1 (April).

_____. 1995. "North American Steel Over the Next Ten Years." In Committee on Economic Studies (ed.), *The Steel Industry in the Year 2005*. Seminar Proceedings. Brussels: International Iron and Steel Institute.

Tenaris. 2010. "Mission." At <ir.tenaris.com/strategy.cfm>.

Thompson, P. 1989. *The Nature of Work: An Introduction to Debates on the Labour Process*. Basingstoke: Macmillan.

Treado, C. Durkin. 2010. "Pittsburgh's Evolving Steel Legacy and the Steel Technology Cluster." *Cambridge Journal of Regions, Economy and Society* 3, 1.

United Steel Workers (USW). 2009. "Steelworkers Form Collaboration with Mondragon, the World's Largest Worker-Owned Cooperative." Media release. October 27. At <usw.org/media_center/releases_advisories?id=0234>.

USWA Local 1005. 1992. USWA Local 1005 unpublished computer records. Hamilton, ON: USWA Local 1005.

_____. 1996. *It Started with a Whisper: A History of the 1946 Strike*. Hamilton, ON: United Steelworkers of America Local 1005.

U.S. Steel. 2010. "About U.S. Steel." At <uss.com/corp/company/profile/about.asp>.

Vaillancourt, Y. 2010. "The Social Economy in Quebec and Canada: Configurations Past and Present." In J.J. McMurtry (ed.), *Living Economics: Canadian Perspectives on the Social Economy, Co-operatives, and Community Economic Development*. Toronto: Emond Montgomery.

Vallas, S.P., and J.P. Beck. 1996. "The Transformation of Work Revisited: The Limits of Flexibility in American Manufacturing." *Social Problems* 43, 3.

Van Alphen, T. 1988. "Steelmakers Join to Develop New Technology." *Toronto Star*, September 17.

Veblen, T. 1954. *Absentee Ownership and Business Enterprise in Recent Times*. New York: Viking.

Verma, A. 1996. "Issues of an Aging Workforce: A Case-study of Slater Steels–Hamilton Specialty Bar Division." April. Aging Research Network at the Centre for Studies of Aging (CARNET). Monograph Series: Issues of an Aging Workforce. Toronto: Centre for Studies of Aging, University of Toronto.

Verma, A., A. Frost and P. Warrian. 1995. "Workplace Restructuring and Employment Relations in the Canadian Steel Industry." In A. Verma, A. Frost and P. Warrian (eds.), *International Conference on Workplace Change: Human Resources and Rationalization in the Global Steel Industry*. Conference Papers. Toronto: Faculty of Management, University of Toronto.

Verma, A., and P. Warrian. 1992. "Industrial Relations in the Canadian Steel Industry." In R.P. Chaykowski and A. Verma (eds.), *Industrial Relations in Canadian Industry*. Toronto: Holt, Rinehart and Winston.

Vieta, M., and A. Ruggeri. 2009. "Worker Recovered Enterprises as Workers' Co-operatives: The Conjunctures, Challenges, and Innovations of Self-management in Argentina and Latin America." In D. Reed and J.J. McMurtry (eds.), *Co-operatives in a Global Economy: The Challenges of Co-operation Across Borders*. Newcastle upon Tyne: Cambridge Scholars.

Villa, P. 1987. "Systems of Flexible Working in the Italian Steel Industry." In R. Tarling (ed.), *Flexibility in Labour Markets*. Toronto: Academic.

Villeval, M.C. 1988. "Destructuring of an Industry and Local Changes in the Wage-earning Relationship." *Labour and Society* 13, 4.

Wainwright, H., and A. Green. 2009. "A Real Green Deal." *Red Pepper: Spicing Up Politics*,

October 7. At <redpepper.org.uk/A-real-green-deal>.

Waring, S. 1991. *Taylorism Transformed: Scientific Management Theory Since 1945*. Chapel Hill, NC: University of North Carolina Press.

Warren, K. 2001. *Big Steel: The First Century of the United States Steel Corporation 1901–2001*. Pittsburgh: University of Pittsburgh Press.

Warrian, P. 1989. "Industrial Restructuring, Occupational Shifts and Skills: The Steel and Electronics Manufacturing Cases." Background Paper prepared for Study Team Two, Colleges and the Changing Economy, Vision 2000. Toronto: Ontario Council of Regents. August.

_____. 1990. "Is the Wolf Coming to the Canadian Steel Industry in 1990?" Paper presented at the Sloan School, Massachusetts Institute of Technology. April 6.

_____. 2010a. "The Importance of Steel Manufacturing to Canada — A Research Study." Ottawa: Canadian Steel Producers Association.

_____. 2010b. Personal communication, June 22.

Warrian, P., and C. Mulhern. 2001. "The New (Economy) Steel: Learning at the Regional and Firm Levels." Paper presented at the Ontario Network on the Regional Innovation System Conference, London, ON, December. At <utoronto. ca/onris/research_review/Presentations/PresentationDOCS/Presentations01/ WarrianMulhern01_NewEconomy.pdf>.

Watson, T. 2006. "Stelco's Second Coming." *Canadian Business Online*, March 27.

Weaver, J. 1982. *Hamilton: An Illustrated History*. Toronto: Lorimer.

Webber, M. 1986. "Regional Production and the Production of Regions: The Case of Steeltown." In A. Scott and M. Storper (eds.), *Production, Work, Territory: The Geographical Anatomy of Industrial Capitalism*. Boston: Allen and Unwin.

Weber, M. 1978. *Economy and Society*. 2 vols. Ed. G. Roth and C. Wittich. Trans. E. Fischoff et al. Berkeley and Los Angeles: University of California Press.

Westell, D. 1992. "Stelco Local Waves Olive Branch." *Globe and Mail*, April 2.

Westergard, J., I. Noble and A. Walker. 1989. *After Redundancy: The Experience of Economic Insecurity*. Cambridge: Polity.

Whitaker, R. 1979. "Scientific Management Theory as Political Ideology." *Studies in Political Economy* 2 (Autumn).

Whittington, L. 2009. "Ottawa May Demand U.S. Steel Sell Stelco." *The Toronto Star*, May 7.

Whyte, W.F., and K.K. Whyte. 1991. *Making Mondragon: The Growth and Dynamics of the Worker Cooperative Complex*. Second edition. Ithaca, NY: ILR Press.

Williams, K., T. Cutler, J. Williams and C. Haslam. 1987. "The End of Mass Production." *Economy and Society* 16, 3 (August).

Williams, W.M. 1986. "An Historical Sketch of the Canadian Steel Industry." *CIM Bulletin* 79 (September).

Willis, P. 1979. "Shop-floor Culture, Masculinity and the Wage Form." In J. Clarke, C. Critcher and R. Johnson (eds.), *Working Class Culture: Studies in History and Theory*. London: Hutcheson.

_____. 1988. *Learning to Labor: How Working Class Kids Get Working Class Jobs*. Aldershot, Hants: Gower.

Wolman, B. 1985. "Quality Improvement Program at Stelco Inc." Proceedings of the International Symposium on Statistical Process Control in the Steel Industry. Vancouver. August 18–21.

Womack, J.P., T. Daniel and D. Roos. 1990. *The Machine That Changed the World: How Japan's Secret Weapon in the Global Auto Wars Will Revolutionize Western Industry*. New

York: Rawson.

Wood, S. (ed.). 1989. *The Transformation of Work? Skill, Flexibility, and the Labour Process*. London: Routledge.

Woods, Gordon, and Co. 1977. *Hamilton–Wentworth Steel and Related Industries*. Toronto: Woods, Gordon.

World Steel Association. 2009. *World Steel in Figures 2009*. Brussels: World Steel Association.

_____. 2010. "World Steel Top Producers 2009." Brussels: World Steel Association. At <worldsteel.org/pictures/programfiles/top_producers.pdf>.

Wright, E.O. 2010. *Envisioning Real Utopias*. London: Verso.

Yates, C., W. Lewchuk and P. Steward. 2001. "Empowerment as a Trojan Horse: New Systems of Work Organization in the North American Automobile Industry." *Economic and Industrial Democracy* 22, 4.

Zuboff, S. 1984. *In the Age of the Smart Machine: The Future of Work and Power*. New York: Basic.

About the Authors

D.W. Livingstone has recently retired as Canada Research Chair in Lifelong Learning and Work at the University of Toronto and is now professor emeritus in the Department of Sociology and Equity Studies at the Ontario Institute for Studies in Education/University of Toronto (OISE/UT). He was head of the Centre for the Study of Education and Work from its inception and director of the SSHRC-sponsored national research network on the Changing Nature of Work and Lifelong Learning (WALL) from 2003 to 2008. He has done path-breaking research on informal learning practices, including the first national surveys and related case studies of changing learning and work practices in the "new economy" (see <wallnetwork.ca>). He was also the principal investigator of the OISE/UT Biennial Survey of Educational Issues, the only regularly conducted, fully accessible survey of public opinion on educational policy issues in Canada (see <oise.utoronto.ca/oise-survey>). He received the 1999 John Porter Memorial Book Award of the Canadian Sociology and Anthropology Association for his book, *The Education-Jobs Gap: Underemployment or Economic Democracy* (Garamond and Westview, 1999, second edition 2004). His other books include: *Class, Ideologies and Educational Futures* (Falmer, 1983); *Social Crisis and Schooling* (Fernwood, 1985); *Critical Pedagogy and Cultural Power* (editor) (Bergin & Garvey, 1987); *Stacking the Deck* (OurSchools/OurSelves, 1992); *Recasting Steel Labour: The Stelco Story* (with June Corman, Meg Luxton and Wally Seccombe) (Fernwood, 1993); *Recast Dreams: Class and Gender Consciousness in Steeltown* (edited with John Marshal Mangan) (Garamond, 1996); *Down-to-Earth People: Beyond Class Reductionism and Postmodernism* (with Wally Seccombe) (Garamond, 2000); *Working and Learning in the Information Age: A Canadian Profile* (Canadian Policy Research Networks, 2002); *Hidden Knowledge: Organized Labour in the Information Age* (with Peter Sawchuk) (Garamond and Rowman and Littlefield, 2004); *The Future of Lifelong Learning and Work: Critical Perspectives* (edited with Peter Sawchuck and Kiran Mirchandani) (Sense, 2008), *Education and Jobs: Exploring the Gaps* (editor) (University of Toronto Press, 2009) and *Lifelong Learning in Paid and Unpaid Work* (editor) (Routledge, 2010).

Dorothy E. Smith is professor emerita in the Department of Sociology and Equity Studies in Education of the University of Toronto (OISE/UT) and adjunct professor, Department of Sociology, University of Victoria. She has been developing for over thirty years the implications of women's standpoint for sociology, problematizing the objectified forms of organization and social relations characteristic of contemporary society and focusing more recently on the significance of texts for the organization of power. Her published books are: with Sara David (ed.), *Women Look at Psychiatry: I'm not Mad, I'm Angry* (Press Gang, 1975); *Feminism and Marxism: A Place to Begin, A Way To Go* (New Star, 1977); with Naomi Hersom (ed.), *Women and the Canadian Labour Force*, conference proceedings (Social Sciences and Humanities Research Council of Canada, 1981); *El Mundo Silenciado De Las Mujeres* (CIDE 1985); *The Everyday World as Problematic: A Feminist Sociology* (Northeastern University Press, 1987); *The Conceptual Practices of Power: A Feminist Sociology of Knowledge* (Northeastern University Press, 1990); *Texts, Facts, and Femininity: Exploring the Relations of Ruling* (Routledge, 1990); with Susan Turner (eds), *Doing It the Hard Way: Investigations of Gender and Technology, Sally Hacker's Collected Papers* (Harper-Collins, 1990); Frigga Haug (eds), *Eine Soziologie für Frauen* (Argument Verlag, 1998); *Writing the Social: Critique, Theory and Investigations* (University of Toronto, 1999); *Institutional Ethnography: A Sociology for People* (Rowman and Littlefield, 2005); with Alison Griffith, *Mothering for Schooling* (Routledge 2005); and an edited collection of studies by institutional ethnographers, *Institutional Ethnography in Practice* (Rowman and Littlefield 2006). She has received numerous international awards for her pioneering research.

Warren Smith began work at Stelco's Hilton Works in early 1967 as a boiler flue cleaner in the Utilities Department. There being a high turnover of stationary engineers, he was asked by Stelco in 1975 to train as boiler operator, making him the first of many non-credentialed employees to fill positions previously filled by engineers. In the 1980s, after a complaint was filed under the Operating Engineers Act by a more highly certified employee, these workers were required to get a third class ticket. He became increasingly active in the union local as steward, assistant chief steward, health and safety instructor and, in 1988, chief health and safety representative in his department. He was elected divisional health and safety chairperson for ironmaking in 1993 and president in 1997. Throughout his time as health and safety chair and president, as well as serving on eight different investigative committees, Warren had unprecedented opportunities to become familiar with most mills and shops in the plant and the concerns of many workers. The 1997 election gave the Smith slate half the seats on the executive and four of six on the grievance committee. In spite of company efforts to undermine his administration in the next three years, his slate went on to win every executive seat in 2000. He was defeated in the 2003 election despite negotiating a contract that was ratified by 72 per cent of the membership. Warren returned to his job as Technician-Energy in the Utilities Department at Hilton Works and retired in 2005. He now works as Outreach Co-ordinator for Chris Charlton, Member of Parliament, Hamilton Mountain.

Index